Crossing the River of Fire

Crossing the River of Fire

Mark's Gospel and Global Capitalism

Wilf Wilde

✚ EPWORTH

Copyright © Wilf Wilde 2006

The Author has asserted his right under the Copyright, Designs
and Patents Act, 1988, to be identified as the Author of this work

British Library Cataloguing in Publication data

A catalogue record for this book is available
from the British Library

0 7162 0599 8
978 07162 0599 9

First published in 2006
by Epworth Press
4 John Wesley Road
Werrington
Peterborough PE4 6ZP

Typeset by Regent Typesetting, London
Printed and bound in Great Britain by
William Clowes Ltd, Beccles, Suffolk

Contents

Foreword

Although *Crossing the River of Fire* has connections with the important English ethical tradition of radical political economy, it differs from it by being substantially rooted in biblical theology. Like John Ruskin and William Morris in the late nineteenth century, it is a strong tract for the times, a critical engagement with the recent invasion of Iraq, interpreted as an exercise of the new empire of global capitalism. Yet, it is much more than that because it takes religion much more seriously. It links with the resurgence of religion: globally, as the furious religion of Christianity and Islam; and, nationally, as the growing recognition of the emerging contribution of religion to local and public life – initially seen as social capital, but increasingly as faithful or religious capital. The latest William Temple Foundation research report, *Faith in Action: the Dynamic Connection Between Spiritual and Religious Capital* (WTF, 2006), clearly embodies this trend.

Reflecting on this combination of factors, which constitute current resurgent religion, we are becoming more and more aware that the historic dependence on the dominant old mainstream liberal tradition of social Christianity and Church is no longer sufficient. Clearly, it still usefully influences recent church statements on economic affairs, from the ecumenical report, *Prosperity with a Purpose* (CTBI, 2005), such denominational reports as *Faithful Cities* (Methodist Publishing House and Church House Publishing, 2006), and regional reports like *Faith in England's North West: The Contribution Made by Faith*

Communities to Civil Society and the Region (2003), to the contribution of individuals, including Brown and Ballard's *The Church and Economic Life: A Documentary Study, 1945 to the Present* (Epworth, 2006). Essentially, these represent faith's solidarity (at times critical) with the mainstream of government and economy. Yet resurgent religion is now generating very different faith stances, which both criticize that mainstream *and* increasingly search for radical alternatives to it. Muslim interest-free banking systems clearly illustrate this trend, but so does *Crossing the River of Fire*. It is not therefore a question of whether you agree with it or not. It is rather a matter of recognizing the significance of such faith-based radical critiques and alternatives in this rapidly emerging global and national context, and how you engage in dialogue with them. This is why this is such an unusual and important but increasingly necessary contribution to Christian social thought and practice in what must increasingly be seen as the global locality of Britain.

John Atherton
Manchester Cathedral

Acknowledgements

My first book is dedicated to my wife Jan. I first knew that this strange mix of theology, political economy and history might work when she read the draft of what became the chapters on Mark's Gospel. Having been influential in my becoming a Christian and having known me for 35 years, she has heard my views evolving. As a busy head teacher in a church school, and a Church of England attendee from a child, she was still being challenged by a view of the gospel that was different. I hope this works for other Christians as for Jan.

It is also written with thanks for my grown-up children, Matt and Rachel, who are very definitely not church attending. Yet I hope that for their generation, who will have to live with the consequences – in Iraq and elsewhere – of the Empire of Global Capital, they too will see the politics and economics of the good news in a different way.

This book would probably not have been possible without the assistance of two saints over the last ten years. Chris Beales has supported me constantly despite his own frantic schedule to build the engagement of faith communities, and of Christians and Muslims in particular, working together for a better society. As I write this, he is on his third trip to Afghanistan. John Atherton has given of his time and intelligence whenever asked and has been more than helpful in suggesting ways to communicate my inter-disciplinary wanderings in this polemic. A trip back home to Manchester would never have been complete without a visit to the Cathedral or the Reebok or to see John and Vannie.

The support of a scholar, Michael Northcott, has also been important. Like Chris, Michael and I go back a long way – to Durham University days – and it has been remarkable to see how our lives have differed and yet converged. Making use of the Bothy, usually at different times, to write in the beauty of the Scottish Highlands has been one passion to share, besides the critique of Empire. His book as a theologian on the American Empire has helped me pin down my own theological message. Since Michael's book came out after most of this had been written, our conversations cannot properly be conveyed in the few footnotes where I have acknowledged him.

Thanks too for Natalie and all involved at Epworth for backing this project.

1

9/11, Jesus and Iraq

'The ground opens ... The scene shifts continually from one end of the Empire to the other, from Britain to Palestine, from Morocco to the Caucasus.' The country 'fell victim to disasters which were quite unprecedented, or had not occurred for many centuries. Whole towns were burnt down ... [The Capital City] suffered severely from fires [and from] a reign of terror.'[1] As the result of 'incendiary carpet-bombing, thousands of small fires joined up to become a giant lake of fire covering eight sq miles. The temperature approached 1,000 degrees and a firestorm became a typhoon of 150 miles per hour against which human resistance was powerless and from which there was no escape ... 40 per cent of the city had been destroyed. The fires consumed so much oxygen, that people suffocated. It is thought that 100,000 people were killed in the raid, 100,000 injured and 375,000 left homeless. Fourteen B-29s were lost: under the 5 per cent loss rate that was acceptable.'[2] 'Flames everywhere. It was like nuclear snow. Hard to believe it was New York City.'[3]

The fires of the two global wars of the twentieth century killed at least 80 million people. Today's global capitalism is not responsible for this killing, but the capitalism and imperialism of the world before 1914 was. As the world returns closer to the global economy of 100 years ago, it is vital that we remember our history. For we now have a new global capitalist empire with aggressive designs, determined to remake the world in its own image.

1

In the first paragraph, alongside a brief description of 11th September 2001, are some other descriptions of the fires of war. The 30 years of war in the middle of the twentieth century was supposed to be war to make the world safe for democracy and be war to end war. By such propaganda do empires justify their next invasion. Here was a 30 years' war far worse in terms of killing than that which ended in Europe in 1648, or the 25 million killed that marked the fall of empire in China in 1644. When empires collide or disintegrate the consequences for ordinary people are vile. In Dresden in February 1945 and Tokyo in March, the fires – the 'devil's tinderbox' – marked the beginning of the end for two empires of the twentieth century. The peoples of Germany and Japan have learnt; the present leaders of the USA and the UK have not. 9/11 has marked the beginning of our new century. On its pretext, an elected emperor – a new King George – has declared war on a distant client state. The excuse that 9/11 gave to the present ruling elite in the USA to attack Iraq – and the support given by the UK government – is not a good start to the twenty-first century.

The first story of empire is taken from a Rome that created the context for the New Testament. It describes the effects of the civil war in 69 CE, where Nero's dynasty, which descended from Europe's first emperor – Caesar – was replaced eventually by Vespasian. Around the same time, the first 'Gospel' of the Church was written by someone we now know as 'Mark'. It was written just as Roman troops, led by Vespasian and his son, 'blitzkrieged' their way through Galilee on their way to crush a revolt in Jerusalem. This tells the 'good news' of a crucified agitator from Galilee whom the Roman Empire had executed in its normal fashion 30 years or so earlier. Like one of his heroes, Daniel, this Jesus was put to the test in the fires of the Empire.[4] This book attempts to help us reflect again on this good news in a world dominated by the Empire of Global Capital.

If Jesus lived in twenty-first-century Iraq

Jesus was born, lived and was executed in a Palestine remarkably like present day Iraq. The naked and brutal realities of power politics in the Middle East have changed little since then though the protagonists and labels have changed. Jesus was born when a Roman client king – Herod the Great – was coming to the end of his life and the end of 33 years of a totalitarian regime. The Palestinians of the first century faced constant warfare, sometimes civil war, a denuded land and exceptionally heavy taxation. The similarity between Herod the Great's regime and that of Saddam Hussein's in Iraq is uncanny. Herod was king by the 'grace of Rome'. Herod was supported by the Romans, as was his father and his sons, as key coalition allies against both the Egyptians to the south and the Parthians[5] to the east – sometimes this was even more important in the midst of Roman civil wars.[6] Herod came out of the local nobilities, like the older Hasmonean regime in Jerusalem,[7] that had looked to the Romans to supplement their own power against rebellious peasantry and other enemies (in this case Seleucid Syria).[8]

Herod had first shown his mettle in this regard by putting down bandits in Galilee, 30 years before Jesus' birth. Landlessness, usually caused by war and debt, encouraged a form of social banditry to thrive in the border regions. Antipater, Herod the Great's father, had struggled with a powerful bandit leader named Hezekiah who operated on the borders between Galilee and Syria. In 40 BCE, after being named king by the Romans, Herod began a three-year campaign, took the ancient fortress of Sepphoris, killed Hezekiah, and extracted a 'huge' 100-talent tax from Galilee for Rome. Herod then conquered Jerusalem with two Roman legions in support and killed the king, Antigonus, the Parthians had helped place on the throne. Antigonus, another king of the Jews, was bound to a cross and flogged before his execution. Herod murdered his own family to stay in power

– at least three sons, a wife, her mother, and two kingly Hasmonean high priests (his wife's grandfather and son). There is no historical record outside of Matthew's Gospel of the massacre of young boys in Bethlehem (2.16–17), but it is perfectly consistent with his known behaviour. Herod often had to use mercenaries – Thracians, Germans and Gauls – to do his dirty work.[9] Herod's regime was established and sustained by a police state that spied on and murdered its own citizens. These spies were still around for Jesus in Jerusalem as Luke (20.20) reports.

Until 1991 the USA's rulers used Saddam Hussein as their favoured client to resist the threat of the Iranian (Parthian) revolution; hence their support for Iraq during the wars against Iran. Hussein's assumption of power, like Herod's, was marked by a continual bloodbath against his opponents. Hussein also put down 'terrorist' movements, which in 1991 had been encouraged, like the Taliban in Afghanistan, by the first George Bush regime just after the Gulf War. The savage slaughter in the Shia and Kurdish revolts was part of a ruthless pattern. The use of chemical weapons against the Kurds earlier in the 1980s, which Blair so often cites as the moral reason for war, gained no criticism from him at the time. Much to the disapproval of Dick Cheney and Donald Rumsfeld, the George I regime decided to leave Hussein in power and then chose to look the other way as aircraft and Scud missiles were used against Kirkuk. Saddam was allowed to remain in power, not because of UN rules about overthrowing sovereign states, but because they preferred the 'Saddam we know' to the opposition they couldn't be sure of controlling.[10]

Imperial rule and first-century Palestine

As in today's Iraq, Jesus grew up in a Galilee where social rebellion was rife. The Galileans had become the 'first of Herod's later subjects to become acquainted with the strong arm tactics of their future king'. Hengel concludes that there was a 'deep longing for freedom in Galilee'.[11] Proud of their history, yet encircled on all sides, the Galileans of Jesus' time would have understood the fight of the Kurds and the Shia for self-rule in Iraq; they would have understood the Palestinian plight of today all too well. Herod's links with Rome were well known then – four of his sons were brought up in Rome and another one lived there. In Galilee, therefore, it was more than just a longing for freedom: there was an intimate connection between anti-Roman and anti-Herod beliefs; just as today anti-American and popular sentiments can easily get conflated.[12]

Herod must have suspected that Caesar would be unlikely to trust Palestine to one ruler. On his death in 4 BCE, all the claimants were summoned to Rome. Rather as the various factions of the Iraqi National Congress looked for US support, or as Iraq was divided into its three former Ottoman provinces by the 'no fly zones', the key was that the decision to split Herod's kingdom, just before Jesus was born, was made in Rome and by Rome.[13]

'Pax Romana' was given a 'divine' sanction by the Empire, just as Bush II held his morning prayer meetings in the White House, or as the Lutheran Church and the Church of England rushed to give God's support to the imperial fight for king and country in 1914. Yet, the 'Pax Americana' like its Roman predecessor has been based on permanent war while claiming to stand for peace.[14] The Iraq war, like the Roman wars, was fought for Empire. It was fought to make sure that the Empire will be in control in places it defines as strategic. Put in the terms of the first century, Saddam Hussein was a totally corrupt client king who owed his original power to Empire. Even without today's political economy of oil, it will not do for client kings to bite the hand that feeds them. They must be put back in their place; otherwise, the whole system will not operate properly. One would expect no less than a war on Iraq from those that command the global American Empire.

The Austrian political economist Joseph Schumpeter, writing

in 1919 on *Imperialism and Social Classes* described Rome, in the years of her imperial expansion:

> There was no corner of the known world where some interest was not alleged to be in danger or under actual attack. If the interests were not Roman, they were those of Rome's allies; and if Rome had no allies, then allies would be invented ... The fight was always invested with an aura of legality ... The whole world was pervaded with a host of enemies and it was manifestly Rome's duty to guard against their indubitably aggressive designs.[15]

Wengst sums it up well at the beginning of his book *Pax Romana and the Peace of Jesus Christ*: 'a disturber of the peace was done away with by legal means, by the power responsible for peace. It follows from this that not only was Jesus' understanding of peace different, but above all that his activity cannot have conformed to the Pax Romana but must have been contrary to it.'[16]

The peace and security of empire

For the Roman Empire, Caesar, like the Pharaohs before him, was divine. He had brought peace to the (Roman) world, after the civil wars that had brought him to power. After the Battle of Actium and generations of permanent war in the Roman Empire, Caesar was proclaimed 'Saviour'.[17] Caesar was also made Lord, Kyrios and Emperor, to whom every minor king had to bow. Unfortunately, because we have reduced the gospel message to one of 'religious' salvation, these titles, which we proclaim about Jesus in Church, have quite lost their real meaning in today's Empire for most conventional Christians. In the New Testament context, however, Jesus' titles in the Roman world did not just make a religious claim, but a politically alternative claim. To proclaim Jesus as Saviour and Lord was in today's terms a political act: to stand against Empire. The Church has too often conveniently forgotten that the Gospel writers deliberately perverted the language of the Roman Empire to make imperial claims for Jesus. We are likewise so used to making imperial claims for Jesus today that we can be unaware of their political significance.[18]

The conventional exegesis of the New Testament has been driven more by Paul's supposed views in Romans 13; obedience to the necessary power of government has thereby been justified ever since. This is a propaganda view of Paul. A group of American Christians, worried about the USA's role in the Gulf War in 1991 and the deaths of so many innocents in Iraq found that, for many in the Church, any critique of the War had foundered on the later distortion of Paul's beliefs. Neil Elliott argues that the Establishment churches have distorted Paul into the voice of the 'sanctified status quo' in a way that Paul himself would have not recognized. To proclaim a crucified carpenter from an obscure province, executed like a slave, as being greater than Caesar, Paul knew to be a dangerous 'folly'. See the beginning of Paul's first letter to Corinth for one example (1 Cor. 1.18–25). Elliott goes on to say that Paul's theology can be liberated from the straitjacket into which so many theologians have put him. Elliott's discussion of the theology of empire in his commentary on Paul's first letter to the Thessalonians, written before the second Iraq war, is particularly apt. For Paul takes the slogans at the heart of Caesar's propaganda 'Peace and Security' and turns them on their head (1 Thess. 5.3). As Negri and Hardt have put it for today's empire in 2000: 'Although the practice of Empire is continually bathed in blood, the concept of Empire is always dedicated to peace.'[19] Elliott argues that the language of Thessalonians is 'politically inflammatory': a 'bitter frontal attack' that 'tears away' the 'pretensions of imperial propaganda'. The rule of God is deliberately counterpoised against the rule of Caesar. Here there is 'an attack on the spiritual core of Empire'. The 'golden age' of God's favour on Augustan rule is not at hand. While Paul is so supposedly supportive of governments and of 'honouring Caesar', it is worth remembering that the Roman Empire repeatedly threw him into prison and probably killed him. For Paul, the Pax Romana is shown to be a fraud, and it kills the true bringers of peace and justice. 'The justice of God is not what the Empire calls justice.'[20] As we look at the case for global economic justice in the next chapters, we should bear this in mind. The warning of the last book of the Bible – Revelation – is also clear: those who compromise with the hubris of empire will be destroyed by it in the end. No more than the Roman Empire, will the age of Bush and Blair and its fight against 'global terrorism' bring peace and security. Today's Global Capitalist Empire will not bring peace or prosperity for all.

Iraq: the Latin American dependency model is globalized

Many have seen through the propaganda about the threat of Saddam and the 'moral' case for his removal. But is a deeper political and economic reality driving this rationale for the US and British elites? Can we start to understand this historically, economically and theologically? Now we know that Iraq did not have weapons of mass destruction and so posed no real threat to the USA or UK. Should we just say that the US 'neoconservatives' were determined to use 9/11 to make Saddam an example and rebuild Iraq as part of their project for the new American dominated twenty-first century? Or should we just say that Tony Blair supported George Bush after 9/11 as part of traditional British foreign policy to keep the special relationship and to stop the USA acting unilaterally? Or should we just say that ideologically our rulers needed 'a war on terror' to replace the war on communism? If the 1990s' exceptional growth was to be replaced by a slower global economy, a new repressive era might be required in the USA and elsewhere: how better than to dress it up as the war on terror?

The role of Iraq is to be the Middle Eastern test case of lessons learned in Latin America – indeed first learnt in the colonial and slave subjugations of the USA itself. As Negri points out, as early as 1823 the Monroe Doctrine was intended to establish the 'right' to US hegemony over the Americas, as colonial Latin America was breaking free from Spanish direct rule. The lesson of nineteenth-century Latin America was of its subjugation to both British economic power and US political power despite the appearance of independent nationalist regimes. Now the same tricks are to be applied to the Middle East. For the 'neoconservatives', Iraq is to become the new US power base for the spread of global capital to the area. Understood in this geo-economic, as well as political sense, the co-option of British imperialism in this process makes perfect sense for both sides. The corporations that dominate the British international presence come from this colonial and imperial inheritance: as was BP to Iran, Shell to Indonesia and HSBC to China. Now the British collude with US power to take their junior place. This is about far more than throwing a few goodies the way of Cheney and Bush cronies. This is not a conservative agenda. It is aggressively imperialist.

So the USA's power elite hope for Iraq will be to establish, as in Latin America, the semblance of an independent state. This provides the framework – under some cobbled together parliament – for global capital eventually to expand its hegemony in the Middle East. A few body bags from the US working classes and more deaths of Iraqis is a relatively small price for the US power elite to pay for this, as long as they can continue to win the propaganda game. In the long run, the US power brokers know that neither Israel nor Saudi Arabia provide suitable long-term bases from which to subjugate the Middle East for global capital. One is too clearly based on a murderous oppression of the Palestinians; the other is too limited as a dictatorial monarchy to have even the semblance of winning its own people, never mind the war for the minds of the Middle East. Iraq is a good opening gambit in the new chess game in the Middle East; not only does it keep the Iranians in check, but it also provides a southern base (note US support from the new regimes in Georgia and the Ukraine) for stripping away the old Soviet Caucasus from its allegiance to whatever remains of mother Russia. Middle Eastern oil and Caucasian oil and gas (don't forget Kazakhstan and Azerbaijan) smooth the wheels of the new imperial capitalism.

Empire and imperialism

Negri and Hardt begin their book on empire with the words: 'Empire is materialising before our very eyes'. Published in 2000, and written at least three years before the war in Iraq, what was becoming clearly evident to them has become evident to a lot more people since 2003. This is not a prelude to an anti-American rant, although US unilateralism is important. For this new Empire is not just an American hegemony, but an implicit US elite tutelage on behalf of global capital. Since 1989, and with support from nearly all the ruling elites of the world, the Global Capital Empire is the new world hegemony. From the perspective of empire, in Rome and under today's capitalism: 'this is the way things will always be and the way they were always meant to be'. For Negri, this is not an empire limited by territory. Therefore, empire is different from imperialism. Imperialism is still based on territory – the extension of the soverignty of the nation state beyond its own boundaries. 'Empire establishes no centre of power and does not rely on fixed boundaries.'[21]

Marx did not use the term imperialism. It is a term made famous by Lenin in his analysis of the economics of global capitalism between 1915 and 1917.[22] So, as we shall see in Chapter 3, Lenin like Solzhenitsyn, was responding to the cataclysm of 1914. It was not a 'chasm' that was impossible to forecast; many in the socialist movement had seen it by 1907 at the latest. In Chapter 3 we look especially at the English and German roads to 1914, but there was more or less an open competition between territorial imperialisms – adding on the Austrian, Russian, Serbian and Turkish; the latter taking the British into Iraq in 1917. The USA, in joining the Great War, also shows the sign of things to come: here imperialism is advanced under the apparent cause of anti-imperialism. Today we have competing nation states more easily subsumed within the Empire of Capital.

The link between Marx and Lenin was the work first of a British Liberal, Hobson, and of an Austrian, Hilferding. Hobson was much influenced by the experience of the Boer War of 1899–1902 and of the US imperial conquest of the Philippines in the Spanish–US war of 1898. Hilferding could already see that Latin America was functioning as a 'virtual colony'. The Monroe Doctrine already functioned then as a version of imperial competition: as the US elite positioned itself against the informal British economic dominance of the Americas.[23] As Curtis shows, since the interregnum of 1918–45, the Monroe Doctrine has been gradually redefined as the superpower learnt to spread its wings, using both IMF and World Bank for this purpose. Informality – but nonetheless empire – rules.[24]

Capital and political economy

Conceptually, Marx had seen that the formal empire of flags and political authority mattered less even in the mid nineteenth century than the rise of capitalism to be the dominant global mode of production. This is ever more true in the twenty-first century. In the nineteenth century, the formal expansion of competing imperialisms predominated over the informal domination of capital. The key analytical tool of political economy in this book is therefore to understand the development of capital; for it sees today's global capital in the classic sense as a complex of social relationships. Today's global capitalism is a triumph not just of ideology, but also of capitalist economic and social relations. It is the job of today's Empire to support and expand these relationships globally. This work then is in what some may see as the old-fashioned classical tradition of political economy. Although developed by Adam Smith, in the twentieth century it has largely been the discipline of Marxists. This stems from a belief that the interdisciplinary analysis of the structures of society and the integration of the political with the economic is an indispensable basis for understanding the structures of global injustice and poverty. It also stems from a profound dissatisfaction with the use of much conventional economics as a propaganda tool to justify the capitalist system and/or the neo-liberal truisms that pass for political and economic analysis both in academia and even more in the popular media.

This book's argument then is that the war in Iraq should be seen as part and parcel of an expanding Global Capitalist Empire dominated by the USA, with British and other corporations in a vital supporting role. It is not purely a new American Empire. The new Empire of Capital embraces Argentina and Brazil, Abramovich and Putin in Russia, the European Union and even 'Communist' China. The Africa Commission is a good expression of this global mentality whereby, it is hoped, Africa will be more efficiently managed and absorbed. In the long run, it is profit and accumulation that rule in this empire. For Negri, capital itself has become an independent power.[25] This is an empire where the mark of the beast is on all: 'who can control the beast and who can fight against him' (Rev. 13.4). It is this empire which we can oppose; not globalization itself. It is this empire that stands in the way of global justice and is happy to fight poverty with a sword.

Even though I oppose global capitalism, it is the highest form of world development we have yet achieved. More people today live longer, are better fed, are better educated and have better health. Yet the poor in our society are more marginal than ever, so are the poor worldwide. The key is to transcend a capitalism

12

that shows a capacity to generate more wealth than ever before, yet also generates bigger inequalities both within and between societies. Increasing monopoly power and increasing inequality has always been a function of capitalism – that's why we need to transcend it. It is the power of global capitalism – not globalization – with which ordinary people must grapple. In the Christian critiques of global injustice, there has never been a sustained theological, theoretical and historical critique of capitalism itself. Much less has an alternative been proposed (other than say the abolition of debt or 'fairer' trade), particularly any alternative that might use that discredited word 'socialism'. The glimpses of a libertarian socialism briefly outlined in the last chapter do not reject the material benefits capitalism has gained for some of us, but works for its transcendence.[26]

Until This First

In 1862, John Ruskin published a critique of the prevailing conventional economics of his day, which he called *Unto This Last*. I was much tempted to call this piece Until This First.[27] For my first book has had a long gestation. It is a work of synthesis, which ideally should have come after at least three other major works. To be sufficiently scholarly, it should have come after: a historical and theoretical critique of the genesis and growth of global capitalism; a justification from Genesis to Revelation of the biblical critique of empire and an assessment of today's theological critiques both of empire and capitalism; and a detailed historical account of the conventional economics which today ideologically justifies capital's triumph. I would also have liked to include the policy implications of a Christian socialism, based on an anarchist and libertarian tradition stemming from Blake and Morris, which are only hinted at in the short last chapter. This is a much shorter and deliberately polemical account full of not totally proven sweeping assertions.

13

Five years after Ruskin, Karl Marx's critique in *Das Capital* was published in German to what was a resounding silence from the generation that called themselves political economists. What, after all, would an obscure German Hegelian philosopher know about economics? Ruskin, on the other hand, whose critique was more moral and cultural than Marx's emphasis on class and expropriation, was pilloried for his efforts. In the first 30 years in Britain, it was Ruskin more than Marx who became part of one major strand of the ethical critique of capitalism. He influenced William Morris, who features so largely in this work, and was of great importance to the formative reading of the Labour movement over the next 50 years. This book is a Communist Manifesto written 20 years before Das Capital is ready.[28] My friends', family's and publisher's judgement, is that this tract for the times demands publication now.

Theology, apocalypse and the gospel

The book attempts to address the political economy and theology of understanding today's empire from a British context. As a political economist who is also a Christian, to understand the historical significance of global capitalism, which I explore in Part 1 of this short work, has of necessity required me to do theology in Part 2. This theology must be seen in the context of a historical and dialectical political economy. 'Apocalyptic' here is not about dramatic end-of-the-world battles, but about unveiling, which is the translation of the Greek word *apokalupto*. It derives from the verb *kalupto* – covered or veiled. *Apokalupto* means to uncover, or unveil the way things are typically held to be. The aim of the theologian and the political economist is to unveil. It is about seeing behind the scenes.[29] As we have learnt over the Iraq War, it is about seeing through the propaganda to the real meanings and messages lying behind the spin of empire. This is as true of economics as it is of religion.[30]

This theology then is not just a timeless spiritual message, set by accident originally in the first century, but a rooted theological reflection on our history, on today's political economy and our experience of God. If we wish to develop a concern for justice in our analysis of the global political economy, we need to show that it is not incidental to our theology, but at its heart. We have taken our theology out into the world of economics and politics; how much does our theology change in the process? We still tend to bring fixed notions, if only the economic world would listen. What we have not done is reformulate our theology. We have to reformulate – in an enlarged narrative – our understanding of the gospel itself.[31] We do not just need a new political economy that leaves our theology and the Church untouched. So, truly understanding a Christian political economy transforms utterly what we mean by the gospel. What is attempted here is to look at this reformulation through a theological, historical and political reading of Mark's Gospel.

It has been good to see the active opposition of many in the Church to the Iraq war. For some Christians, as with the campaigns for global debt relief, trade justice and Make Poverty History, the unveiling of the war in Iraq has led to an increasing radicalization.

The implications of US imperialism have been profound for the potential development of Latin America. The role of the Church in Latin and Central America in opposing poverty, dependency and the tyranny of capital has led it into a clash with oligarchies and empire, which, at times, has been nothing short of murderous. Crossing the River has truly been a matter of surviving the fire for many in Latin America.

The aim of this book is to help Christians go back to the radical theological roots of the biblical stories against empire. It is the power of global capitalism – not globalization – with which we as Christians must grapple if we wish to preach the gospel in the 'contemporary' world. It is global capitalism that rules in an empire that now makes one marginalized just to be a 'liberal' in the USA or a 'socialist' or anti-capitalist anywhere. The Iraq War tells us a great deal about the Global Capitalist Empire. Our own 'Christian' 'Socialist' leader has allowed the ruling party of New Labour in the UK to be incorporated in a project of US hegemony: the occupation of Iraq under the guise of liberation. The spin that took Britain to war also tells us a great deal about the New Labour project and its active accommodation to and incorporation within global capitalism. Since Iraq, New Labour's subservience to the American and Global Capitalist Empire is clearer. Its subtext – for a Christian Socialist growing up with the disillusion of the 1960s and the defeats of the 1980s – is to find space and practical policies for speaking about socialism again. Three or four terms of being in power is worse than nothing if it sets back the cause of socialism for another generation or more.

A Labour Party bound and gagged?

When William Morris analysed the British ruling elite in 1877, he attempted to warn the 50-year-old socialist movement in Britain that the elite 'would deliver you bound hand and foot forever to irresponsible Capital'. Morris also warned of the British ruling class who 'ruined India, starved and gagged Ireland and tortured Egypt'.[32] More than 100 years later, it is the tragedy of the British socialist movement that I write this piece not to warn for the future but in despair over the present where a Labour government has followed in this imperial tradition. Morris's worst fears over state socialism and over British imperialism have been realized in the successful taking of power by the New Labour project, for most of the mainstream Labour movement has been bound and handed over to global capital.

The real political economy of neo-liberalism is not about the efficient running of the 'market' economy, as it is usually presented. It is about who runs the global economy and in whose interests. The Labour Party which was created in part to fight the mammon of global capital has not only become its servant, but has even celebrated its own mental and physical subordination. Nowhere is this clearer than in Blair's subordination to Bush in the interest of being the junior partner in the USA's present global hegemony.

Marx writing on the British Empire in India, 150 years earlier in 1853, put his finger on what Iraq in 2003 shows us: 'The profound hypocrisy and inherent barbarism of bourgeois civilization lies unveiled before our eyes, turning from its home, where it assumes respectable forms, to the colonies where it goes naked.'[33] The abuse of power by the ruling elite in the USA, in collusion with the New Labour regime in the UK, has been revealed in Iraq in all its assertive nakedness.

To understand the plight we are in, we need to pin this down in the hard history and dirty politics of rich and poor. For we live in a system geared to profit, which has dispossessed most people of the earth from their common treasury and made them dependent on selling their labour for much of their waking time to new masters – geared to empire, war and finance. We need to understand these masters who have bound us to global capital, and what drives the society they run. For of course, these new masters will pretend, with all their honeyed words, that they are our servants.[34] When we are frequently told at the beginning of Blair's sentences to 'look' and 'I say unto you' with tones of religious conviction, or when George Bush II tell us that his light of America is the light of freedom shining in the darkness, we should indeed look, hear what is said and consider their deeds. If ever there was a case for darkness masquerading as the light; here it is.

Today's revived Christian Socialist Movement has been trapped too by the state and by the politics of New Labour. For far too much of the last ten years, the Christian Socialist Movement has been a propaganda tool to glorify the 'successful' politics of three terms in office or as a gravy train for aspiring MPs. Christian socialists need to free themselves from this ultimately destructive embrace and look for alliances with the wider socialist movement inside and outside of the Labour Party. In 1893, Keir Hardie helped found the Independent Labour Party to help break Gladstone's embrace; by 1914, he had seen that the Labour Party had become a part of the Establishment. We have returned to the issues that Morris confronted in the early 1880s, with the bitter experiences of the last 125 years.

Crossing the river of fire

In 1881, in a lecture on the prospects for architecture, William Morris spoke of a 'river of fire' that will be hard to swim across. His own conversion from Gladstonian liberalism and from English romanticism to the British socialist movement of the 1880s and especially to a Marx-inspired revolutionary socialism was taking place at the same time. It was addressed especially to his own friends who he felt were standing on the brink of the river in their critique of Victorian industrialism and urbanization – specifically Matthew Arnold, Thomas Carlyle, William Ruskin and George Rossetti. For Morris, crossing the river of fire was a picture of the hard path of renouncing his class and moving over – given the huge division in Victorian society – to the side of the working classes. He saw the British Empire as a tyranny that only leads to 'commercial war'.

I have borrowed Morris's imagery and given it my own twist. First, Morris has not been given sufficient credit for linking his moral and aesthetic critique with a materially based analysis of political economy, much influenced by Marx. This work too attempts to link theological ethics and political economy. Second, this tradition goes all the way back to a liberating theological protest tradition, linked to both Old and New Testament, from Amos and Daniel, to Mark, Paul and John the Revelator. Third, because much of the Christian and other anti-globalization analysis of the last decade in Britain has been akin to Ruskin – a moral critique that lacks a detailed understanding of the real workings of the global capitalist empire – their analyses of the debt and trade justice issues are naive and policy proposals inadequate. It is only what Morris called a gospel of discontent; lacking a fuller gospel that better understands today's political economy. Despite its potential and real radicalizing impact, it has got to the brink but stopped well short of the economic and theological critique of global capitalism that is required. This means it falls short of understanding the extent of the powers we face; it lacks in short a theology of the cross and the resurrection.

The river of fire idea emerged when I was writing a conclusion to my commentary on Mark's Gospel. For it struck home that Marx had come to a critique of capital via an earlier critique of philosophy and theology. Apart from Hegel, one of his early inspirations was Feuerbach – the fiery brook. Marx attempted to earth his praxis into a critique of political economy. Marx himself had to cross over his own Feuerbach to reach a critique of capital. Many campaigning Christians may today have a similar river of fire to cross, for we too need a critique of theology and a critique of political economy.

September 11 and the Iraq War have unveiled that the Global Capitalist Empire often means war; as it did in 1914 and again in 1931. Millions of people in the twentieth century died from war – literally hundreds of thousands in the fires of Dresden and Tokyo – because of the pursuit of empire. The true gospel is about the real suffering caused by imperial power; it is also about the resurrection hope for what Morris called the 'days to come beyond'.[35]

Part 1

Global Capital and Political Economy

2

A Political Economy of Development:
The Americas

From China and Rome to European feudalism

Capitalism has had a long prehistory. Why did it develop in Britain first and then in Western Europe and North America rather than anywhere else? It is certainly not because Europe and North America have the oldest history of human development and therefore the longest time to build up an acceleration to 'take off'.[1] Nor was it because of European inventiveness; because the Chinese had made many of the same technical advances almost 500 years before. Nor should capitalism be confused with industrialization or with urbanization: China had both and the ancients the latter. Rome, in Jesus' time, had a population of maybe one million while other Roman Asian cities (like Ephesus) were larger than classical Athens (which had around 250,000). This compares with the much smaller towns of medieval Europe, where even major trading centres like Venice and Milan were no larger than 40,000 to 50,000. In China, the discovery of rice variants that permitted two crops a year from well-irrigated land led to intensive growth and a higher population; China developed a flourishing urban culture and highly advanced technology much earlier than in Europe. The first paper money was issued in 650 CE, 1,000 years before Europe. As early as the tenth century, the T'ang capital was said to have two million inhabitants. Such development encouraged textile and iron production. Industrialization under the Sung dynasty in the twelfth century meant that China was already producing as much iron as Europe at the start of the eighteenth century.[2] Only with the growth of London in the seventeenth century did the European cities begin their climb to match the scale of the Chinese. Most of the arguments for the beneficial wealth effects of today's global capitalism stem from the relative assessments of the increase for the average Chinese (and to a lesser extent, the average Indian). Ironically, political control in the most un-democratic large state in the world, with its own weapons of mass destruction, is still vested in the 'Communist' Party's modern variant on the oriental mandate from heaven. The US military – for one – is well aware of this demography.[3]

The thesis here is that the genesis of capitalism requires a his-torical analysis of the change in social relationships. Capitalism developed in Western Europe as a result of a peculiar Western European feudalism. As Perry Anderson shows, this in turn was itself a synthesis of the slave mode of production in classi-cal Rome and Greece, with the communal mode of production brought by the Germanic invaders. This was not replicated in Eastern Europe, which had not experienced the slave mode of production internally at this point, but exported 'Slav(e)s' to the more developed centres in what would be called today's Middle East.[4] The older civilizations of the East on the Eurasian land-mass had other forms of rule – an Oriental despotism, if you will – that precluded Western style feudalism, with the important ex-ception of Japan.[5] Much of the neo-liberal but also the 'Christian' analysis within the Jubilee and trade justice movements often misses or underestimates the vital importance of this long-term historical dimension. Consequently, the critics of debt and advo-cates of fair trade have no complementary theoretical analysis of capitalism, offering alternatives that are not thought through or are simple-minded appeals to the world leaders who sit astride the present Global Capitalist Empire.[6]

The global economy and capitalist exchange

In the nineteenth and twentieth centuries, the West liked to think of itself as 'advanced' while the east and south were backward. For most of the world's history, the reverse was the case. To the ancient world, barbarians inhabited the forests of Northern Europe. To the great ancient civilizations, Northern Europe was either an irrelevance or an earlier supplier of metals or slaves. In the classical period within the Roman Empire, for example, the eastern half of the Empire had the more developed economy, numerous cities and more wealth.[7] For most of history until the victories of colonialism and then European industrialization, produce flowed mainly from east to west. Early colonial expansion, of course, was partly driven by the Western desire to find better routes for this trade. The West was in deficit in its balance of payments to India until the eighteenth century[8] and until the mid nineteenth with China.[9] In much of the early spread of capitalism to the rest of the world, primitive forms of accumulation – like the lust for gold in Latin America or the taking of slaves from Africa – aided the accumulation of capital in Europe and in North America. So, the global economy has been around a long time, the question is whether the sheer quantity of integration in the early twenty-first century makes for a qualitative difference.

Noam Chomsky argues that what he calls the present 'global system' and the 'emerging international economic order' is the result of the last 500 years of history – he starts with Columbus arriving in America in 1492. Most importantly, 'gaining an understanding of what these last 500 years has meant is not simply a matter of becoming aware of history, it is a question of becoming aware of current processes'.[10] It is important to realize when speaking both of the history and of today's global capitalist economy that the system as a whole includes a complex relationship between capitalist, semi-capitalist and pre-capitalist relations of production. Since roughly 1500, what we could call mercantile capitalist relations of exchange have usually linked them.[11] The distinction between capitalist internal relationships and a capitalist world market is important for two reasons. Capitalist relations of production have not become universal until much more recently. First, it more fully explains what is going on in today's 'South', where capitalism is becoming more firmly established. The history of the last 20 years has been to see these internal capitalist relations more fully developed, particularly within Asia and Latin America; a process that is ongoing. Second, it shows that although Africa or Latin America could blame their problems for the ways in which they have been incorporated into the world market, it may only be of late that capitalism – that is capitalist relations of production – has ruled internally, if at all.

To understand global capitalism is not only to analyse the dynamics of the system – for which globalization is a jargon word – but also to understand that it is made up of a series of capitalisms, each with its own history and political story to tell. The capitalist world economy has a driving force that stands apart from any particular expression of it. That driving force is profit and the accumulation of capital. The capitalist system is not just the sum of the parts, but it can only be made sense of in light of the development of the parts.

Marx and global capitalism: a generational difference?

I was first introduced to Marx in late 1971, the same year in which I became a Christian and David Harvey began his own capital reading group in Baltimore. Harvey begins the discussion of 'globalization' in *Spaces of Hope* by pointing to the difference a later generation brings to a reading of Marx. Then many radicals coming out of the protests of the late 1960s came to Marx with a great enthusiasm. In the USA, this was driven by civil rights and Vietnam protests; in Western Europe, more by disillusion in the social democratic models of the West. After the bloody suppression of the Hungarian uprising in 1956, and of the Prague Spring of 1968, there was a continuing exodus from Communist Party orthodoxy. After 1989, Marxism in theory and practice has appeared to the academic Establishment in politics and economics to be in terminal decline. The theologian, Timothy Gorringe, writing in 1993, had to apologize for having Marx as a 'dialogue partner' in his work *Capital and the Kingdom* on economics and ethics. Harvey goes on to point out that in the 1970s it was harder to get an abstract theoretical work like *Das Capital* to speak to many of the issues the 'new left' US radicals faced. Harvey suggests that a reading of Lenin was required on imperialism, of Gramsci for the understanding of political power and hegemony, of Miliband or Poulantzas for theories of the state and the development of welfare, of the Frankfurt school (like Marcuse) for an understanding of bureaucracy and ideological legitimacy; never mind environmental issues increasingly coming to the fore. Such a 'host of mediations' required an 'act of faith' to get from *Capital* to the present day.[12]

Marx, of course, wrote through a period of unfettered capitalism; much more akin to our times again since 1989. Harvey emphasizes that today the *Capital* text 'teems with ideas' for our current problems. It reads as a 'devastating critique of neoliberalism run riot'. The paradox thereby stands out. In academia, in the late 1960s and 1970s, Marx was sought after, but harder to make directly relevant intellectually. Now *Capital* is so 'pertinent' yet, 'scarcely anyone cares to consider it'. The refuge for the increasingly geriatric 'new' left has been in cultural and philosophical studies, where the historical grounding of Marx in political economy can be neglected. In an academia where literature, postmodernist philosophy and cultural studies are taught as a major way into Marxism, modern students are not presented with the intellectual equipment to 'deconstruct' political economy's dominant principles. So, neo-classicalism and neoliberalism rule in the economics faculty, which is broadly left to go its own way. Stiglitz's and Sen's critique, heralded by Christian Aid, Ann Pettifor and John Atherton,[13] lags behind that of Hobson, a liberal social reformer whose more thorough critique of imperialism was published in 1902.[14]

Globalization was long ago subject to a commentary by Marx and Engels in the *Communist Manifesto*. Like Chomsky, they too start with 'the discovery of America, the rounding of the Cape ... the East Indian and Chinese markets ... trade with the colonies, the increase in the means of exchange and in commodities generally gave to commerce, to navigation, to industry, an impulse never before known'. Written in 1848, the revolutionary consequences of this new capitalism are summarized with an eloquence not surpassed by globalization analysts 150 years later. Marx largely (but not entirely) focused on the transition from feudalism to capitalism in Europe and especially in the most advanced capitalist nation – and leading imperial nation – of their time: Britain.

The capitalist revolution

I challenge anyone to find a better description of the global political economy at the beginning of the twenty-first century:

> Constant revolutionizing of production, uninterrupted disturbance of social conditions, everlasting uncertainty and agitation ... The need of a constantly expanding market for its products chases [capital] ... over the whole surface of the globe. It must nestle everywhere, settle everywhere, establish connections everywhere. [Capitalism] has through its exploitation of the world market given a cosmopolitan character to production and consumption in every country ... All old established national industries have been destroyed or are daily being destroyed. They are dislodged by new industries, whose introduction becomes a life and death question for all civilized

nations, by industries that no longer work up indigenous raw material ... In place of the old wants ... we find new wants ... The cheap prices of its commodities are the heavy artillery with which it batters down all Chinese walls. ... It creates a world after its own image.[15]

Marx is no economic determinist here. He is well aware of the importance of logos as well as prices, of image and propaganda as well as raw materials, production and new industries. If Marx's breadth of vision was filled out by Weber's emphasis on the psychological/religious 'spirit' of capitalism, it was not because Marx and Engels were unaware of other factors but placed a different emphasis on the role of the economic in their dialectical understanding; as indeed does Heslam, a Christian writer.[16]

Marx went on to publish the first volume of *Das Capital* in 1867. He built upon the ideas of the earlier – largely British – classical economists, showing that the use of surplus labour (above that required for subsistence) was the crucial determinant of economic development and the shape of politics and ideology. His point was that under capitalism, the socially produced surplus is controlled by the minority who own capital. So the key questions in this part of our analysis will be: how is the surplus product of any given society produced? Who controls it? And what do they do with it once they've got it? He argued that capitalist relations of production are different from those of any other forms (or modes) of production, because the extraction of the surplus is hidden. If you were a serf working on the lord's land, or paying rent directly in kind (or increasingly in later years in England after 1350, in cash), the extra coercion required to extract the surplus was plain, even if it was nominally supported by legal and political structures. With other forms of 'primitive accumulation' – warfare, raiding and plunder – the surplus extraction is obvious, whether it be supported 'legally' by governments (as in the Crusades) or not. In capitalism, on the other hand, there appears to be a free exchange. The early indigenous growth of the capitalist mode of production in Western Europe is a story of the surplus being increasingly economic in form as serfs, peasants or artisans were stripped of their land or their other means of production – often violently. Capitalism, as defined here, is not a spirit of enterprise, or production for the market (which could include peasants or slaves), nor a set of production techniques. It corresponds to a set of social relationships. Crucially, it is dependent on the major (but not the only) productive activity in society being on the basis of a wage contract. Employees sell their labour and cannot long survive without doing so. This is why, ultimately, the exchange is not free: it is forced, but hidden and unequal – for those without capital are much weaker than those with it.

Colonialism and native peoples: the world we have lost

Marx drafted a long-term work plan, which had further books on foreign trade, the world market, the crises of capitalism and the state. In Chapters 2, 3 and 4, I shall fill in some of these gaps – not in a theoretical way but with some historical analysis of global trade developments since 1500, the struggle over British-inspired free trade after 1846, the development of protectionism from the 1870s particularly and the deflationary agricultural and the general crisis of the 1920s and 1930s. This runs alongside an updated view of empire, influenced by Negri and Hardt, who see the function of the US state on behalf, not only of US capital, but also of global capital in general.

Harvey argues that Marx placed colonialism as his last chapter in *Capital* Volume 1 for a reason.[17] For it was in the colonies that any (neo-classical or neo-liberal) theory that capital was the reward for abstinence, entrepreneurship or harder work was shown in fact to be a propaganda myth. The work of primitive accumulation was instead largely driven by the sword: conquest and exploitation. The 'pretty fancy' of a Robinson Crusoe world, so beloved of neo-classical economics, was 'torn asunder' by the actual colonial experience of expropriation. Capital comes into the world 'dripping from head to foot, from every pore, with blood and dirt'.[18] Marx's analysis of British colonialism in Ireland, of empire in India and of the breaking down of the Chinese walls with the arguments of 'free trade' led him to these conclusions.

Much recent Christian analysis has side-stepped these issues and has instead looked to analyse the 'unequal exchange' in trade; this can of course occur but does so in the contexts of historical, sociological, economic and political power, which are frequently not analysed in enough depth. At another level, Ulrich Duchrow and Franz Hinkelammmert's recent critique of the 'global tyranny' of capital lays great stress on the function of private property. This stresses, alongside an analysis of Latin America in particular, the struggles of indigenous communities to hold on to their ways of life against the increasing encroachment on 'non-capitalist' lands and property. They cite the Zapatistas' revolt in Chiapas, where an indigenous people bring a pre-capitalist experience, politics and mentality to the pressures upon them. For the authors, it seems that it is capital's attitude to property that lies at the core of their different ideology. But it is precisely because, for example, the people of Chiapas have a different non-capitalist mentality that their attitudes to property are potentially so different. When the colonizers started to arrive, some Native Americans sometimes 'gave away' the land: it did not belong to them, so signing it over in their minds was a meaningless gesture – even if it was not so for the incomers. The key to the mode of production understanding is to see that when non-capitalist, or pre-capitalist social formations sit alongside the capitalist 'mode of production' the contrast between the two economic and value systems is clearest. It is at the point of transition when the conflict becomes the most explicit.For threatened native peoples, another world is possible because they are living in it; for them, as for the native North Americans today, at some point, it becomes impossible to bring back. For West Europeans, this is only a world we have lost. So, our alternatives have to build on the benefits of a highly productive capitalism. [19]

Surplus extraction in Spanish Latin America

When Duchrow and Hinkelammert look at their alternatives, it is not perhaps surprising that writing from Latin America carries an added emotional heat. For in Latin America, 9/11 means the terror attack on a democratically elected government in Chile in 1973. The simmering rage about what has been done to the people's movements in Latin America is well justified and too often forgotten in the analysis of the 'Western' impact on the Orient or the Muslim world. If Jared Diamond can argue that America was the last continent to be settled by humanity, the modern global era begins with the incorporation of the Americas into the global economy. So let us begin our development journey here.

As we shall later see that Eastern Europe's experience of the late Middle Ages was the mirror image to that of Western Europe, so too was Latin America's experience the opposite of the healthier trends in North America. The key to understanding the difference lies in their histories – specifically the history of their incorporation into the capitalist world market and the consequences for their internal political economies. Indeed, in his short history dominated by guns, germs and steel, Diamond picks up another date to remember in American history: what in English dating we could call 16/11 (November 1532) when the Inca emperor first met Pizarro at what Diamond calls the 'collision at Cajamarca'.[20] Put at its starkest, the key to Latin America lies in the Conquistadors.

The Conquistadors introduced two elements into the surplus

extraction equation that have dominated Latin America ever since: the first is that they came looking for gold; the second is that the conquest of the native empires of Incas and Aztecs was grounded on the same principles as the Spanish and Portuguese reconquest of Iberia from the Moors. 'Spain (and Portugal) were no strangers to conquest and colonisation when they reached the New World.' The Castilian monarchy attracted manpower from the north of Iberia into the underpopulated lands of the south by granting land and liberties to the new settlers. The further south, the fewer the settlers and the larger the estates (known as latifundia) became. With poor land, the new aristocracy found it easier to gain income from tithes than from directly engaging in agriculture themselves. Both the Muslim peasants who remained and the new Christian smallholders were happy to pay a tithe for 'protection'. The reconquest of Iberia therefore 'gave the Castilians the experience of settling defensively amongst a subject people of a different race and culture'.[21]

To put this more analytically, the fundamental orientation of the Latin American colonies was to the external extraction of surplus (measured in silver); more literally, the riches of the Americas mostly went to Spain to prop up the Spanish Empire. The silver trade was built up in the 1550s to become the most important export for the entire colonial period. At its peak, Spanish America accounted for around 20 per cent of Spain's revenues, and was the asset around which further loans could be raised.[22] The degree to which treasure ships were attacked by English and French 'privatizers', sanctioned by hostile governments, shows its importance. The colonial revenue flow, rather than enhancing Spanish development as in the British case, had major implications for the slow and late capitalist development of Spain (which led to Franco). It also had extremely negative consequences for Latin America.

The takeover of the Aztec and Inca empires

The two major empires of South America – those of the Aztecs in Mexico and the Incas in Peru – provided ample settled labour, already used to provide a surplus for the bureaucratic priestly elite, which rested rather precariously on top of the Latin American social pyramid. Both had ruling classes that had only come to power themselves in the fifteenth century, not long before the Europeans arrived, although their civilizations had been growing for at least the previous 500 years. The Aztec and Inca rulers were military emperors, who needed constant expansion, supported by an aristocracy of warriors, priests and administrators. Power was centralized and the rulers ordained with divine authority. The more advanced native societies already had a sharp division between the rulers and the ruled. The aristocracy lived off conquest. The masses of commoners were agricultural labourers and there was a large slave class from conquered tribes. Dominion was characterized by tribute levied on many kingdoms. The rapid fall of these native rulers under an external shock stems, it would appear, from the stagnation of productive resources that was already occurring. Pre-Columbus America had not experienced much technological progress; it lacked iron, the wheel, ships and discursive writing. As these societies had become more developed, it was not agricultural productivity that had advanced, but more effective devices for exploiting labour and absorbing the produce of vanquished tribes.

So, the timing of the Spanish arrival was fortunate, as these empires were already past their 'sell-by dates' and were surprisingly easily toppled by tiny invading forces, using superior weapons, but also using internal conflicts to their favour. It was not difficult then for a more advanced military elite to come in and take over from the native rulers; rather like the Norman conquest of Saxon Britain. The Spanish colonists of South America had a ready-made empire to take over. Some of the native kingdoms and discontented parts of the ruling elites even made pacts with the Spanish. A civil war had already been raging in Peru when they arrived.

This is not to say that a great deal of devastation was not brought by the South American conquest. The accidental introduction of European diseases virtually wiped out whole populations, particularly in the Caribbean islands. Apart from the Church sometimes – and hence the crown – there was a complete disregard for the natives' welfare. One estimate is that the population of Central Mexico fell by 90 per cent. In Brazil, in the sixteenth century, the death toll in the coastal areas controlled by the Portuguese, was between a third and a half of the native population. In Peru, the demographic decline was not halted until the early eighteenth century.[23]

The 'conquistadors' were easily corrupted from the beginning. The lust for gold propped up in turn a Spanish Empire that was falling behind in the Western development race. The surplus extraction from South America therefore always had an external orientation – in Latin America's incorporation into the world market. Much of the surplus drained away – first to Spain – and then to the big neighbour to the north, whose own internal dynamics were much healthier. Yet, the Europeans by no means destroyed everything they found. In terms of the extraction of a social surplus, they built on much of what was already there.

The colonial client states and the global economy

In the east of South America, the Portuguese colonialists found an economic development at the level of slash and burn agriculture, or of nomadic hunter-gatherers. Brazil's economic development until the mid twentieth century has been dominated by the way in which labour was exploited for a surplus and the commodities upon which the new settlers chose to accrue it. In 1500 Portugal, via its ownership of Madeira, was already the largest sugar producer in the world and with prices rising sixfold in the sixteenth century, sugar was the natural choice. Unlike the more settled west, the death of much of the native population led to the import of slaves, given Portugal's control of the West African slave trade. By the end of the sixteenth century in Brazil, 70 per cent of the plantations' labour force and perhaps 33 per cent of the total population were slaves. In north-east Brazil, where the sugar was best established, 50 per cent were slaves. Around 40 per cent of all slaves in the Americas went to Brazil.

The booms and slumps to which Brazil was to be subjected for much of the next 400 years, rather like much of Africa today, followed on from the economy's dependence on one or two primary products. Whatever the nature of the internal relationships, Brazil was immediately subject to the whims of the international economy. By the end of the seventeenth century, as Britain developed sugar in the West Indies, sugar prices halved, as did sugar exports from Brazil. From then on, the inward-looking, poverty-stricken subsistence economy of both the north-east and the native 'Indians' was actually a creation of the international economy and not some pre-existent state.[24]

The conquest of Latin America was not achieved under a free enterprise model; initially the adventurers needed a strong state in support. The new Spanish-American aristocracy was given legitimacy by the Spanish crown and the entire silver trading system was predicated on the authority of the Spanish state – to organize the supply of labour, the royalty rights and its monopoly purchase. Yet, even by the end of the sixteenth century, the strain was beginning to tell on Spain. Her agrarian exports became less and less important to the colonists. As Spain began to lag behind in the ability to supply manufactured goods, Spain became 'little more than a middleman' in the economic exchange between America and Europe, which was taken over by foreign, largely British and then North American merchants. By the late seventeenth century, after exhausting wars of independence against

Portugal and the Netherlands, Spain was 'no longer the supreme power in the world'. Yet, she managed to cling on to her American Empire for another century or more. By the eighteenth century, Spain 'now presented the curious spectacle of a metropolis that needed her colonies more than they did her'. The new white oligarchy in South America accepted their colonial status, until Spain itself was in difficulty, as the price for the benefits of colonialism which they enjoyed: Spain's very weakness had given her colonies more relative independence. Only the French invasion of Spain in 1808 finally led to Spanish colonialism's demise. In turn, this sparked and justified both British and US intervention. The contradiction was even more marked in Portugal's case. With British support, their empire in Brazil lasted until the end of the nineteenth century and in Africa, until the twentieth.[25]

Underdevelopment in Latin America

For the first half of the nineteenth century, the old structure of trade in South America was disrupted as the old provinces of empire fought out the boundaries of the nations and who should rule within them. The second half of the century saw the enhanced development of Latin America's export economies. Trade no longer had to pass through Spain or Portugal, as intermediaries. As the leading manufacturer of the age, Britain began to take on a monopolistic position in trade with Latin America. Other minerals had replaced precious metals and sugar. By 1840, Chile had already become the largest copper producer in the world; it had fought Peru and Bolivia in two major wars, the second time with British help, to win control of nitrate deposits. New dynamic export areas emerged – not only in Argentina and Chile, but also with oil from Mexico and Venezuela.[26]

However, a tradition of four centuries of internal and external looting gave the nineteenth- and twentieth-century Latin American governments an enormous legacy of neglect and backwardness to overcome, even assuming they had progressive nationalist intentions. The implantation of semi-feudal 'latifundia' estates, with impoverished peasants (often of native extraction) ossified social relations in the countryside until well into the nineteenth century. When it came, industrialization caused further fractures in already unequal and underdeveloped economies and societies. Consequently Latin American industries did not develop a base in local mass consumption for the new working classes, which would then require an extensive capital goods industry to make the machinery necessary for manufactured consumer goods. Instead, production, like the surpluses, was focused externally, based on the area's incorporation into the world market. Satisfying the luxury consumption of the elite often required imports. The basis for continuing debt and balance of payments difficulties was laid very early. By the 1960s, this process was described as 'under-development' for a continent massively rich in resources and labour.

So the broad answer to the surplus questions in Latin America is as follows. The surplus was extracted first by naked force and then by primitive accumulation from various types of pre-capitalist formations – slavery and peasant latifundia. The surplus went first to the Conquistadors who were nevertheless linked by Spanish colonialism and empire into the developing capitalist world market. In the nineteenth century, surplus extraction passed increasingly to first the British Empire and then increasingly to the USA. Significantly, US imperialism was able to have a commanding position in Latin America without direct colonial rule, as the Monroe Doctrine explicitly claimed. Instead the USA manipulated client dependent regimes and client ruling classes, which shared some of the surplus. The focus of extraction was still externally driven: the surplus went outside Latin America and was not reinvested. There was very little trickle down to the classes below and very little surplus for them to invest; truly, they had – and have – nothing but different forms of chains. If Moorish

Spain had been the model for the Conquistadors, Latin America was to become the model for the global American Empire starting in the Americas in the nineteenth century and elsewhere, beginning with Cuba, Puerto Rico and the Philippines in the late 1890s. After 1917, the American Empire was slowly to become the world's dominant power.

Argentina: symbolic success and failure

The symbolic story of late nineteenth-century Latin America was the apparent success of Argentina from 1880 to 1914. In 1870, Argentina seemed to have as much going for it as the USA. Its GDP per capita was only slightly lower; it had mineral resources, plentiful land and European immigration. Between 1880 and 1914, Argentina sustained the kind of growth more common in the tiger economies of Asia in the mid twentieth century: of at least 5 per cent per annum. Alejandro, the Argentine economic historian, has estimated that income per capita tripled between 1880 and 1930. By 1900, Argentina was one of the richest nations in the world. On Maddison's estimates, it still had the fourth highest GDP per capita in the world.[27] So, it is vitally important to understand the persistent economic and political crisis of Argentina in the next 100 years. Usually presented as a recent financial crisis caused by debt and the banks, Argentina is an excellent case study of Latin American issues, yet it has been particularly poorly covered in the British media. Argentina has also been one of the rallying calls of those on the debt and trade justice campaigns in the West, but since the early twentieth century, it has pursued the kind of protectionist and import substitution policies now often recommended for the poorest developing countries. These policies did not reverse what became a precipitous decline, nor did they prevent Argentina's reincorporation into the imperial world order.

Military victories against Paraguay in the north (which had

itself broken away from the old Spanish colony of Rio del Plata) and the Pampas natives to the south expanded the territory available for cattle, sheep and cereals. The ranching economy of Andalusia, which was to shape the 'cowboy' economy of the grasslands of Texas and northern Mexico, was now also shaping the Pampas. Britain became the major customer for Argentina's wheat and meat, available for export thanks to steamships and refrigeration. Argentina imported manufactured goods in exchange for foodstuffs. British business established a commanding position in the Argentine economy, owning the railways, the telegraph, meat processing plants and many banks and merchant houses.

Spanish power in what became Argentina had been under threat from the British from the late eighteenth century. The war of 1793 gave Britain the sole right to carry slaves to the Spanish colonies and in 1806–7 both Montevideo and Buenos Aires were attacked by British forces. With the consequent fall of Spain, a 'Liberal' Junta seized power in Argentina. This represented the power of the local elite and excluded non-whites.[28] However, whatever the appearance of independence, Argentina functioned as an economic colony of Britain until 1914. The agro-industrial processing surplus gave Argentina (and Uruguay) a fundamentally external orientation. Even as late as 1937, Argentina provided 65 per cent of Britain's imports from South America, while Britain remained the largest foreign investor.[29] But as the demand and prices of agricultural products fell in the 1920s, Argentina's dependent export economy was then set for a long period of extended decline. Not surprising then, the stress by some Latin American theorists on their dependent or peripheral status locked into a subordinate position on the capitalist world market. The policies and crisis of the post-1989 era can only be understood in the context of the great frustration felt about this decline.

The lopsided political economy of Argentina

The River Plate basin was not a crucial area for the Spanish colonial occupation – there was no obvious mineral wealth or precious metals. The early settlement, particularly in the north, tended to be along Brazilian lines and, in 1822, 25 per cent of the population of Buenos Aires was black. The Liberal Argentine Republic of the nineteenth century remained under the control of local aristocrats and merchants. Although in theory Argentina passed an Immigration Act in 1876 modelled on the US Homesteads Act of 1860, the actual clearing of the natives from the Pampas reflected their control; the land grants did not, as in some places in the USA, create a class of independent small farmers but large estates owned by aristocrats. Thus, Williamson argues that the 'roots of Argentina's society still lay in the sixteenth century'. Consequently, when the meat processing economy of Argentina grew, with the attendant docks, rail, light industry and services, the new immigrants poured into the cities and not onto the land. The foreign-born population in Buenos Aires in 1869 amounted to 50 per cent of its population. The frequent question for Argentina for the next 150 years was how the landed elite were to incorporate the restive urban proletariat and an insecure middle class, while keeping their own economic (and perhaps political) power intact.[30]

The first decade of the twentieth century was a vital one for Argentina. The labour and trade union politics of Argentina until 1914 followed the European trade union debates and style of syndicalist militancy, borrowing not only from Britain, but also from the stronger anarchist traditions of Italy and Spain. Between 1900 and 1910 for every two immigrants that arrived, usually from a background as poor agricultural labourers, one came on a temporary basis and returned home. What became the newly settled proletariat was concentrated largely in the food processing and refrigeration industries in Buenos Aires. Out of this hectic growth came a militant working class: the first general strike was as early as 1902. Levitsky calls the Argentine proletariat the 'largest, best organized and most cohesive in Latin America'.[31] If the economic mother country moved to the Liberal Party, the solution in early twentieth-century Argentina was the Radical Party – an all-class alliance of dissident aristocrats, the middle class and some elements of the working class. After another general strike in 1910 and the electoral reform of 1911, Argentina had universal suffrage before Britain, and the Radicals stayed in power until 1930. As Williamson points out, the problem of Argentina from 1912's franchise reform was what he modestly calls a 'lop-sided political economy'.[32] Political and economic power no longer coincided. Economic power remained with the rural elite, but political power meant an attempt to use the 'democratic system' to extract benefits from their economic monopoly. If the economy is booming – as it was to 1914 – this can work; if there is a global and/or local recession, the state is likely to 'tear itself apart'. The working class was divided too: outside Buenos Aires, there were 600,000 rural workers and 725,000 seasonal workers – all outside the union power base. The Socialist Party could take over from the Radicals in the capital but not elsewhere. The other key was often the urban-based middle class: in good times it tended to side with the urban workers; in bad times, with the landed elite.

Tragedy, the military and industrialization

The Argentine boom lasted until 1921; with a falling working day, unemployment falling from 14 to 7 per cent and real wages rising. The Radical Party first came to power at the high point of the boom under President Yrigoyen in 1916. The Radicals appealed to all those who opposed the oligarchy with credit support for small farmers and increasingly powerful trade unions. The general strikes of 1918 and 1919 were too much for the middle-class elements in the Radical Party, which tracked right and left in an attempt to keep the coalition together. The peak of the radicalism came to be symbolized by the 'Semana Tragica' – the tragic week of the general strike in January 1919. A march of 200,000 workers was attacked by the police and army, killing 700 and injuring 4,000; more were shot in protests in Patagonia.[33] The American continent was to show a great capacity for violence against working people when power and wealth were threatened. As the boom faded, the Radicals first cut public expenditure and then, in 1928, President Yrigoyen looked to oil nationalization to thwart the syndicalists, while at the same time trying to blunt the trade unions. When no one class is able to rule clearly, the military usually ride to the rescue. This was the case in Argentina in the Great Depression: the army overthrew Yrigoyen in 1930. The comparison for Latin America and much of Africa should not be with the Britain of today, but with Cromwell's post-1649 military dictatorship after the English Civil War. Policy in favour of the majority of course is the recommended course of the trade justice movement's idealism about government in the 'poor countries'. As we shall see, what this naively ignores is the class structure of these political economies. What is worse is its poor grasp of history: the kind of policies usually recommended for Asia and Africa have been tried all over Latin America since 1914. This is not to recommend retreating into some conservative notion that the state should not get involved: as we shall see, the state has always been involved – it has usually done so as a client kingdom of the powerful global empires. When the client state attempts to bite the hand that feeds it – whether in Cuba or Iraq – it usually gets crushed or destroyed, just as the Roman Empire destroyed Israel.

The years 1919 and then 1930 mark a watershed in Argentina's history. From here on the lopsided political economy was to work a terrible vengeance on the hopes of ordinary Argentines. Economically, the major result was the decision of a part of the old landed oligarchy to go for industrialization. Yrigoyen's Radicals had tried to show their independence from Britain: first kicking up a fuss about British-owned rail rates in the midst of the troubles in 1919. But they had backtracked and, by 1928, had been persuaded to commit to buy more British manufactures. In 1929, the British ambassador still referred to Argentina as an 'essential part of the British Empire'.[34] When the military came to power, they hoped to utilize the US against the British. US isolationism in the 1930s and US banks' low foreign lending drove the Argentine military back into imperial preference. In keeping with an increasingly protectionist world, Argentina was at first excluded from the Ottawa Agreement of 1932. With the threat to Argentine beef by quota and tariff, the military were only too keen to sign on to a new pact in 1933. An import substitution policy in textiles, electrical goods and processed foods followed, alongside nationalizations to develop indigenous industry. Profits prospered as wages fell around 20 per cent between 1929 and 1932. A protectionist import-substituting industrialization was the main plank of the oligarchy and military.

Peronism, roots and history: 1930–55

Despite the traditions of the earlier generation, the new industrial workers of Argentina had little trade union representation at first. There were 229,000 metalworkers by the end of the 1930s, but only 4,000 trade union members. In 1930, when another trade union confederation was founded – the CGT – it called upon 200,000 members out of 4.5 million workers. But industrial growth now moved apace. By 1941, 40 per cent of industry had been built in the previous ten years. The cotton industry, which produced only 8 per cent of domestic demand in 1930, produced 31 per cent in 1934 and 58 per cent in 1939. Manufacturing accounted for 50 per cent of the labour force in 1946 against 30 per cent in 1936. Rural workers flocked to the cities.

From the mid 1930s, the Socialist Party reasserted its role within the CGT, while the Communist Party attempted to organize the rural sugar workers in Tucumán. Traditionally in Argentina, the rise of the new radicalism under the name of Perón has been associated with the new workers – migrants from the rural areas coming into industry for the first time. In the space between one imperial power waning and another rising, there was certainly a short-lived Argentine industrial boom. Real wages rose 25 per cent between 1930 and 1944, compensating for the post-1929 losses. A feel-better factor, bringing together both the older union movements and the new, culminated in the huge mass mobilization in favour of Perón in one of the most memorable dates in Argentine history: 17 October 1945. Perón, in turn, managed to pull a corporate state together, which brought in the leadership of the trade unions, alongside the new industrialists and, in the beginning, even some elements of the agrarian elite. A new radical Gladstonianism – Argentine style – was born. Perón's main campaign slogan called for social justice, and his wife, Eva, came to represent even more closely Peronism's populist appeal to the poor. At first, Perón was sustained by a boom and his populist policies. One of his first acts was to nationalize the unpopular British-owned railways in 1947. Perón co-opted the union leaders – and union numbers shot up with this encouragement, from half a million in 1945 to two million in 1950. The share of wages rose from 44 per cent to 60 per cent of GDP. A Peronist became head of the CGT. Munck calls the process from 1930 the 'Peronisation' of the working class. To keep the coalition in place, however, Perón had to face both ways at once. Perón was forced to do deals to attract the USA to invest in the oil industry in Patagonia. He began to denounce strikes from early on, if they were not under his control, imprisoning strike leaders in the key refrigeration plants. There were clashes between metalworker Peronists and Communist-led workers in the key plants in Rosario. The 1951 rail strike was declared illegal and the industry put under military rule.[35] Argentina had serviced its debt and kept free trade through the 1920s. It had kept its currency reserves in London in the 1930s – with the peso pegged to sterling – and, with the post-war boom, by 1947 Argentina had paid off its national debt. Being debt-free, however, is never a solution in itself. Wheat exports in particular started to be squeezed both by European and US protection. In 1949, with the devaluation of sterling, export income fell 30 per cent. With too much demand on the state to solve the economic problem, yet with no more output supplied, one result is roaring inflation – which reached 35 per cent per annum in 1949.

Argentina re-incorporated: 1955–76

By 1951, both the agrarian and business elites had begun to leave the Peronist coalition. In 1955, the military, the old landed oligarchy and the new industrial capital all combined against Perón. The political analogy is of England in 1848. The benevolence of the first Peronist era was over, never to be resurrected. Another Radical government (1958–62), supported by the US-sponsored Alliance for Progress, as its answer to the Cuban Revolution, clashed with the trade unions. There were three general strikes in 1957 and three more in 1959; days lost in strikes peaked in 1959 and real wages still fell by 25 per cent. The workers themselves were badly divided as the Socialists and Communists felt they had seen the trade union movement taken over by the Peronists. In 1946, Perón had dissolved the attempt to create a British-style Labour Party. By 1955, the Communists too were in favour of Perón's removal.

One way in which the Argentina of the 1960s differed increasingly from that of the Peronist era was in the growing influence of US capital. In 1958, US companies accounted for 14 of the top 100 manufacturers and had 30 per cent of manufacturing sales in Argentina. In 1968, they owned 60 per cent of Argentina's top manufacturing firms and accounted for 60 per cent of total sales. US capital investment in Argentina increased from $350 million in 1950 to $472 million in 1960 and $992 million in 1965. At the same time, a more capital-intensive industry with lower demand for labour meant that smaller firms were closing and militants were sacked. Yet, car production increased 50 per cent in the 1950s. The story of these two decades then was of Argentina's reincorporation into the sphere of global – and specifically US – capital. Nor was privatization an idea unique to Mrs Thatcher and the 1980s: in 1955 plans to introduce it for Buenos Aires transport and in 1961, on the railways, led to strikes. Not surprisingly, with the pressure of incorporation, the Peronist Justice Party programme of 1962 reads like that of much of the trade justice movement today (or of the British Labour Party in the 1980s): the repudiation of debt, nationalization of the commanding heights of industry and banking, a state bank and protection from imports. The Peronist party was banned from taking part in the 1963 elections.

Following the Brazilian coup of 1964, and as internal pressures built, the military intervened again in 1966. The generals planned to stay in charge for 20 years to complete their 'modernization' (four terms for New Labour). What prevented it was the Argentine equivalent of 1968: an uprising in the motor city of Cordoba in May 1969 called the 'Cordobazo'. In an Argentine expression of shop floor power, the workers confronted their own unions splitting the CGT, built barricades and used dynamite. There was a general strike in Rosario and the sugar sharecroppers in Tucumán and the Chaco came out too. As the oil crisis broke, only the Peronists seemed able to pull Argentina together and Isobel Perón won 62 per cent of the presidential vote in 1973; promising afresh to nationalize the US transnational corporations, subsidize local business with an income social pact and tax agriculture (which meant tax the elite). As killing started on all sides, she sacked the mayor of Buenos Aires because he was 'soft on terrorism'.[36] This was 30 years before 9/11.

Argentina's dirty war: 1976–89

The old tactics of Peronism would no longer work without a boom to sustain them. With inflation in 1975 hitting 185 per cent, peaking at 30 per cent a month, and after a general strike in 1975, the military returned in 1976. The issue was increasingly becoming: why should anyone bar the military ever be able to rule in Argentina, or for that matter in Latin America as a whole? With inflation at 400 per cent in 1976, real wages fell by 50 per cent in the next two years. For Munck, as the share of GDP going to wages fell from 50 per cent to 30 per cent, this military government attempted to break the political mould set since 1930 with an economic policy also based on agro-exports. For Williamson, neo-liberalism in Argentina effectively meant 'declaring war' with full US support, to crush the popular movement that had been placated in Argentina since 1912. In the Argentine instance, the state only had brute force left. The 'dirty war' mainly hit trade unionists and socialists – strikes were made illegal and the CGT was abolished. Five major trade union leaders were assassinated in five years and disappearances became routine. Of 100,000 shop stewards, 10,000 were dead or in prison by 1979. As in Britain, but far more brutally, the homogenous working class was broken.

Despite all this, Argentina's 'lopsided' political economy and an oil crisis had got its debt back from nothing up to $43 billion by 1983. The usual analysis of the 'debt crisis' looks at the oil-generated bank lending but forgets that it was lent to places like Argentina because they could no longer afford oil imports. The attempt of one part of the Empire's periphery to break free (in the Middle East largely, but also in Venezuela and Mexico) had merely saddled an older once-successful part with unsustainable debt. Between 1976 and 1986, 15,000 industrial firms were to go bust. Manufacturing employment fell by nearly 50 per cent in big factories. Three-quarters of the new jobs created were white collar, in banking, retail or personal services. In other words, the trends observed in the advanced West have all been seen before. But in Argentina, the overall economy rested on a tiny base, so the dependence on the 'informal economy' started to become dominant. A new urban poor sat alongside a newly created middle class.

The Radical Party under Alfonsin came back in 1983 after the disaster in the Falklands, launched to provide a patriotic diversion to yet another oil price induced crisis in the early 1980s. Rather like the British Labour Party in 1987–92, the loss of the election in 1983 caused a crisis within Peronism. It was the first free election they had ever lost, getting 40 per cent of the vote in 1983, but only 35 per cent in 1985. With inflation at 28,000 per cent, with GDP back at the 1974 level and with a fiscal deficit of 12 per cent of GDP, Argentina faced yet another crisis.[37]

Even most Peronists were prepared to back desperate measures. Carlos Menem's electoral success of 1989 meant that someone who appeared to be a Peronist and a populist could now adopt neo-liberal policies in the new climate of the 'democratic' Latin America of the 1990s. Patronage was important in a society where despite GDP growth of 7.7 per cent per annum in 1991–4, measured unemployment rose from 8 per cent to 18 per cent between 1989 and 1995. Most of this had come after the Mexican debt crisis of 1994.

Menem: Peronism and patronage

Menem had been a regional party boss and he knew how to crank up and consolidate the Peronist political machine. The urban poor became clients to whom patronage was given. For one commentator, the Peronists became a 'party of social work'. Menem ruled by decree – 545 decrees to be exact, when Alfonsin had used ten. The oil industry and pensions were privatized. Menem also promised to cut federal 'waste' – 700,000 jobs were to go in

20 days by decree.[38] Peronism under Menem still depended on its machine politics to control the State and to keep the working class loyal. In his first three and a half years, Menem faced little opposition. Trade unionists became increasingly critical; as one put it: 'Not only does it negotiate with the enemy, it negotiates badly.'[39] In 1983, the trade unions had 38 per cent of the places on the party executive; by 2001, they had 13 per cent. The Peronists won elections in 1991, 1993 and in 1995; the 'Olivos Pact' was signed, which enabled Menem to run for a second term as president. Yet evidence of Menem's corruption was growing: his brother was reported to have accumulated $1 billion in Uruguay within three months. The extent of privatization under Menem was even greater than that in Brazil under military rule, raising $31 billion.[40] This was a style of Reaganomics and Thatcherism without Thatcher or Reagan; it shows that both in Britain and the USA, we have personalized the issues, when in fact the real issue is ascendant global capital. But, by 1999, Menem could not get acceptance for a third term.

Argentina's neo-liberal era: 1989–99

Despite Menem's 1989 campaign hints of defaulting on foreign debt, US funds flowed into a neo-liberal Argentina, rising from $3.2 billion in 1991 to $11 billion in 1992–3. Led by car production, exports to the new free trade area, Mercosur, had also risen by 70 per cent by 1994, accounting for 30 per cent of exports. Brazil was now Argentina's biggest market. Cavallo, the finance minister, developed a reputation for prudence. Yet after the Mexican crisis and the sharp rise in unemployment, the cost of funding the budget deficit grew from $1.3 billion to $5.6 billion in 1995–6. Most importantly under the Menem–Cavallo reign, the peso was made convertible into US dollars on a fixed one-to-one ratio, while the independence of the Central Bank was enshrined. This was six years before Ed Balls won Gordon Brown to this view for Britain and followed indeed the dying economic act of the Chilean military dictatorship. The tie to the US currency was a sign of absolute desperation: it chose to defeat inflation in a way that would inevitably lead to an economic crisis if the dollar rose. This had worked in Hong Kong for nearly 50 years, it was said. The key was, however, that Hong Kong had been successful as a US and British entrepôt in the Far East. In Argentina, a small unsuccessful economy was to tie the peso to a big successful one for a decade. In 1994–5, Argentina's exports were saved by the appreciation of the Brazilian real, because Brazilian interest rates had risen to 60 per cent, in response to the Mexican crisis. From early 1996, however, the dollar also began to rise; Cavallo, perhaps hearing the death knell, resigned over health spending. The final economic crisis in Argentina was precipitated by Brazil's devaluation of the real in 1999. After the currency crises in the Far East in 1997–8, the capital and foreign exchange markets started to mark down economies like Brazil, where the fiscal deficit had also been rising.

Politically, this was accompanied by Menem's fall. In 1997, the Radicals had united with Frepaso to form the Alianza, a coalition of largely middle-class centre-left groups, strongest in Buenos Aires. In Rock's analysis, the narrow victory in 1999 of Alianza's presidential candidate, Fernando De la Rúa, reflected the divisions of the Peronists, who retained a large majority in Congress and the provinces. The new government raised the age of retirement for women and reduced the minimum state pension. Bringing back Cavallo, the tax savings – 2 per cent of GDP – were eaten up by debt-service costs. In the October 2001 elections the Alianza vote collapsed and the biggest jump in voters was in 4 million spoiled ballots. Withdrawals from bank deposits reached $500 million per day in late November, and $1 billion in early December. As a result, the government and banks imposed a 'corralito', literally a 'little fence', to limit cash withdrawals, effectively blocking access to the savers' own money. After protest marches, a state of siege was declared and in the demonstrations on the hot nights that followed around 30 were killed.

Ironically, with some anti-globalization campaigners arguing for the reinstatement of fixed exchange rates in the new world of casino capitalism, in Argentina the IMF actually supported a fixed-rate system to the 'tune of tens of billions of dollars right to the bitter end'.[41] This is not to say that the IMF was compassionate: in words often used by Gordon Brown, it bemoaned 'insufficient flexibility' in the Argentina labour market, just as effective unemployment was to rocket upwards to at least 40 per cent.

They all must go: 2001–05

As the economy now collapsed for much of the middle class, 50 per cent of the population were on the official poverty line – some 19 million people. Seven and a half million, could no longer afford sufficient food. There were reports of children starving in Tucumán. In 2002, the government defaulted on debt of at least $130 billion. Public services disintegrated.

The marchers had blamed the whole political Establishment and were led under the slogan 'they all must go'.[42] As Rock points out, at least the fall of De la Rúa did not result in a military coup. Although the country went through five nominal heads of state in ten days, the transitions observed legal niceties. In December, De la Rúa had called for armed intervention against the rioters. The military commanders refused to obey until instructed to do so by Congress. That order never came. One benefit of 20 years of democracy was that the military had been kept busy overseas – from Iraq in 1990, to Croatia, Somalia, Cyprus, Kuwait, Haiti and Angola – as the Argentine government had been busy trying to win most favoured status with the USA.

It took until May 2003 for a new president – Kirchner – to re-start negotiations with the IMF. To win public support, he began the trial of 'corrupt' judges and the sacking of top military. The

Congress passed and then extended a ban on mortgage foreclos-
ures and the seizure of debtors' cars; forced employers' payments
to a trade-union run health scheme; and claimed that foreign
banks' head offices should be responsible for new deposits in
their Argentine branches. The Congress's actions and the continued threat of Argentina reneging on its debt has kept relations
with the IMF frayed.

By 2003 there were hints of an economic recovery in Buenos
Aires: 'to rent' or 'for sale' signs gave way to internet cafés. Yet
still 'businesses that take twenty-four hours to set up can dis-
appear in twelve', and 'misery itself has been institutionalized'.
Shanty towns have sprung up for ex-suburban families who sort
through the dustbins in upmarket areas. The 'piqueteros', road-
block activists for workers' rights, are more or less tolerated.
Selected workers' organizations have sometimes been allowed to
take charge of unemployment funds in a bid to stave off social
violence. Public disillusion remained; as one cab driver put it to
Edgar Cozarinsky, we are just 'waiting for the first foul-up'.[43]

The case of Argentina shows all too clearly the dangers of a
superficial global analysis that lacks a detailed look at the local
political economy of class and political forces, often with over-
simplistic notions of debt and trade reform. Here an old agro-
export economy still controlled by a landed oligarchy and industry controlled by the USA had combined to block sustainable
long-term development. Argentina had gone a whole century with
no land reform and it desperately required structural change by
and for ordinary people. Successive military and civilian regimes
used both internal and external power to block change. Cancelling debt or better prices for the exporters of beef or cars would
not be more than short-term measures. As workers now occupy
abandoned workplaces, more fundamental structural changes
on the land and in industry will need to take place. This is not
about political will, corruption or efficiency – it is about who
holds political and economic power.

From Latin America to the USA

Against this non-ideal type of Latin American development, it is quite easy to develop its ideal opposite in the USA. The pilgrims came to North America to build a 'New World'. After the initial thanksgiving for survival, the surplus was in the hands of a growing farming class, who reinvested for the future. This is not to say that primitive forms of accumulation were not employed; slavery was important in the early settlements of Virginia and the Carolinas. But the presence of forced African slaves spoke only too clearly of the impossibility of trapping and exploiting sufficient numbers of the indigenous North American (Indian) population. Exposure to Western diseases killed many and there was simply not enough labour to plant on the potential temperate farmlands. Here the surplus was extracted locally, internally driven and invested first at home. The American dream implied an independent yeoman class of owner or at least tenant farmers. The surplus was therefore – in concept – more widely spread and more egalitarian. By the mid nineteenth century, with an imported population of millions and slavery finally removed as a block on capitalist development, the USA was ready for its own rapid industrialization.

This stronger economic base produced enough independence, even before the removal of British colonial rule, for the people both to desire and be able to elect their own government and for the first development of a modern parliamentary democracy. The point here is to see the economic base that supports the possibility of an effective 'democracy'; many Latin American governments have and had the correct constitutional models, but the economic orientation and consequent political and class realities did not make a 'Northern' model of parliamentary democracy viable until as late as the 1990s. With local and global recession always threatening, the sustainability of this 'Washington consensus' and of its parliamentary model is always being challenged in South America.

Even more, if the historic consequences of black slavery have been dreadful in the USA, how much worse in Latin America (and indeed for the white slaves in Russia, still serfs until 1861), where the external political economy has been far less propitious for the slaves' eventual absorption. The extent of the devastation for the common people in Latin America shows in real terms how important it is to answer their development and justice issues with a historical depth and feeling normally conspicuously lacking in most shallow, and a-historical neo-liberal analyses, which assume some kind of 'Robinson Crusoe' society in Latin America, with a similar history to that of North America, when it is not and never has been. When piled high with further ignorance about the history of US imperialism in the Americas, it usually succeeds in adding insult to injury; so Latin America fails because of 'corrupt' governments and a 'mañana' mentality, when there is not the least attempt to start to analyse why this politics and psychology may have appeared in the first place. Explanations based on the personality of politicians (Perón in Argentina) or of the failings of state intervention (which suit the usual capitalist propaganda) look at the superficial responses, not to the underlying structural problems.

The dark side of the American model

There is just enough truth in the bright side of the successful North American model of development for the story to be told without embarrassment. There is, however, a darker side; this is true without even calculating the benefits to the USA from its global Empire, or sifting through the propaganda about the ideological manipulations of American foreign policy in particular (as Chomsky does so well). The American dream was established at a murderous cost to many American people – never mind the great extent of its violence against foreign oppressed peoples, from Mexico to Vietnam and beyond. The massacre of Native

American peoples and the appalling and continuing consequences of the dehumanization of the American slavery system are well established. A tiny, wealthy and powerful elite has always ruled the USA. The economic and political power of the early colonial rulers was based on black slavery and on white servant labour. Despite the pretence to a representative democracy, the elite always feared the common people. Land, money, violence and racist propaganda were all used to make sure that this power was not threatened. The wealth and power of this American elite was from the beginning based on a brutal and massive exploitation of the majority of the population. Violence against protest and therefore against the common people in the USA was endemic from the very start, and in the nineteenth century it was used particularly against urban workers. Religion's role was to either justify the existing order or suggest spiritual solace.

America was never the land of the free. However, one of the important victories of the anti-colonial revolution was that it enabled the settlement of land beyond the Appalachians, which the British had always opposed. A land with 20 per cent of its population slaves in 1770 could then open up the possibility of at least tenant farming for another 30 per cent of the population. In 1900, 25 million (out of 75 million) Americans lived off such farms. The violent cost of establishing what is often called 'the new capitalism' in the USA after 1860 needs to be emphasized: the Civil War took 600,000 lives (the equivalent of 5.5 million in today's population). The rapid rise of American monopolies and imperialism followed swiftly on from rapid industrialization in the North and after reconstruction in the South.

In the increasing imperial power that was the USA in the second half of the nineteenth century, a further civil war was still being fought on behalf of capital. The multinational American working class was fighting increasingly violent and bitter battles against its new capitalist employers. The USA's experience may be more akin to that of Germany, where a later industrialization and an earlier concentration of capital led to the early growth of a socialist movement. In 1900, the two largest socialist movements in the world were in these two countries. Zinn's list of revolts and killings goes on and on. The American labour movement's defeat and buy-off between 1873 and 1941 is a vital part not only of American history but of global history too. It is a story of how violence, money, ethnic divides and propaganda can be combined to defeat the common people. It is a story not of the victory of a feudal landowning and nascent capitalist class as it was in Britain after our Civil War, but of a highly modern imperialist class and power, which still rules global capitalism today. It is worth understanding this story well since it is little told – and particularly not in the USA, where the powers that be have no interest in reminding anyone of how violent a history it has.[44]

Hurricane Katrina

In September 2004, Mike Davis, whose book *The Prisoners of the American Dream*, explores the attack on the working classes of the USA wrote a prophetic piece called 'Poor, Black and Left Behind'. As in the rapture of dispensationalist evangelicalism explored by Northcott, it predicted the departure of the white middle classes and the consequences for a flood-ravaged New Orleans. After 9/11, Davis's *Dead Cities*, looked back on the 'flames of New York' in H. G. Wells and at the incipient violence, the hidden racism and the realities of the underclass of the USA, which were laid bare for many more by the non-embedded television coverage of September 2005's Hurricane Katrina on the Gulf coast States.[45]

Much has been written on the 'cultural' failure created by the slave mentality of the US South. Poor black people – alongside the white trash – in the USA are then conveniently blamed for their failure to participate in the end of history and the global triumph of capitalist liberal democracy. 'Third World America' is put alongside other Third World failures. The unjust use of power, with the potential and frequent recourse to violence to uphold, is what links the poverty of Africa with that of the poor of New Orleans. As the famines in Africa have been much generated out of the barrel of a gun, so the poor blacks left behind in the US underclass are to be rescued from their failure to be ready for the rapture at the point of a gun. The National Guard is sent in like an official posse to find the 'looters'; the lynching this time is carried out by character assassinations on prime time television. If the slave mentality has penetrated the black consciousness, the fear of the black, other, Hispanic or marginalized peoples of the USA has deeply penetrated the official consciousness of the USA's global elite and its client middle classes. The sacredness of property – water and food and dippers rotting in abandoned Wal-Marts – must be preserved at all costs. So the 82nd Airborne, fresh from Tikrit, invades New Orleans in full combat gear, guns at the ready, looking like the SS, using the same impenetrable sunglasses of a police state to hide the glare of the empty streets. The Empire eventually moves in to New Orleans or to Fallujah to find it has conquered a swamp.

The hotels outside the devastation zone are filled with bureaucrats while the people who could have used them are told to pay their own way, with the market of course reflecting the new pricing realities from gasoline pumps to hotel rooms. The sports stadiums swamp up as the hotel chains increase profits. 'Business as Usual', Churchill remarked in 1914. Business as usual must reign supreme, because any suggestion that it does not is anathema. And the churches of America are called upon to do their normal charitable philanthropy.[46]

The lay theologian Ched Myers describes his experience of the unmasking, from the shadows, of a similar largely Hispanic and black underclass. Writing in 1996, he describes 'a war on my doorstep', a 'tidal wave of fury and rage'. In the riots of 1992, after the failure to punish white police for beating a black man, Los Angeles was to be 'scorched by the fires of rage erupting from the nightmare of Empire'. Myers concludes that for the under-class there were 'no more lies they can tell themselves. No more dreams to fix on. No more opiates to dull the pain.'

Like the floods of New Orleans, the riots of Los Angeles briefly gained the attention of the elite, George I and II both used the National Guard to make Los Angeles and New Orleans object lessons in how the elite deals with a 'great disruption'.[47] As New Orleans prisoners spilled out onto the super-highways, still wearing their Guantanamo Bay orange prison gear with gun-toting guards all around, the scene was symbolic of the black side of the American Dream. In the Global Capitalist Empire, the strongest evidence of the contradictions of global capital does not only lie with the poor of Africa, it can also be seen in Los Angeles and New Orleans – if the oppressed masses of the USA can see they too are in chains.

3

1914 And All That:
English and German Imperialisms

1914

When Alexander Solzhenitsyn wrote his historical novels on the decline of holy mother Russia, and its transformation into the Stalinist Union of Soviet Socialist Republics, his pivotal point for understanding Russian history was his novel *August 1914*. There is little doubt that the outbreak of war in 1914 is a key turning point in global history. It marks what for Hobsbawm is the beginning of the short and murderous twentieth century, which he ends in 1991 with the breakdown of Russia's despotic Empire.[1] Focusing on this particular period is vitally important in understanding where we are nearly a century later, partly because we have recently seen the propaganda for another imperialist war – in Iraq – and, unlike 1914, where there was little popular support to 'stop the war', it still goes on. The war of 1914–18 was a 'great' and destructive 'world' war, but is still important today because of the insights it gives us into the political and military implications of the global expansion of capitalism, particularly after 1870. In all the memorials and remembrances to the suffering, little of the history has highlighted the relationship between capitalism, imperialism and globalization. As we have looked at the Americas to understand something of political economy and the global accumulation of capital, this chapter looks instead at two other major capitalisms – at the English and German historical experiences –to understand afresh the political, economic, sociological and cultural roots of the imperialist war of 1914–18.

Another historian of the 'Great War' correctly points out that it was 'a clash of world empires'.[2] It is impossible to escape the conclusion that whatever the apologetics written about the logistics of railway timetables, the European empires' fight for the division of the new spoils of the expanding global capitalism of the late nineteenth century led to the devastation of the Great War. It was not the capitalist states that fell in this catastrophe, but the variety of absolutist empires still remaining in this 'new' capitalism in Austria, Germany, Russia and Turkey. All crashed under the pressures of a total war. Another empire, the British, was to implode over the next 50 years and yet another – the sixth, the USA – was eventually to gain world hegemony. The Great War started the process of what eventually became a triumph for the newly emerging Global Capitalist Empire (centred on but not limited to the USA).

For the British Empire, it was a critical episode in our 'long retreat' from world economic and territorial domination. The victory of 1918 was a pyrrhic victory. The Empire was territorially bigger than ever before, but the cost in dead, in loss of economic power and in financial debt was a toll that few in 1914 were predicting.[3] The British imperial economy has never recovered its 1914 pre-eminence. The state's influence is now so pervasive that it is hard for many to think of a serious dismantling. With the wider franchise, the political nation had changed too. Taking government expenditure back to its 1914 level of 8 per cent of GNP looks impossible and unthinkable. The old 'Liberal' state was abolished during the Great War; never to be recovered. A new 'security' conscious state came into being, which operated rather more against the people than against the 'enemy'. In the first nine months under Liberal rule, the Prime Minister provided only one survey of the war's progress to the House of Commons and this was followed by no debate.[4]

The 1914 churches as the prophets of Baal

In 1914 England and Germany were the nations of the two largest Protestant churches in Europe. The twentieth century has seen an enormous decline in both countries' nominal church attendance. It is a social and demographic experience they both share, which sets them apart from the experience of the other large traditional Protestant church – that in the USA. Although the decline in England's church does not exactly date from 1914, it certainly starts to accelerate in the era of imperialism. Can there be any connection? It was bad enough to see two ruling classes plan an imperial war. Yet what made it worse for the church was the divine sanction it gave to such a squalid affair. Seen on the British side as the defence of Belgium, it may appear reasonable. When seen against another major Protestant church with impeccable theological credentials, falling in line with its own imperial Establishment, the whole theological enterprise begins to smell. It was 1914 that, like Solzhenitsyn, Karl Barth took as the turning point for his critique of the liberal German theology of the universities. Seeing the doyen of German theologians, Adolf von Harnack, a friend of the Kaiser, lead 93 intellectuals into vocal support for the war, Barth wrote his famous commentary on Romans to 'begin with God anew' because 'liberal theology had unmasked itself' to be a servant of empire. William Temple, relatively a liberal for his time, who became Archbishop of Canterbury in the Second War, supported British involvement in the First; he complained that the Germans had made a God of the State.[5] In 1914 the leadership of the British church had done exactly the same. They had made a particular idol of the British Empire. The Church, and the Church of England in particular, which so often was led by the same elite that took us to war, was equally responsible for translating the economic and power realities of imperialism into the propaganda message of God, king and country.

Ordinary people had good reason for cynicism with the Church after 1914. Here are the prophets of Baal prophesying exactly what the 'kings' tell them to prophecy. There is no space to pursue all the historical and theological implications here, but it is worth noting that in 1914 – in both England and Germany – Establishment Christianity sold out so completely to the existing order of empire that one wonders how mightily the Church has been compromised and for how long. Is this one reason why the common people could at last begin to see through it after 1914? There is a sad twentieth-century history the churches in England and Germany share – for the dreadful lack of prophetic discernment. The Church leaders were from the ruling class that made the war – and in England, I include so-called radicals like Gore, Tawney and Temple – and they could not see beyond their own class upbringing and environment. The theology of empire largely espoused by the churches in England and Germany in 1914 certainly seems to have helped both reap what they have since sowed. In the twenty-first century at least, the Church has learnt to be more wary of God being brought into the service of king and empire.

For those who had eyes to see, the war did not suddenly appear like a 'chasm in the road'. As early as 1907 the Second Socialist International made peace the theme of their Stuttgart Conference and in 1911 after the Agadir Crisis it declared that capitalism made war 'inevitable'. In 1914, not all were fooled by the theology of empire. Keir Hardie, in particular, had been warning about the dangers of war after the Russian alliance had been signed in 1907.[6] So God was speaking in a still, small voice to some: which God was the mainstream Church listening to in 1914? What kind of letter would the writer of Revelation send to the churches of England and Germany in 1914? The power of empire to manipulate and enforce its ideology will constantly re-emerge in this book – today with the potential manipulation even of seemingly radical movements like Make Poverty History. To understand

how the churches were so easily won over requires us to understand more of the history of how English and German imperialisms were made. We shall then briefly look at the consequences
for Iraq after its conquest by the British in 1917.

The myth of peaceful English evolution

It is a myth that English capitalism evolved peacefully, as a
natural development from a peculiar English pragmatism and
consensus. It is a myth that ignores the realities and the politics
of English history. There was nothing particularly peaceful or
naturally inevitable about the creation of English capitalism. It
ignores too the creation of a British Empire not only out of slavery and the subjugation of India, but out of the absorption and
conscription of other nations within the 'United Kingdom' – in
Wales, Scotland and Ireland. It is a myth that originates from the
mid nineteenth-century domination granted by the Workshop
of the World to the British Empire. As the comforts of the Victorian Age accumulated for the new middle classes in England,
it is perhaps an understandable myth, as they observed the continued upheavals – of 1848 and of 1870, for example – common
elsewhere in Europe.

The establishment of a modern capitalism in Europe has cost
the British and British imperialism dear. Every twentieth-century
war memorial still bears tribute to it. In short, modern English
capitalism, which now has its part in the new global capitalism,
has not been a peaceful pragmatic evolution. It has taken a lot of
bloodshed and a great deal of struggle to create the modern capitalist economy and state that we take so much for granted today.
This is as true of Britain, as it true everywhere else.

It is a myth that would have fitted the United States better since
in the North there were only the Native Americans to fight and
not the slow death of an ancient aristocratic feudalism. In 1865,
however, the USA knew what the British had forgotten about in

their own revolution 200 years earlier. The Americans of 1865 had just lived through their own murderous civil war. Many of the immigrants to the Americas brought with them too the memories of the hardship and poverty of other absolutisms and the early birth of capitalism in the rest of Europe.

Nor has the development of British capitalism always been gradual; there have been times before of huge dislocation, rapid take-offs and revolutionary situations. Those who wish to portray the present as somehow totally different from the past – so therefore we have a New Labour for a 'new' capitalism – will use their own myth makers and spin-doctors to play down the revolutions of the past. The struggle over how to tell the story of the English Civil War and of the English Revolution is a good case in point for these revisionists. Hill criticizes the tendency of post-1970s revisionist history to see no long-term causes in the Revolution or to deny that a revolutionary upheaval had taken place at all.[7] This has political and ideological consequences for all ensuing analysis.

Likewise, via A. J. P. Taylor in particular, the view of the Great War as an accident of railway timetables has turned attention away from longer-term causes like colonialism, imperialism and capitalism. Today we have similarly clever apologist pieces, like Ferguson's pathetic attempt to bury the 'Marxist' approach in the dustbin of history, which end up with the helpful thought that the pity of the Great War was that it was caused by 'human error'. Stephen Poliakov's 2003 BBC play *The Lost Prince* repeated these themes for today's popular consumption. Here was a genteel world where kings and kaisers and tsars, who were all related, managed to involve a few other people in their family squabbles, while rustic peasants supported their rulers and clever advisers ate lavish dinners. Here was the public school consensus of the British political classes, so beautifully parodied in *1066 And All That*, where the 'Great War' is 'this pacific and inevitable struggle' and the world is 'made safe for democracy'.[8] The same propaganda game has been played out again since 9/11 2001.

Rewriting and distorting the past provides an ideological legitimacy for New Labour's economic neo-liberalism and resurrected Fabian neo-imperialism. New Labour has learnt the lessons of Orwell only too well: 'Who controls the past controls the future. Who controls the present controls the past.' Those of us on the 'lost left' who oppose New Labour have every reason to be watchful and angry as the history of ordinary people is being written afresh to legitimize Britain's junior role in the global imperial partnership. To understand our present problems – globally and theologically – we continually need to think historically. For so much of the contemporary analysis of debt, trade and Iraq, for example, has lost a structured history. Here is an attempt to 'think the present historically in an age that has forgotten how to think historically in the first place'.[9] In this chapter are some pointers to understanding, in the British and German cases, the interrelationships between capital, empire and globalization. These historical pointers can then lead us on to a better understanding of the British role in the 2003 Iraq War.

The state and the rise of English capitalism

There is another Victorian myth that the 'British model' of capitalist development is of a laissez-faire state, little involved in the creation of a powerful capitalism; unlike France, Germany or Japan. In fact, the early success of English capitalism owes a great deal to the early centralization of its feudal state and therefore of its early capitalism. It took France and Spain until the fifteenth century to gain the internal political cohesion to establish an absolute monarchy; it took Germany and Italy until 1870. England had this in essence by the tenth century.[10] The creation of the English state did not come from a natural evolution, or from a pragmatic consensus, but from the consistent threat of Viking invasion and from a Conqueror, who laid much of the land waste. It has taken much bloodshed and many struggles to create the surpluses and accumulation on which the modern capitalist economy and state have been based and that we take so much for granted. Extending its feudal domains took the English ruling class all over Europe. The risings of the common people in the feudal era – the best example being that of 1381 – were a necessary part of the breakup of serfdom, before it was formally abolished in 1645. The absolutist state of the Tudors and Stuarts developed out of an aristocratic civil war (the War of the Roses). The 'Mother of Parliaments' fought for its powers in a Civil War. The era of early agrarian capitalism (where 'sheep ate men' via enclosures) produced a huge social dislocation. The primitive capitalist accumulation that partly laid the basis for Britain's industrial domination of the nineteenth century was at times savage and cruel.

The limitations of the Norman aristocracy's ability to control the entire surplus of feudal England were set by a strong tradition of common law inherited from the older Anglo-Saxon order and by the continuance of an independent peasantry in the north and east, particularly stemming from Viking settlement and rule. Serfdom was never as strong thereby in England as it was in its West European heartlands. The growth of the wool trade and the development of London as a trading and mercantile centre acted as a further pull towards commercial relations on the land and the development of artisan production in the towns. This widened the share of the surplus in a way never possible in Latin America, or in Eastern Europe. The key to English development apart from the early centralized state was the manner in which the English landed aristocracy, without the need for a large standing army after the defeat of the Armada, had turned capitalist in its orientation. The Protestant Reformation played a key role in the widening nature of surplus extraction in England. The surpluses previously accumulated by the feudal church were reallocated to the rising gentry and were used by Tudor absolutism to tie the gentry into the new state. Protestantism, anti-popery, patriotism and Establishment could conveniently become the propaganda vehicle for the English Empire.[11] The final defeat of the northern earls under Elizabeth set the seal on the spread of capitalist relations on the land in the sixteenth and seventeenth centuries. This made the English 'commercial aristocracy' more likely to fight Stuart absolutism, but not at the cost of its economic power. Ownership of land was still important and hardly disturbed by the Civil War; from 1688, it was only a factor of production in the new capitalist enterprise. The eighteenth-century landed estates dominated the countryside, as the aristocracy continued to hold many of the formal offices of political power until the twentieth century.[12]

The English and German models

The characteristic English landholding system of aristocratic rentiers, tenant farmers and proletarianized wage labourers on the land, which had emerged by the eighteenth century nevertheless made for a wider spread of sharing in the agricultural surplus than elsewhere in Europe. The dominance of London, developed further by colonial trade, provided further avenues for a broader enrichment. For the English bourgeois revolution that took place in stages between 1641 and 1867, the widening of surplus accumulation domestically and the encouragement of colonial expansion would go hand in hand. In England, the coalition of aristocracy, gentry and rising middle class promoting surplus extraction was wider and more efficient than the aristocratic reaction that ruled in France until 1789, but nevertheless turned against any attempt to widen it further between 1645 and 1653, 1790 and 1820, in 1838–48 and again between 1906 and 1926. The aristocratic embrace of British capitalism, even more with its imperial consolidation in Wales, Scotland and Ireland, left it only half way to a genuinely meritocratic capitalism. It is the irony of

New Labour that it continues the Thatcher revolution of trying to make complete the final stages of the bourgeois revolution.[13]

The contrast with the German experience shows the uniqueness of the English model. For not only did the centralized German state arrive considerably later, it was also brought about under Prussian tutelage,[14] which gave German society a militaristic bent until 1945. A united German state arrived on the scene with industrialization and modern monopolies already well developed. Barrington Moore's path-breaking work for the modern era, written as long ago as 1966, uses an analysis of the social conflict between lords and peasants to understand the later political development of dictatorship or democracy. He has a wonderful quote on the results of the military tradition for German society: 'One cannot find in English history the counterpart to those German conservatives whose parliamentary representatives rose in demonstrative applause to (one) ringing challenge … The German Emperor must always be in the position to say to any lieutenant "Take ten men and shoot the Reichstag".'[15]

Tawney had good reason to make the sixteenth century – sometimes known by later historians as 'Tawney's century' – a key link to twentieth-century developments.[16] Ironically, it makes even more sense in Germany than in England to focus on the sixteenth century. For in England the sixteenth century also needs to be placed alongside seventeenth-century developments; or to be more precise, the agrarian relationships that Tawney also stressed, need to be seen before and after the Civil War. The rise of English absolutism tied to the new agrarian capitalism, symbolized first by Henry VIII and for which Charles I is later blamed, was politically and militarily defeated by 1649. English agrarian capital, however, remained economically untouched.

'Turning Swiss': the Peasant War in Germany

The German model and all that led to 1914 and 1939 has to be seen not just in the context of the new united Germany of 1870, but in what kind of Germany had been created during the class and regional struggles over surplus extraction since the sixteenth century. The key to German history and to that further east has been the relationship between the rulers and the peasants until the twentieth century. The pressures from the peasantry, particularly in south Germany, which lived off the trade routes into Italy and further east, stemmed from what is usually forgotten – the only successful peasant revolution in Europe before 1789: that of the Swiss. The Swiss – as Zwingli pointedly reminded Luther – had made their own economic revolution and Protestant Reformation.[17] This always carried a more militant 'Anabaptist' and egalitarian strand, which became dominant in the peasant uprisings throughout Southern Germany in the 1520s. The German Peasant War, as it became popularly known, is described by Blickle as the 'mightiest mass movement in European history before 1789'. Barrington Moore who describes 1524–6 as the most important mass peasant movement of early modern times stresses the contrast with English developments. He concludes that partly because of this defeat the possibility of a liberal democracy in Germany was cut off for centuries.[18]

The roots of the German economic model, set as an alternative to that of the Swiss, can be traced back at least until Luther's time. For it is clear that the Protestant Reformers in Germany sat between the forces of reaction on one side and the peasants' radical 'Anabaptist' protests on the other. As with Henry VIII in England, the German princes used the Lutherans in their fight against the Spanish-controlled (Holy Roman) Empire and thereby the Pope, whom the Habsburg kings at this point controlled. As a rule of thumb, Luther's (Magisterial) Reformation was a reformation made in the towns to suit the urban bourgeoisie, to eventually be ruled over by princes fighting for space within the Holy Roman Empire; the Radical Reformation was made by the peasants, sometimes in co-operation with the lower classes in the towns, often led by the intellectual clergy. The clash of these interests made for the persecution of any radicals, to which the label 'Anabaptist' was often applied.

Blickle reaches the same conclusion as Engels and Barrington Moore via a more theological route. Blickle argues that the old view of the 'Peasants' War' was that the peasants had risen, misunderstanding the message of Luther. It was Luther's own view. Blickle comments that this opinion was 'not only self serving but wrong'. Using the Swiss experience, the Swabian Twelve Articles, and the message of Muntzer in Thuringia, Blickle argues 'Luther created neither the demand for change nor even its religious expression. It was Luther, not the revolutionaries of 1525 who misunderstood.' From then on the Radical Reformation that arose out of and supported the Revolution of 1525, and which Luther helped create, was to be largely incompatible with the Magisterial Reformation – not only in Switzerland, but even more so, in Lutheran Germany. Nor did Luther, a monk whose strong point was not politics or history, have any knowledge – until told of it – of the Hussite movement in Bohemia a century earlier. As in Bohemia, the Catholic States like Bavaria and Austria sided with reaction and empire because the radical threat from the example of 'turning Swiss' was akin to turning Bolshevik in 1917.[19]

The second serfdom

Blickle's argument is also vital in its implications for the church, for he concludes that, what he calls the communal reformation of the Anabaptists was 'taken away ... from the communities and made a matter of State'. In other words, the German states did what Henry VII was to do in 1532–9. 'The Anabaptists (so-called) sought to save a remnant of the communal reformation by withdrawing from the realm of this world' (as did the English puritans, after 1653 and increasingly after 1660) 'but the rulers mercilessly exterminated them'. This was particularly noticeable in all the 'Catholic States', not only in Bavaria and Austria, but also with the Protestant movements in France, Spain, Italy and Poland.[20]

The murderous defeat of the peasants in Germany, supported by Luther and enshrined in the Diet of Speyer by 1529, established both the possibility of an enhanced absolutism and the continuance of a reactionary aristocracy in power. The crushing of revolt not only had major consequences for the nature of the Established Protestantism that resulted, but for the princes whose power Luther had encouraged in his determination to resist the peasants.

When Engels, writing in 1850 when the German bourgeoisie had just been defeated in the revolt of 1848, had asked himself who profited from the revolution of 1525, he concluded that the 'Princes' had gained most. And the 'Big Princes' – eventually Prussia and Austria – were to gain most of all. The way was set for the unification of Germany to take place under the rule of the Big Princes. The route to 1914 and to 1939 – and the route to Nazism – was set as far back as 1525. Engels' analysis is borne out by contemporary accounts. Blickle also argues that, in the ruling classes, the major beneficiaries of the failed revolution were the 'territorial rulers', who gained at the expense of the empire, the territorial nobles and the monasteries. Politically, he argues the peasants disappeared for 300 years.[21]

It was also Engels who was one of the first to point out that extra power to the princes led eventually to what he called the 'second serfdom'. Rather than the English model that increasingly commercialized the owner–tenant relationship, increased surpluses were forced off formerly free peasants by increasing the pressure and turning them into serfs. This was particularly the case for the Prussian aristocracy – the Junkers – and elsewhere further east and ran alongside increasing grain (rye) production for the European markets in the eighteenth century. Eastern Europe thereby experienced the exact opposite response to the feudal crisis from that of the West. Its relative backwardness was compounded. Anderson comments that for some peasants in the east, a second serfdom is not strictly accurate, for here free peasants, who had often moved into the freer lands to the east, were to be increasingly tied from the fifteenth century onwards. The second serfdom does, however, describe a second 'wave' of serfdom – now in the east – lasting until the eighteenth or nineteenth centuries. This accompanied the increasing intrusion of the west into the eastern economy and the decline of serfdom in the west. This also led to a different function for the aristocracy; it had not become capitalist in the English way. It continued to extract its gains in the old way. Barrington Moore calls the period the 'manorial reaction' and describes Prussia as the 'Sparta of the North,' 'a militarized fusion of royal bureaucracy and landed aristocracy'.[22]

The marriage of iron and rye

The merchant and middle classes, who had been increasingly dominant economically in England from the sixteenth century, in Germany were incorporated into the political structures in a more repressive way. The abolition of German serfdom – indeed, its abolition in much of Central Europe – had been spread on the back of Napoleon's revolutionary peasant armies after 1789.[23] The natural reaction of the German aristocracy and growing middle class, without their own 'bourgeois' revolution, was to look to reaction – as in 1848 – to safeguard their interests. Here Barrington Moore – no Marxist – sums up Engels: 'a commercial and industrial class which is too weak and dependent to take power and rule in its own right ... throws itself into the arms of the landed aristocracy and royal bureaucracy, exchanging the right to rule for the right to make money'. Barrington Moore compares England and Germany thus: 'At no point did Germany go through an experience comparable to the abolition of the Corn Laws [in Britain in 1846]. ... The whole coalition of Junker, peasant and industrial interests around a programme of imperialism and reaction had disastrous results for German democracy.'[24]

As German industrialization gathered apace after 1870, the marriage of the old aristocratic surplus and the new capitalist one became known as the marriage of iron and rye as both were given tariff protection. But the German response to the advent of imperialism and monopoly capitalism was not purely about reaction. The marriage of iron and rye, as the alliance of princes and big urban bourgeois had been in the sixteenth century, was necessary to quash 'popular discontent' and to 'carry through the political and economic measures necessary for modernization'. Bismarck was thereby the epitome of conservative modernizers, who also brought the German welfare state into being, while the German Social Democrats (SPD) remained illegal. The example of Bismarck is a historical refutation of any thesis from Blairite New Labour that 'modernization' carried out in the service of capital is automatically 'progressive'. The difference then, apart from a colonial empire, between Germany and England between 1870 and 1914 was that England had an aristocracy controlled by capitalism, while the Germans had a new and vibrant capitalism controlled ultimately by an aristocracy, based on the land and on militarism. The aristocracy then controlled the surplus in Germany until 1914 and even the leading capitalists aped their prestige and their 'von' prefixes. Dahrendorf, looking afresh at the phenomenon from the vantage of the 1960s, followed Weber by concluding that in Germany 'the traditional leading stratum (as he calls it) managed to turn the rise of the entrepreneurial middle class to its own uses'. British bankers and industrialists aped their landowning betters too, but their relationship to the land and the peasantry (there wasn't one in England) was fundamentally different.

Gerschenkron pointed out that after 1848 the Junkers also increasingly brought the remaining peasantry into their political coalition as it was the popular discontent of the big German proletariat they feared. Bracher also sees the way the German bourgeoisie were bought off in 1848: 'National unification … was a sequel to the crushing of the liberal revolution of 1848' that succeeded in absorbing the bourgeoisie into 'a pseudo constitutional, semi absolute, feudal, military and bureaucratic state'. Dahrendorf also stresses the Reichstag's function before 1914 as a popular facade to hide the autocratic fabric of the new Empire; Dahrendorf, struggling with his terms, calls pre-1945 Germany an 'industrial feudalism'.[25] With this brief internal historical context, we can now return to the outbreak of the Great War in 1914.

The plunge to war: German imperial aims

The successful reunification of Germany under Prussia in 1870 and the defeat of France changed the balance of power in Europe. Bismarck planned 'a rule of trois' – the three Absolutisms of Austria–Hungary, Germany and Russia – and concluded a formal treaty with Austria in 1879. The problem was that Russia and Austria were competing for mastery in Central and Eastern Europe, as well as the Balkans, largely to determine who would benefit from the spoils of the even weaker Ottoman Empire. The Habsburgs had therefore lost sight of the long-term advantages of the reactionary absolutisms holding together, as they had made common cause to defeat Napoleon's revolutionary peasant threat. Instead, as early as 1870, Marx predicted another war between Germany and France, but this time, France, he said would be in alliance with Russia. The Franco-Russian treaty was signed in 1893 and left the four empires equally tied. Winning over the fifth, Great Britain, became vital to both sides. If not able to win over Russia, Germany worked consistently for a neutral Britain and the Kaiser, as the first grandson of Queen Victoria, was still hoping for this right till the end, in August 1914. Despite the scramble for Africa in the 1890s, the imperial powers' interests had often coincided; in the opening up of China, for example. Around the time of the Boer War, between 1898 and 1901, the British and Germans discussed a colonial deal in Africa, with vague promises of German gains in any fallen Portuguese territory in return for German abandonment of claims in the Transvaal, but the price of the deal for the German leadership was British neutrality in Europe. Britain signed up with Japan in 1902 to protect her Asian interests instead.

In 1907, a new German government had come to power under von Bulow with a rhetoric of nationalism, anti-socialism and colonial expansion. The aim of successive German chancellors was to continue the Bismarckian policy of creating national unity by external aggression. Ironically, the new nationalist coalition was needed to counterbalance the Junkers who saw less need for a navy to fight British colonialism or for tax increases. Although parliament had no power over ministers, the Prussian elite was worried about the rise of the SPD, the largest 'socialist' party in the world and after the 1912 elections the largest party in the Reichstag, with a third of the vote. It now seems clearer with historical hindsight that, by the end of 1912, two crucial developments led the plunge to war. The first was that the Kaiser and his leading advisers had decided that war against Russia (and thereby with France) was 'inevitable' within the next 18 months, largely to pre-empt Russia's recovery from the lost Japanese War of 1905. There was increasing talk of a 'preventative' war in conservative and military circles. There was a spectacular increase in German army estimates. The next chancellor, Bethmann-Hollweg, needed the Reichstag to vote through the military budgets – the SPD voted through the first increase in income tax in July 1913 – and planned to blame war on a Russian attack.

The second development was the increasing weakness of the

Ottoman Empire and the rise of the southern Slav States, like Serbia, which also threatened the Austro-Hungarian Empire. Their success in the Balkan war of 1913 and his apparent ability to deal with the Austrians, via the Germans, was to deceive Grey in 1914. By then, the German rulers were ready, even with only one ally. Austria's defence was therefore seen as central to German interests and the Austrian Empire was desperate to crush Serbia. The talk of a short decisive war came first out of Germany; for the rulers of old imperial Prussia knew that a long war would be socially dangerous. So it proved.[26]

The Weimar Republic

In this way, the Weimar Republic, as with the abolition of serfdom, was an externally imposed creation in 1918, as the old Prussian-based Empire collapsed. But in 1918, the Junkers and their landholdings did not collapse with the Empire, as they did with the Russian invasion in 1945. Even without the Versailles treaty and the Great Depression, the Weimar Republic was going to struggle. The bourgeois had no experience of rule, and their time was rather like that of the brief middle-class 'parliament of the saints' in seventeenth-century England. The new Weimar Germany started with a virtual civil war until 1921. Under the pressures of global recession in 1933, it rolled over and died. The aristocracy and the big capitalists meanwhile thought they had a tool in Hitler that they could manage.

Bracher's summary is a good one:

Many people still believe in the theory that the National socialist tyranny sprang into being almost overnight and quite inevitably as the result of the distress caused mainly by economic difficulties arising from Versailles, inflation and the economic crisis ... In fact, however, this is no adequate explanation ... for the character of the regime.[27]

Think too of those who voted for Hitler – not just voting for a Germany 'betrayed' in 1918, nor just for jobs – but particularly of the peasantry, the increasingly squeezed artisan classes and the petty bourgeois, who had been in alliance with Junkers and capitalists before. In a Germany split between the big capitalist battalions of monopoly imperialism and the large trade union dominated Socialists and Communists, the old middle orders felt trapped and powerless. Hitler came from this class and could articulate its fears all too well. It is not surprising either that Hitler's roots were in Bavaria and Austria where the original counter-revolution had been pushed through in areas deeply embedded with old imperial beliefs. Fischer points out that although it is normal to stress the 'reactionary' petty bourgeois support that Hitler gained, the Nazis competed effectively with the Communists for working-class support, and indeed gained votes across class, regional and church boundaries, although not uniformly so. In the March 1933 election – the last under Hitler – the Nazis gained 17.2 million votes (44 per cent of those voting), a bigger mandate than that for Blair in Britain in 1997. The rest, as they say, is history.

As German historians and sociologists like Ralf Dahrendorf have since argued, starting with 1918 and the problems of Weimar does not explain the history and structure of a German society that so easily led to a fascist, nationalist and militaristic solution. As India and China head down an increasingly nationalist path, the need for this kind of structural analysis is ever greater. At a massive cost in death and suffering, the defeat of Nazism finally abolished what Dahrendorf calls the imperial German past: 'what came after was free of the mortgage that burdened the Weimar Republic'.[28] The success of West Germany's parliamentary democracy has to be seen in this context.

The implications for the German church also took until the post-1945 era to become clearer. If, in 1914, the huge and influential SDP in Germany had caved in to nationalism and imperialism (bar Karl Liebknecht and his partner, Rosa Luxemburg), the

German church found it even harder to break with 400 years of the Lutheran definition of two kingdoms, which left the state free to choose war as long as it didn't offend 'religion'. It took until the Barmen Declaration of 1934 for what became the Confessing Church to make the difficult decision to break with the Lutheran Church's authoritarian tradition. Similarly, with Bishop Bell of Chichester deliberately overlooked by Churchill for Canterbury after he had opposed the carpet-bombing of Germany, it took the Church of England until 1982 to explicitly reject Thatcher's rejoicing at the killing of young Argentine conscripts in the Falklands.[29]

British imperialism and the road to war

Alongside the economic drives for imperialism – of cheap raw materials, new markets and a potential outlet for 'surplus' population – Semmel's work sees the internal social and propaganda effort by the governing classes in both societies to establish a mass popular base for imperialism. 'Social imperialism' made its first appearance in the UK with Disraeli. It was explicitly linked to empire by Disraeli as the Queen was unveiled as Empress of India in 1876. The franchise changes of 1867 and 1884 and any material – welfare – benefits were to be given to secure support for an often aggressive imperialism. The aim was to 'incorporate the working class into the imperialist system'. Schumpeter called it 'People's Imperialism'. It is no coincidence that Semmel's analysis of the rise of imperialist policies in the UK after 1895 borrows from a German work on the eventual rise of the Nazis.[30] To the English eye trained to see the Liberal moves of the early twentieth century as the first 'socialist' measures, the real nature of such reforms is better understood when it is seen that an arch-conservative like Bismarck was behind them in Germany.

It is vital to see the connections between the imperial struggle with Germany and the policy of leading Fabians and Liberal imperialists from the 1890s. One of the Fabians' first resolutions spoke of the 'comfort of the few at the expense of the many'. This sounds so Blairite that one wonders if the modern spin-doctors have looked it up. Like Blair today, they too wished to 'modernize and reform' the state from above by centralized direction, and at first looked to influence the Liberal Party as a way to 'permeate' the institutions of government. They succeeded: it was their kind of imperial thinking that lay behind the determination of Asquith, Grey and Haldane, first appointed to the Liberal government of 1894, to plan for the ultimate showdown with Germany. George Bernard Shaw and the Webbs argued in favour of both the Boer War and World War One.

At the time, John Burns, one of the organizers of the London Dock strike of 1889 and the most working-class member of the later Liberal government argued the South African war was 'for gold, for capitalist domination masquerading in the guise of freedom and franchise'. Price describes the Boer War as 'the purest example of Imperialist War' taking place in 'an orgy of patriotism'. Like all imperial wars, it was to be justified on the 'dubious grounds of moral responsibility and strategic necessity'.[31] The parallels with the justifications for the invasion of Iraq are only too clear.

The diplomatic war game

Permeation was working in ruling circles: Grey was to recommend the entente with France and Russia in 1902, two years before it became Conservative foreign policy. Britain had sided with Germany in 1870–1, as it was assumed that a French victory over Prussia would give too much power to France. At root, the British decision to intervene in 1914 was based on the same logic in reverse; it was assumed that British intervention was needed to defeat a German/Austrian victory over France and Russia. The German economy was a greater challenge to Britain after 1870.

British imports of steel had risen from 8 to 45 per cent of exports between 1875 and 1913, with Germany as the major supplier. Yet, Britain exported twice as many machine tools to Germany as she imported. Britain was Germany's biggest market; Germany was Britain's second biggest.

Nevertheless, the pressures were not a simple-minded 'economistic' imperialism. Diplomatic realignment against Germany began on the imperial stage and after the Boer War. It coincided with a huge increase in war debts and greater limits, by Gladstone's standards, on Britain's ability to spend its way to continued naval supremacy. The Kaiser's intervention apparently in favour of the Boers in the Kruger telegram of 1896 grated, as did Germany's increasing desire to gain colonial territory. Likewise, the first move towards France was first and foremost a 'colonial bargain'. The British and French had colonial disputes in West Africa, on the Nile and over Thailand. After war in the Sudan in 1898, the basic deal with France was to give Morocco for Egypt. If Grey was happy with French gains in Morocco to be set against new German territory, the Germans were not. The Kaiser's appearance in Morocco in 1905 to claim equal rights with the French was deliberately designed to test the strength of the new Anglo-French entente. It succeeded in making the British ties with France all the stronger.

Many liberals saw the Russian autocracy as a traditional British enemy, after all we had fought them in the Crimea in the 1850s. The movement towards Russia started like the French as an 'imperial arrangement' to parcel out spheres of influence in Persia and Afghanistan, as a means of protecting India. The Foreign Office policy was to keep an uneasy balance between discouraging the Russians in the east, while not pushing them to take an increasing role in the west, specifically in the Balkans in support of the southern Slavs. It was also worried about two dictatorships – Russia and Germany – coming together to forge an alternative imperial deal (shades of 1939!).

A Liberal government (shades of Blair and Bush's neo-cons) went ahead with an Anglo-Russian entente in 1907 despite the opposition of many both in Russia and in the British command in India. Kitchener, then in command of the Indian General Staff, wanted to declare war on Russia if there was any further Russian advance towards India. When Austria annexed Bosnia in 1908, Germany promised that it would mobilize if Russia did so. All the pieces were in place for the imperial struggle to come.

From 1906 to 1914, British imperialism and domestic social reform were nearly as closely connected in the new Liberalism as they had been in Bismarckian Germany or were to be in the Nazi Reich. British foreign and defence policy was made by a small elite who constructed a 'shadowy edifice' of 'compromise and half truths'. It was an elite that often conferred little with Parliament or public and had an overriding preoccupation with rising German power. Parliamentary debates only occurred after treaties and key decisions had already been made. Grey, foreign secretary from 1906 to 1914, had said as early as 1895 that he was 'afraid that we shall have to fight sooner or later', while in 1903 he described Germany as our 'worst enemy'. Joll comments that Grey was obsessed by Prussian militarism;[32] he now had his chance to lead the UK into what he too had long seen as inevitable.

While keeping German expansion in check by use of the naval blockade, the strategy of maximum gain for minimum cost was quickly shown to be bankrupt as the British Expeditionary Force was virtually wiped out at Ypres and as trench warfare began in the west in November 1914. The real strategic battle of 1914–16 was not between the generals who ploughed our dead into the Western Front and the 'Eastern' campaigners like Churchill, but between the old nineteenth-century notion of a limited war to limit Continental power and the need for a total war to achieve an imperialist victory in the new technologically-driven monopoly capital era.

1914 And All That: English and German Imperialisms

An imperialist war takes us into Iraq

It is easier to see with the benefits of the experience of the new global capitalism of the 1990s and the twenty-first century that the war of 1914 was in fact all about what I shall call the theology of empire. The story that war would be over by Christmas probably started in Germany. The German military needed it this way so they could then turn east. (Of course, this is exactly what did happen in 1940.) The myth of a quick war was allowed to run by a British government, although the War Office had concluded in 1912 that a war with Germany would last at least three years. Kitchener's army was not intended to fight the war in 1916; it was to inherit the peace in 1917, after the French, Russians and Germans had battered each other to bits (the historical precedent was 1815). With a longer war, British global strategy and aims came explicitly to the fore by 1916. Perhaps it was no coincidence that the first engagement of the new World War One came in West Africa. For the costs now being suffered, British strategy effectively swung to gaining territorial compensation: in Africa (at German expense), in the Middle East and Islamic world (from Germany and Turkey) and in Central Asia (from a weakened Russia). No wonder that the joke was in St Petersburg that the British Empire would fight to the 'last Russian'. It was to do this once again from 1941 to 1945. The new War Cabinet of Lloyd George's new coalition of December 1916 tells the story; it was christened the Imperial War Cabinet.[33]

Rather like the British inheritance in 1815, it was the new American Empire that in both 1917 and in 1941 intervened and mopped up the major benefits of the peace. By 1918 the USA had taken over Britain's role as the world's largest creditor nation, as the British had borrowed heavily in the USA to pay for the war.[34] The route to Britain's financial problems was set by the hubris of empire. Part of the new gains of this imperial war were to be oilfields across the Middle East in areas of the defeated Ottoman

Empire, especially in the new creation of Iraq. Rory Bremner's 2003 TV exposé of the old propaganda on Iraq was excellent; it's a shame that the propaganda both before and since, which went to hide British imperial planning for the Great War, was not unveiled too. A million British men died in the pursuit of this Empire. And please don't tell us that we fought for our 'moral responsibility' towards Belgium. Again, joint French and British war planning had always assumed a potential attack through Belgium.[35] Like empty chemical warhead containers, what a wonderful pretext it provided.

Oil and the breakup of the Ottoman Empire

The post-9/11 attempt to reincorporate Iraq into the sphere of global capital has its origins in the breakup of the Ottoman Empire. It is also to the roots of this old rule that some of the Wahhabi-influenced Saudis and others appeal in the name of a modern political Islam.[36] The needs of empire ruled supreme for British policy on the Ottomans. After taking over Egypt in 1882, further attempts to break into the fringes of the Ottoman Empire in the Middle East were precipitated by the discovery of massive oil deposits in Iran in 1908. The imperial competition both for territory and for oil was most acute between Britain, France, Russia and the USA – nominally allies after 1914.

The British as ever feared Russia taking too many pieces from the Ottomans: hence saw Iran as a buffer and divided it between them in 1907, 1914–18 and again in 1941–5. The same stand-off between Britain's Indian Empire and Russian expansionism created Afghanistan as another buffer state. Disraeli, anticipating Chamberlain, had ever claimed 'peace with honour' after the Berlin Conference had limited the expansion of Bulgaria, supported by Russia. Balkan Christians at this point would be sacrificed, despite Gladstone's scruples, as the price of keeping Turkish support against Russia, as in the Crimean war. As the Turkish

Empire grew weaker, Britain was first able to support the foundation of Kuwait in 1896–9, and then drew the boundaries between
Saudi Arabia, Kuwait and Iraq in 1922.[37] There was also conflict
with the US over oil. Although the USA at this point produced 80
per cent of the world's oil, it only had a twelfth of the reserves. The
British and French had in 1916 carved out the Middle Eastern oil
reserves and respective spheres of control: the British were to get
Palestine, Jordan and Iraq; the French, Lebanon and Syria. Apart
from the oil, the main territorial dispute had been over heavily
Kurdish Mosul, which the French allowed to go into northern
Iraq. The US elite were furious: they were even implicated in
raising the standard of Arab nationalism and anti-imperialism
(British that is) in Shi'ite Karbala especially. They were eventually cut into the deal in 1920.[38]

War was not declared against Turkey as a German ally until
November, but troops were sent in October 1914. Ferguson
points out that in 1914 120 million of the world's Muslims, out
of a total of 270 million, lived under British, French or Russian
rule.[39] The Turkish Sultan in his role as caliph, with the Kaiser's
explicit encouragement, declared a jihad immediately. After taking Basra, the British had a disastrous campaign. Nevertheless,
when Baghdad was taken in March 1917 the army proclaimed
itself as liberators.[40] Kitchener had promised independence but
only within the British 'protectorate' umbrella. The Ottomans
had largely left the holy cities of Najaf and Karbala alone; indeed
in 1915–16 there were strong protests against Turkish conscription. When a jihad was declared against the British in Iraq in
Karbala in 1921, the first bombing and gassing of the Kurds was
suggested by Churchill, as colonial secretary, to create a 'live-
ly terror'. The RAF practised its aerial bombing campaigns of
1943–5 first on Kurdish Iraqi villages in the 1920s. The policy
was still sanctioned by the minority Labour government of 1924.
Kurdish leaders were shot without trial. As with Rome in first-
century Palestine, and as with British imperial policy in Africa

or the Spanish in the Americas, whole villages were destroyed for not paying tax. As with the USA in Vietnam, new weapons were experimented with in the 1920s in Iraq, especially rockets and fire bombs with delayed action and white phosphorus. Bomber Harris learnt his trade here by suggesting that bombs should be dropped in every village that 'speaks out of turn'. The RAF liked the bombing as it was cost-effective. As the RAF was used against Turkish troops in Kurdistan in 1922, the threat of such British weapons of mass destruction kept a resurgent Turkey from reconquering Iraq. As Simons concludes, it was 'the RAF which was the midwife of modern Iraq'.[41]

Seven years after the 'liberation', in 1924, the British set up the first constituent assembly in Iraq. This was followed by parliamentary elections in 1925 and the first of two military treaties, the second with a Labour government in 1930, giving the British bases near Baghdad and Basra respectively. In this period, the UN mandate was 'manipulated' to provide a 'legal cloak of respectability' to effective colonial rule. Even when Iraq joined the League of Nations in 1932, its foreign and domestic policies of landlord and largely Sunni elite rule was sustained by the British military and dictated to by Britain; not unlike Iraq in 2005 under the USA (except for the Sunni rulers, who have thereby formed the major part of the violent opposition). Such an unstable client regime faced six coup attempts between 1936 and 1941. When war broke out, a pro-German coup of March 1940, threatening to cut the oil pipeline to the Mediterranean, was put down with British troops from Basra in April. The king remained in power until 1958 with a regime where two-thirds of the cultivatable land was owned by 2 per cent of the people. Fifty families owned 20 per cent of the land while the bulk of the population was landless.[42] Under Eisenhower, the US State Department attempted both in Iran (after the overthrow of Mossadeq and the reinstatement of the Shah) and in Saudi Arabia, alongside Israel, (in what was known as the British 'Iraqi solution') to use the client relationship to put pressure on the more nationalistic states – then Egypt and Syria. The British used Iraq to invade Iran in 1941 and kept a military base there through the unrest of 1951–3.[43]

The Ba'ath Party, which first came to power in 1958, consolidated in 1968 and by 1979 had spawned Saddam Hussein, owed its origins to the protest against British rule in the 1920s. It began in Syria and was also viewed suspiciously by the French who saw the British and the Americans using it to undermine their position. The first Iraqi Ba'ath Party members did not appear until 1951 and even in 1958 there were only 300 members. The Ba'ath vision was Pan-Arab but, akin to Latin America, it was based on an attempt to create a viable national capitalism with social welfare for the masses. As it came to power, welfare expenditure doubled as land occupations and riots took place in Kirkuk. Once they had adjusted, the Americans and the British found the Ba'athists were useful for their virulent anti-communism. Indeed, the persecution of the Iraqi Communist Party, which had organized the small urban industrial workers, dominated the 1960s. The problems and benefits revolved around oil. The 1961 counter-coup came a few days after the announcement of a new national oil company; but the Ba'athists eventually nationalized in 1973; a policy only reversed 30 years later by the USA. But even the army coup of 1963, which led to a virtual state of war against the Kurds, had involved nationalization of the banks and industry (which were small); the key elite control of the land was untouched.

Tikrit is famous historically not only for being the birthplace of the Kurd Saladin, but, after the Mongol invasion of 1394, for its memorial of severed heads. This would also be a fitting memorial for the Tikriti faction's domination of the Ba'ath Party. As deputy general secretary of the party from 1966, Saddam Hussein was head of a security state, which he modelled on the SS. Purges usually took out whole families. The oil wealth then enabled Saddam to build up a private sector, with multi-millionaires beholden to him, while then squandering the oil proceeds on palaces and wars against Iran and Kuwait. The CIA links with Saddam had been maintained through the 1980s with the George I administration agreeing weapon licences right until the day before the Kuwait invasion. The hope even at this late stage of pulling Iraq into the US orbit had led the Bush I strategists to assume that Iraq might just take the disputed islands in the Shatt al-Arab waterway. The Bush imperial family took ten years to undo this miscalculation. In the meantime, US imperialism, which had spawned Bin Laden from the struggle against communism in Afghanistan, had spawned a terrorist as head of state in Iraq.[44]

Another 1914?

As the new global economy and financial markets in the 1990s returned in a more intensive way to the world of the 1890s and of the late nineteenth-century British Empire, it is worth remembering that the world after 1890 came to an end in 1914. As we have been reminded in the last few years, shares can go down as well as up, and busts can follow booms, despite Gordon Brown and an independent Bank of England. (The Bank of England was very independent in 1925.) Likewise, health warnings should be attached to academic works on globalization, especially if they are written by Blair's philosopher courtiers like Giddens, to remind us that global empires can lead to global wars.[45]

Such thoughts do not usually populate mainstream publications, so in the weekend before the G8 meeting at Gleneagles and before the London bombings, where most of the media scrum was focused on Live 8 and Bob Geldof, it was good to see Will Hutton singing to a different hymn sheet than Hilary Benn. For Hutton was pointing out that hidden in the debate about climate change, for the US and Chinese elites, is a twentieth-century preoccupation with energy security. As the China National Oil Company bid for Union Oil of California in cash with money borrowed from the Chinese government, Hutton pointed to the secret undeclared struggle by the two powers over oil resources, noting that the US navy 'controls the sea' and US warships regularly shadow tankers taking Middle East oil to China – just to remind the 'communists' who is really in charge – rather like the British in 1865, you might think. Hutton did not mention that this struggle has even slopped over into places seemingly so far away as Darfur and the Sudan because it is China's claim on a chunk of Sudan's oil – and the revenues thereby given to the Khartoum government and its military campaigns in the south – that have made any settlement in the Sudan more difficult.

Hutton then goes on to compare China with Germany at the end of the nineteenth century. He argues that China has played this cleverly by giving its great power rivals – how odd to see such terms re-emerging during a G8 – a stake in its growth. Four hundred of the top 500 US companies manufacture in China; Wal-Mart, its biggest retailer, made its inroads on Chinese supplies; and China accumulates reserves while funding US debt. In the light of my work, this would seem more of an indication of US cleverness. Maybe Bush and the neo-cons are not quite the mad hatters they appear – they can leave that role to Geldof. For in fact, this is a classic sign of the Global Capitalist Empire at work – the key is the incorporation that binds the Chinese elite, like it binds Blair or Mbeki. The recognition of some mutual interests, however, does not necessarily prevent war.

Stuck in the middle of Hutton's piece is then an amazing sentence: 'the open question is whether it will end in another 1914'.[46] Hutton may not know it but he has stumbled on the debate between Kautsky on the one side for the mainstream German SPD and Rosa Luxemburg and Lenin on the other, between 1907 and 1914. Kautsky defended the theory of 'ultra imperialism': that the great powers were so integrated, that it did not make economic sense for the bourgeois classes to make war.[47] This may well have been true, but in Austria, Germany, Russia and Turkey there were more than the bourgeoisie involved. Today global capital and its attendant bourgeoisie rule more universally. Just as the London bombings revealed that going to war in Iraq made attacks on Britain more likely than before, so Hutton is right to pose the old question, does capitalist imperialism make another war inevitable?

After sanctioning the joint intervention with the George II regime in Iraq, Blair has nakedly revealed himself to stand full square in the Fabian tradition of elitist rule, imperialist intervention and support of big capital, which characterized the late nineteenth-century power game that led to 1914. As it was in the 1890s, so it is now. As new Liberalism was the Fabian adjustment to the global capitalism of the 1890s, so Blairism and New Labour is the new Fabian adjustment to the global capitalism back in place since 1989. The first led to the Boer War and the Great War; the interlude depended on the Cold War against 'communism'; the second has now launched the 'war on terrorism'. The first at least was launched for the sake of British imperialism; the second exists as the propaganda ambassador for American and global capitalism.

4

The History of Making Poverty in Neo-Colonial Africa

The end of history?

When I first heard the Make Poverty History slogan it sounded oddly familiar. Instincts also told me, before I knew of all the NGOs who had signed up to it, that there was something insidiously wrong. At its simplest level, even if all its aims were achieved there was no way at all that poverty would be ended in 2005. Why lead with such an impossible outcome, which superficially seems to be driven by left-wing infantilism? I recalled that the World Bank's campaign slogan was 'End World Poverty', which actually is a better summary of the cause. Maybe it doesn't have the media-friendly snappiness of the 2005 slogan, but at least 'Let's End World Poverty' actually says on the tin what most campaigners actually mean. Does the Make Poverty History brand tell us subtly something about this campaign which is not at all what it appears to say on the tin? Nor will it do what it claims.

It took further thought to recognize that it was oddly similar to a symbolic academic article published in 1989: Francis Fukuyama's *The End of History*. Fukuyama, who is now self-proclaimed as one of the world's best-known academics, had provided the academic justification for the recent triumph of liberal capitalist democracy and the defeat of the communist bloc.[1] Here was the final gloss for all those Kremlinologists, like Fukuyama, who had been busy planning the evil Soviet Empire's fall. A philosopher could use Hegelian logic and language to claim that a universal history had reached its final culmination in the US model.

What better than to have an American citizen of Japanese extraction justify the new world order with Germanic thoroughness and logic? What better for this social theme to be launched for the first time at the University of Chicago, for it proclaimed the apparent triumph of the economic doctrines of Milton Friedman and the Chicago Boys who had plied their trade from Chile to Pakistan? Now all that was required was for the 'great disruption' of the social effects of globalization and modernization to be managed by our benevolent rulers.

We need to know more about what game is being played out here and whose interests are being served. Fukuyama's own history reveals rather more than his book about the motivations lying behind his work. Fukuyama's Harvard PhD had been on the Soviet 'threat' to the Middle East.[2] As Chomsky has alerted us, he then served the US State Department for both Reagan and George I regimes, concentrating on the security 'threats' from Iraq, Afghanistan and Iran. In 1980 he was advising the new military dictatorship in Pakistan. In 2001, he was to back the war against Iraq and looked at a clash of civilizations even more fervently than Huntington, the original mentor of the theory.[3] Fukuyama also worked for Paul Wolfowitz, who as policy guru for the Pentagon was one of the first 'neoconservatives' to write of a US foreign and defence policy based on pre-eminence and pre-emption. It was Wolfowitz, Rumsfeld and Cheney who put Iraq on George II's agenda on the evening of 9/11; Blair's coalition-building was a front. As Wolfowitz is so connected to the US Empire's strategy for global capital, it can hardly be a coincidence to see him newly installed at the World Bank. With a degree in Classics and involvement in the New American Century think tank, Fukuyama knows all about running empires.[4]

A new neo-colonialism?

The argument here then is that there is a hidden neo-colonial history to the making of poverty in Africa and elsewhere that is akin to the veiled histories of Fukuyama, the Make Poverty History Campaign and Blair's Africa Commission. The language of the NGO campaign unconsciously gives away its true nature, for the language of compassion is to be manipulated to serve the interests of neo-liberal global capital. The Make Poverty History Campaign in 2005 has the odour of the kind of propaganda effort that started straight after 9/11 to justify the US and British invasion of Iraq. Now most of us know the lies and manipulation that went on to justify that, but I have seen no NGO publicly raising doubts about this campaign. Indeed, the ability of the non-elected NGOs to sing from the same hymn sheet on public platforms has all the worst elements of a New Labour Party rallying around Blair and Brown at election time. Yet, the NGO development lobby is being manipulated on its own ground. The beggars have been so starved of the rich guy's attention, that they are delighted to be given some money and media attention at last. For this, like the Pentagon's shock and awe, is their baby: never mind, if the big boys come in and spin it for their ends, it is still a good cause – doubling aid, cancelling debt, changing trade rules, and good governance – which liberal compassionate people could possibly be against that? The answer is to beware of an Orwellian agenda where a genuine enthusiasm to help the poor, especially in Africa, is being manipulated by the power elite to serve their own and other corporate interests – including the money-raising interests and publicity of the NGOs themselves.

If a hidden agenda to support global capital is partially visible in the philosophical language, its practical leadership is also revealing. The language here is reminiscent of New Labour's first symbolic foray when in government. From Clare Short's Department of International Development in 2000, came 'Eliminating World Poverty: Making Globalization Work For the Poor'. The arrogance of this managerial caste is laid bare in this techno speak. The section titles tell us that we need to know about the global elite's belief in its ability to manage globalization – 'promoting' efficiency and reducing corruption; 'harnessing' private finance and 'capturing' gains from trade. If, as Rawnsley has argued, a small cabal has captured the Labour Party and thereby the British government, it now believes it can manage the world. No wonder it has been forced into bed with the world's only unilateral power. Here three years before the Iraq affair, when Blair was actually to embark on five wars in six years, is laid out the need to 'reduce violent conflicts' for a 'rules based' international trade. While it is accepted that two thirds of world trade goes through transnational corporations, not a critical word on this form of capital is uttered at all.[5] As Mandelson (that champion of spin) has discovered, you might as well manage the wind as attempt to manage the Chinese economy or global capital from Europe.

Much of the development discourse of the 1990s sounds remarkably like British colonial discourse after 1882. This should not surprise us. As a renewed globalization takes over, the propaganda in favour of the White Man's Burden reaches a crescendo with the simplicities of the African Commission. As Graham has also pointed out, a coalition of reliable African leaders has been rolled out, all with strong IMF and World Bank links, to further a new neo-colonial scramble for Africa. We can best understand this potential future by looking at the past 130 years of colonial inheritance.[6]

The colonial state: tribute and corruption

The old African empires, like those of the Incas and Aztecs, were built on tribute from the periphery. Rodney argues that the tribute system in Africa was a major means of mopping up the surplus product. With relatively low population densities, there was little other way to gain control of the surplus. Unlike in feudal Western Europe where serfs were tied to their lords, no African feudalism developed. There was too much open land so there was always more land for settled peoples to move into; likewise this gave more space for both hunter–gatherers and nomadic pastoralists. In many ways, the African state and military are still living off the same system. However, the tribute system was only stable as long as it could be extracted: otherwise arbitrary and tyrannical rule resulted – not a bad description of some African regimes in the twenty-first century. Churchill, who knew all about colonies and empire, described the past and present well: 'Dictators ride to and fro upon tigers which they dare not dismount and the tigers are getting hungry.'[7]

McCarthy points out that once the colonial powers established themselves in Africa they taxed the Africans to pay for their own subordination. What was even worse, the hut and poll taxes were specifically designed to force Africans into the cash economy: hunters, pastoralists and self-sufficient peasants would otherwise have no need to work in the 'white man's' economy. This principal economic dislocation caused by the imposition of a colonial despotism was to force the African population either into the position of semi-proletarians – migrant and temporary workers in their own lands – or to be peasant producers of cash crops. No wonder he notes that the taxes were deeply resented – they were symbolic of a transformed lifestyle imposed on them by force of arms. If taxes did not work, other weapons were employed: to build the railways, forced labour was introduced and, as in the Caribbean, sometimes it was indentured labour brought from

India. Africans have long been conditioned to live under corrupt governments imposed on them from the outside, taxing and taking tribute. Colonial power was built on such 'corruption'. 'India is held in thraldom by an Indian army maintained at the cost of India.'[8] Marx's summary of this fundamental trick of colonial and imperial rule is fundamental to any historical and political understanding of African governance.

Africa's role in global capitalism

Looking to the contemporary situation, it is worth stating clearly at the outset of this analysis: not all poverty, or all of Africa's problems are caused by global capitalism. Ironically, where poverty is most acute – in Africa – it is often where capitalist relations have spread least, not most. Here again specifics matter. It is not just colonialism in Africa; Malaysia and Hong Kong were colonies. Nor is it just 'corrupt' governments; though many are corrupt. We need to analyse the specific form of Africa's integration both within the old imperialism and today's global capitalism. The key here is that the nature of Africa's economic incorporation was to leave it as a producer of basic commodities and raw materials – the prices of which have been in relative decline for more than a century. Two cash crops alone – coffee and cotton – often dominate. For example, all of the major East African states we shall look at briefly in this chapter have coffee export economies. Coffee accounts for over 90 per cent of export earnings in Uganda; for 60 per cent of Ethiopia's external earnings; for 40 per cent in Tanzania; and 30 per cent in Kenya. Since the 1990s, coffee sales values have fallen absolutely by 30 per cent in Ethiopia and Kenya and have halved in Uganda.[9]

This African incorporation reflects its relatively low level of development in the nineteenth century and the lateness of the national development option. What most countries in South America were trying by 1820, most of Africa did not reach until the 1960s. This low level of economic development goes a long way to explain, in Eric Williams' phrase, 'too many pigs trying to get at the trough'. Africa does not produce enough, and in some places food literally goes to those with the guns. All the ethnic, religious and national tensions are overlaid on this fundamental economic fact: there is not enough surplus produced and power too often comes from the barrel of a gun.

African poverty may not simply be a consequence of global capitalism, it is however partly a consequence of European slave raiding, colonialism and continuing imperialism. All that can be attempted here are a few historical examples of the internal development implications. It is a truism that in the 'scramble for Africa' European colonial powers created countries with no more legitimacy than a European compromise around lines on a map. In the worst case, Somalis were spread around five countries. It should not be a surprise therefore when the governance of such states appears a totally artificial construct originally created by the colonial powers and strapped onto the backs of ordinary Africans, usually with client elite Africans (often chosen ethnic-ally by the ruling power) to do the strapping. No wonder then that African governments are 'corrupt'; they are borrowed im-positions from both the colonial and pre-colonial regimes before them. Only Ethiopia escaped colonial rule and it was subject to a British and two Italian invasions.[10]

Sen links famines to war – and the major immediate issue in Africa is often war. This is often a handy excuse for the self-styled global managers. Apart from the anti-colonial wars in Angola, Mozambique and South Africa, McCarthy points out that most of these wars have been secessionist. This follows on from the creation of arbitrary states whose tribute systems today are de-pendent usually on the control of any precious natural resource; for example, Katanga and Zaire (copper) or Biafra in Nigeria (oil). As in Latin America, the economy has been geared to extraction for export: first to slaves and then to resources.

Rural infrastructure has always looked outwards. Only in South Africa, with its extensive settler community, is there an integrated structure. Indeed, there is little inter-African trade. Like the cities of antiquity, the urban areas of Africa live on the backs of the country people, and agriculture has done best in Kenya, the Ivory Coast and Malawi where the ruling elite has a substantial rural interest.[11]

Egypt: colonialism and debt

When I was a young Christian I read *Who Moved the Stone?* Frank Morison wanted to show that the resurrection was a Christian myth and ended up being converted to the view that Jesus did rise again, as the New Testament claimed. Fieldhouse in his *Economics and Empire* sets out to show that economics had little to do with the establishment of empire in the nineteenth century. Apart from revealing the paucity of this academic perception of economic history, he ends up by showing that a subtle blend of what he calls 'politics' mixed with some 'economics' in fact does explain how the British Empire got itself embroiled in the scramble for Africa. For the proper historical discipline of political economy, distorted by twentieth-century academia into two tiny boxes, is perfectly capable of analysing this mix of long and short, economic and political objectives. Nowhere is this subtle blend of economics and politics better shown than in the story of the British Empire's takeover of Egypt. The domino effect, which the British taught the Americans so well in Asia, was also vitally important in Africa: because Britain took on Egypt, she was embroiled in the Sudan; because of the Sudan, she took the protectorate in Uganda; once Uganda was secure, Kenya looked a good place for white settlers. By 1918, having defeated Germany in East Africa in the 'Ice Cream war', why not take Tanzania too and the link-up Rhodes had always wanted right through Africa would be virtually complete.

The problems of Egypt in the 1870s were certainly generated by 'economics'. After Napoleon had broken the old despotic owner-ship of the land, Egypt under Mohammed Ali had broken away from a weakening Ottoman Empire in 1805. What Fieldhouse uncritically calls the 'modernization' of Egypt began under a new 'Khedive', especially after 1867. By the 1870s this meant the increasing integration of Egypt in the European economy. Forty per cent of the scarce fertile Nile valley land was soon given over to cotton.

Between 1863 and 1875 exports, largely of cotton, increased more than threefold. The driver as in many underdeveloped nations before and since was the state. Their capital was largely in the form of – yes, you guessed it – debt. This was of course the 1870s not the 1970s. Egyptian government loans increased to E£90 million, six times the level of yearly exports. With interest on Egyptian debt, being of higher risk, running at 12 per cent versus the normal 6 per cent, two thirds of Egyptian government revenues went towards repaying debt by the early 1870s. Sounds familiar then. The outcome is also akin to Mexico's in the 1980s; in 1869 Tunis went into default. In 1876, Egypt defaulted, both to French and British financiers. French engineers had built the Suez Canal, but 80 per cent of the trade going through the Canal was British. Fieldhouse makes much of the economic argument that intervention was not driven by the bondholders. So for him, the first interventions in Egypt were 'political' – not 'economic' – to protect the Empire, thereby managing to ignore the huge 'economic' benefits to Britain from India.[12] Clearly, the British ruling class was able to see beyond an immediate financial issue to the wider strategic and geopolitical ramifications, which of course were ultimately hugely 'economic'. This is quite akin to those apologists who look at the immediate issues of July 1914 (which were not openly 'economic') and promptly forget all the lead up from 1870.

US style, a so-called anti-imperialist, like Gladstone, was

actually in charge after 1880 when the final decision was made to intervene. Never have the pressures on the executive committee of the ruling class been more clearly shown to override personal peccadilloes. It is interesting to compare Gordon Brown's impeccable public support over Iraq, when his own hero Jimmy Maxton went to prison as a conscientious objector in the Great War. Whatever his personal feelings on imperialism, and with the succession and party unity in mind, he has subordinated his own views to the need to support Blair.

Protest and invasion

In 1875, under economic pressure, the Khedive sold 7/16 of the shares in the Suez Canal; with Disraeli the main driving force on the British side. In 1878, the crops failed and there was famine. The Sultan's attempts to recoup money by cutting army pay in half and by increasing tax only led to protests, led by the military. By May 1882, British and French warships had begun gunboat diplomacy and in June a nationalist uprising broke out with over 700 killed; more noticeable in Britain, because 50 Europeans were killed. The nationalist Colonel Arabi, now in power, anticipating the Jubilee Campaign, had decided to repudiate Egyptian debt.[13] Gladstone sent in the troops as a 'temporary' measure to 'restore law and order'. The disparity of a nineteenth-century 'shock and awe' campaign was quickly revealed as the Egyptian army lost 10,000 men in their resistance to the invasion; the British lost 57. Between 1882 and 1907 the British stated 27 times that they planned to leave. While pretending to act in concert with other powers, Gladstone actually acted unilaterally. The temporary stay in Egypt was to last 74 years.[14]

The renewed nationalist protests in Egypt after World War One could hardly have come as a surprise to the British elite. Besides the anger in the Arab world over the great betrayal of their independence hopes, there were other internal reasons for the discontent that resurfaced in 1919. The British had reintroduced forced labour; they underpaid the peasants for their cotton, as world prices rose in the war and an increasing population was pushing a discontented and increasingly landless peasantry into the cities. Egypt was now importing a third of its wheat to sustain cotton production for the Empire. A third of these revenues still went to paying off debt. Until a parliamentary monarchy was set up in 1922, Egypt was ruled under martial law for nine years.[15] Given such a tradition of the violent repression of protest, continued by Nasser and maintained by Presidents Sadat and Mubarak, it should not be a surprise that some of the most militant of the 'Muslim Brotherhood' have come out of Egypt.[16]

Sudan: the problem of the state

Recent British Christian interest has often focused on the Sudan, particularly on the work of Amnesty and other NGOs during the many civil wars. Sudan has lost at least a third of its population displaced or in war and suffered four major famines since 1984. The dead number up to two million. The agenda of the politics of 'genocide' may have been too easily captured by the right-wing American Christians' dislike of Sudan as a past supporter of Osama Bin Laden. Even so, Sudan is a good case study of the problem of state formation in Africa. Sudan is the biggest country in Africa with one million square miles (compared to Britain's 93,000); India is only 170,000 bigger. Yet where the Indian population is nearly a billion; the Sudan has only 30 million.

Slavery

Sudan has also been troubled by slavery and by slave raiding from its earliest history. The early treaties between Nubia and Egypt were sealed by an exchange of slaves. The word Sudani in colloquial Arabic means a black slave. Modern raiding from north to south has an ancient history; the Darfur-based Sultanate raided the south in the seventeenth century, for example. Sudan's huge size has always made governance difficult. The divides amount to far more than that between north and south, or Arab and African, Muslim and Christian; there are many peoples and ways of life that spread from pastoralists to modern urban traders. It has over 50 ethnic groups and 115 languages. It was not until the nineteenth century that the south came under the control of a state based in Khartoum, originally established as an army garrison by Egypt. The new Egyptian regime raided the south from the 1820s. The Mahdi state, in power from 1881 – an early 'nationalist' and 'Islamic' movement – also needed the slave trading to fund its arms needs.[17]

The British spun their move back to the Sudan by requiring the 1885 killers of General Gordon to pay for their own 'redemption', as one bishop put it. Since it was ten years later, and the Mahdi himself was already dead, we must look elsewhere for a real explanation – namely to colonial competition. With the French coming from the west on the Nile at Fashoda, the Italians would no longer provide a block to German expansion from Tanzania in the east, after their defeat by the Ethiopians in 1896. The Sudan now seemed a back-door route into Egypt.

British colonial rule in the Sudan

When the Mahdists were overthrown in 1898 at Omdurman (with 27,000 Sudanese killed in the battle), the British were also aided and abetted by local rulers in the south. As with Spanish imperial rule in the Americas, the British colonial state in the Sudan then built on the older exploitative patterns. Under colonialism, the transition to old-style rule was quick in the north, but in the south 'pacification', as in Iraq, continued right through the 1920s. The imposition of colonial rule led to successive uprisings by various Dinka peoples and bombing from the British air force was common.[18] Ruth First shows how the Sudan carried a 'double load' – of disunity between north and south and of being a pawn in the colonial conflict: 'Little of any significance … in Sudan's politics did not have some root in externally prompted conflict.' The British colonials compounded the old problem by keeping the north and south apart for administration, further bequeathing a 'perpetual source of division'.[19]

In the 1870s, when Gordon was the Egyptian adviser, he had suggested laying claim to the whole of East Africa. When General Kitchener conquered the Sudan his army was Egyptian and was 75 per cent funded by Cairo. Between 1898 and 1924 Sudan and Egypt had been run as one country. This ended with further outbreaks of Egyptian nationalism between 1919 and 1924. When Sudanese troops rebelled on the assassination of Egypt's governor general in 1924, Sudan's 'Defence Force' was made independent from the Egyptian army. The next British plan in the 1920s had been to create a super East African state including Sudan, Kenya and Uganda. A white settler elite and the Uganda landed chiefs would be reliable allies against the nationalist threat.

Independent Sudan

In the south of Sudan, the customs of native and indigenous law were stressed, but the south was closed to Islam to stop the spread of a resistance ideology and English not Arabic was made the official language. Missionary work had been in competition with those working from Uganda and schooling was also tied to conversion: 'no baptism, no schooling'. Only after 1946, when the first decision to make Sudan independent was made, was much education given to prepare for a new administration. The division between north and south was immediately reflected in elections in 1953: the regional winners being from different parties. Both the north and Egypt wanted a 'united' Sudan and although the south was more anti-British than pro-north, the Egyptians won support for their view by funding all the new parties. By 1954, of the 800 civil service posts only 6 were held by southerners.[20]

Sudan amazingly was the first African state to be given independence by Britain in 1956. This had little to do with the Sudan and was again mainly to do with the British in Egypt. An army coup had toppled the limited parliamentary monarchy in 1952 and Nasser's 'Arab socialism' was clearly in command by 1954. But the divisions between north and south Sudan were not the main British concern from 1953 to 1956. As one British civil servant put it 'a possible civil war in the South and administrative chaos (did not) weigh so much as the apparent certainty of serious disorders and war … in the (Egyptian) canal zone in a week or two's time'. This war – at Suez – did, of course, break out in 1956.

Given the Sudan's divided history, it was virtually the least prepared of any of the British African colonies to govern itself. Sudan's self-determination was now granted in order to subvert the Egyptian claim to it. Independence was a tactic for overall imperial control. The first civil war began at the same time. Sudan's civil wars – the longest in Africa bar Angola – stretch back then, like so many, to the coming of independence. Around 75 per cent of the population was in the north and around 30 per cent of the population was neither Arab nor Muslim. Yet the southern army was led largely by northern officers – the first mutiny and killings came in 1955.[21]

Before the recent advent of oil, cotton was the pivot of the economy and the Gezira scheme was its key. By 1956, it covered 1 million acres and 62 per cent of Sudan's exports were of cotton. Markakis describes schemes of mechanization like Gezira as the 'penetrating wedge of capitalism'. Here landlords owned as much as 40,000 acres each and the government would threaten to use the army to pick cotton, if in the 1960s the Communist-led labourers ever stirred up any trouble. Up to 90 per cent of the population, however, was excluded from the capitalist wedge.

When there was an attempted Communist coup in 1971, it was put down by troops. Sudan still contains the largest percentage of nomadic pastoral people anywhere in the world. Large-scale irrigation, usually for commercial crops, as in Gezira, can rob other areas of water for pasture and lead to droughts. The government overthrew the traditional land rights of the southern pastoral peoples in 1970, trying to coerce a new labour force for this mechanized agriculture. In the midst of Sudan's war, what we are now witnessing is the steady destruction of the pastoral way of life. The colonial regime had destroyed the old economy of Africa, while the neo-colonial one was not able to replace it with anything like a sufficient alternative.[22]

Military coups: 1958–69

Having moved in to take some of the British role in Egypt after 1956, the USA also looked to the Sudan to back a 'responsible military'. The US elite was clearly worried that there would be an Egyptian takeover without the army in command. Recent US governments have been busy condemning the 'genocide' in Sudan; not many mention that this military, like the Taliban, was initially funded by the USA in 1957 first to oppose Egypt and then Ethiopia and Libya. As with British colonialism, the Cold War politics of the US elite bears its own chunk of responsibility for genocide in the Sudan.

The first assembly in 1958 was dissolved by a military coup rather than allow a decision on a federal solution. As its first act the new regime banned all political parties and demonstrations. As it did in Egypt after 1959, US loan money arrived. Again, after another coup in 1964 a round-table conference was halted in 1965. The first large-scale massacres date from this time. The development efforts of the 1960s had doubled debt, while foreign debt had gone up ten times. This is all long before OPEC-induced debt.

By the 1970s, the Sudan was also to become the plaything of both the Cold War and of African geopolitics. This was also long before Osama Bin Laden took any hand in things. Colonel, later President, Nimeiri's regime in 1969 was another military 'socialist' regime that the USA backed (visits from George I when vice president and tele-evangelists being the highlights) against the Soviet-backed Ethiopians. Much of the fighting was close to the Ethiopian border, with the Ethiopians and Libyans supporting the south and the north helping Eritrea as retaliation against the Ethiopians. Both Amin's Uganda and the Israelis also joined the fray.[23]

Debt service now took 70 per cent of exports, while imports of arms took another 15 per cent. In some desperation Nimeiri, like Nasser in the early 1950s, had seen the need to co-opt the Islamic movement. In 1977, a deal was agreed bringing in the leader of Sudan's Muslim Brotherhood and the Mahdi's great-grandson (Sadiq Al-Mahdi). Although Nimeiri had done a deal in 1972 giving some autonomy to the south, its problems would not go away and at each breakdown the ferociousness of the civil wars increased. When a referendum in the south was aborted in 1982, two army mutinies followed in 1983. Despite pleas for a halt, US-supplied military hardware enabled the president to attack the south with greater ferocity after 1983.

John Garang's life 'personified Sudan's bloody civil war'. Born into an illiterate family of Dinka cattle herders, the US influence on the Sudanese army is all too evident: Garang was educated in the USA, eventually taking a PhD in economics at Iowa and advancing to the rank of colonel with infantry training in Georgia. Yet, in 1983, the Ethiopian Derg announced Garang as the leader of the south's revolutionary army (the SPLA). This was largely seen as a Dinka movement, and by many of the Dinka people as their own government. As it was supported by the Ethiopians, themselves fighting separatist movements, its official line was a southern 'revolution' for a united, democratic, secular state.

This added to the antagonism of the northern Islamists. As the SPLA spread into new areas in Nubia and Southern Kordofan (where land clearing for cotton had also gone on apace) and became more efficient at organizing resistance, government troops found it easier to attack defenceless villages.

In 1985, Nimeiri was overthrown and in a parliamentary election Sadiq, whom he had arrested in 1981, became prime minister. Negotiations broke down with the SPLA over the potential imposition of shariah law. By this time, the SPLA and the NGOs had virtually taken on the role of governance in the south. The official northern government then recruited Baqqara militias to fight the Dinka in the late 1980s. The principal motive was as much economic as ethnic: between 1983 and 1985 the Baqqara had lost land to mechanization and cattle. The attempted subjugation of the south then reached new heights as an Islamic regime became entrenched after yet another coup in 1989, masterminded by Sudan's Muslim Brotherhood. The new dictator, General Omar Al Bashir brandished a Koran and a Kalashnikov, as a symbol of jihad. Although the SPLA effectively conquered Equatoria Province in 1990, its position was weakened temporarily by the collapse of the Derg's regime in Ethiopia in 1991. Up to 400,000 refugees in Ethiopia were forced back into the Sudan. This meant that the central government could try and split southern political and ethnic alignments by manipulating relief supplies. Government and rebels were fighting; so too Dinka fought Nuer and Dinka fought Dinka.

Control of the oil tribute

The stakes were raised by the modern form of tribute corruption: the discovery in 1978 of oil in the south. When oil production began, the government cleared a 40-square-mile area around the oil facilities. By 2004, the Sudan was producing 300,000 barrels a day of crude. This makes the Sudan the fifth largest oil exporter from Africa (only Angola, Algeria, Libya and Nigeria are bigger exporters). Oil already accounted for 75 per cent of exports in 2000 and the government budget had increased ten times since 1995: ample funds to keep the military well supplied. The northern definition of the south carefully excluded the oilfields. Nevertheless, the prospects of serious money clarified the need for yet another 'peace'.

In the January 2005 peace agreement Garang became one of Sudan's vice presidents; the highest post ever attained by a southerner. Garang's untimely death in a helicopter crash in August 2005 has raised doubts over the agreement; the suggestion being that President Bashir's regime had no intention of sharing power or wealth. If, in early 2005, Garang personified peace: 'his death will sharply test which legacy will prevail'.[24] The legacy of slave raiding, colonial divide and rule, US military Cold War games, commercial capitalist farming and the conflicts over ways of life and perceptions of society will prevail for a great deal longer. And yet again, oil may be the key.

Kenya: settlers and land

In Kenya, what appeared to the incoming colonial administration to be empty uplands were in fact the nomadic lands of Masai and Kikuyu pastoral peoples. These were simply taken on the coming of the railway in 1901 and sold to white settlers at knockdown prices. The new settlers were given a virtual monopoly (around 80 per cent) of the best potential land in the highlands, and by the early 1950s this amounted to around 7 million acres. The settlers were not peasant farmers; the average land holding was 2,400 acres. They needed the taxes of the state to force the Africans to work on 'their' land. By the 1920s, 50 per cent of the Lou and Kikuyu worked for Europeans. Contracts were served under the pain of prison if broken. Together these two peoples represented 33 per cent of Kenya's African population (20 per

cent Kikuyu and 13 per cent Luo). As the African population increased – it had reached 5.2 million by 1948, versus 30,000 Europeans – so did pressure on the land and on wages. The latter were
pushed down to a minimum. The settlers' mixed farms sold their
maize back to their workers; even the wages went back to the
Europeans. As in Latin America, there was a low demand and
thereby little local manufacturing, although there was a demand
for luxury-end imported consumer goods (often from India)
from the Europeans. As in Argentina, the main domestic industry was in food processing (though in Kenya, it was originally
only for domestic production not export). This was a monopoly
based on protection which served to make Nairobi the local centre with both Tanzania and Uganda the peripheries.

The land problem led to one major form of early Kikuyu protest in particular: squatting on 'white' land. The European farmers often turned a blind eye to this – the squatters provided useful
labour and were usually bound by serf-like contracts tying them
for 180 days a year. 'Kaffir' farming was also allowed: share-
cropping or even formal short-term tenancy for cash. Despite
half-hearted attempts to stimulate African peasant production
after 1945, all remembered that legislation had been introduced
to forbid squatting in 1918. As late as 1931, a million acres was
still squatters' land. Through the 1920s, as prices fell, settlers demanded more work for fewer benefits. Landless Africans pushed
to the towns led to a general strike over wages in 1939. As Kenyan
independence loomed, the colonial government was careful to
make sure that power was given to men like Kenyatta who represented the few relatively large Kenyan landowners. Kenyatta's
main opponent was conveniently held in remote internal exile for
ten years. During the 'Emergency' from 1952 large numbers of
landless Kikuyu were deported from the Central Highlands and
Nairobi – and often supported the Land Freedom Army formed
in 1960. Thirteen thousand were killed in what was effectively
a civil war. Having removed the political and military threat,

a controlled peasantry was now allowed: restrictive legislation was abolished and encouragement was given to peasant farmers, largely back in the Kikuyu heartland. Small peasant landholdings increased from 5 million to 14 million acres by 1964; 55 per cent of the increase came in coffee.[25]

Christian Aid introduces the Kenyan problem with the line: 'in the colonial period Kenya started cotton production'.[26] Besides the key export of Kenya being coffee, this blandness completely misses Kenya's colonial history. Nothing on how the peoples were pushed onto marginal land, taxed and forced into cash crops. Nothing even on how such African economies have become so dependent on one or two cash crops as a partial consequence. Now it is all about fairer trade and debt relief. Yet, a new crony African elite remains in charge of the land. With protection for Kenya, who benefits? On such poor historical analysis, bad policy is made. Meanwhile, to understand the early cotton economy, there is an excellent case study next door to Kenya in Uganda.

The client state of British Buganda

Uganda provides an excellent case study of the way the colonial inheritance has structured Africa's consequent economic and political problems of underdevelopment and corruption. The Uganda that was created by the British Empire at the turn of the twentieth century to support its strategic interests from Egypt down the Nile was put together from what had been up to 200 distinct political entities and over 60 languages. The unification of Uganda was carried through by the British backing of the kingdom of Buganda. This was a mutual collaboration not just an imperial imposition: Buganda used British weapons and support to overrun rivals. This meant the new Uganda was built around a client state, which had major internal consequences for landholdings within Buganda and for any unity within the new 'nation'.

The struggles in the Sudan also had a major impact on the north of Uganda in the nineteenth century, as they have again particularly since Amin's coup of 1971. The Khartoum-based raiders that plagued southern Sudan also put north-western Uganda – the provinces of West Nile, Acholi and Madi – under effective Egyptian control from 1863 to 1879. The Egyptian State attempted to 'nationalize' the slave trade and imposed heavy taxes in grain. The struggle to control the flow of slaves – for the slave traders joined the Mahdist rebellion of 1881–98 against Egypt – caused immense disruption both to trade and to settled agriculture in the north. Unlike the invaded and disrupted north, the fertile and better-watered south of Uganda had a more settled agriculture, which created contradictions for the colonial power. The 'Lancashire' cotton lobby quickly saw the possibilities of using Uganda to produce cotton as an alternative to dependence on the USA. The extent of the troubles in the last decade of the nineteenth century persuaded the Empire to do a deal with the Buganda chiefs, who got 50 per cent of the land: once firmly based here, harsher terms could then be imposed on the rest of the new Uganda. The chiefs became willing servants of the colonial power, for they enforced the new state's tax system. As later in Kenya, the Ugandan peasant was encouraged to work and not to be indolent by tax. In 1900, a hut tax was established; in 1905 it was supplemented by a poll tax. The aim was to give the peasants three options – to work for the government, to labour for the new European plantations being established or to grow their own cash crops. Since most naturally enough opted for the latter, the 'native' chiefs were to use persuasion on the peasants to get them to work on plantations. When this failed too, legislation was passed to re-enact the historical forms of forced labour: the peasant was then legally forced to work on the plantations for a month a year; later, this was raised to two months. The special treatment for the chiefs was enshrined in the 'gun tax' – only those with less than 500 acres had to pay it. Jorgensen calls the phase till 1922, when forced labour was abolished, one of primitive capitalist accumulation. Indeed, in Buganda in this period most of the surplus was extracted by the chiefs, but much was paid in tax to run the colonial administration.[27] The very fact of a more settled agricultural labour force used to working for its chiefs meant that, unlike Kenya, the Ugandan peasants could grow the new cash crops, undercutting European attempts to establish plantation agriculture.

Cotton in Uganda

The key to getting the Ugandan cotton industry off the ground, however, was transport. More unrest in Egypt in 1893 led to the decision to build rapid access from the East African coast. With the Ugandan Protectorate established in 1894, the railway was built on the same gauge as the Egyptian, thus aiding supplies for the British victory in the Sudan in 1898. When rail reached Kampala in the same year, transport costs for cotton export fell dramatically. Once peasant cotton agriculture was established it tended to be favoured by the cotton lobby against the other cash crop plantation owners, who complained to the colonial authorities in vain.

By 1907, cotton had already become Uganda's largest export; in 1916, it accounted for 49 per cent. Peasant cotton production for cash mushroomed each time the British State imposed its taxes – the largest rises followed increases in tax and/or chiefly rent – in 1906, 1910 and 1920. In territories other than Buganda, chiefs were appointed and were paid salaries, on top of rents and tithe income, by the colonial state to enforce cotton cultivation and quality control. The push to cotton was so fast in Busoga that there was not enough land planted to food – with shortages in 1908, 1914, 1918, 1920, 1927 and 1928. The lower classes were under pressure. There were 17 tax revolts in eastern Uganda between 1903 and 1911. There was a rising in Toro in 1919. Punitive

British pacification expeditions, as in Iraq and the Sudan in the same era, were yearly features. In Buganda, the chiefs' wealth, power and status was becoming less acceptable, while the population of around a million in 1888 was down to 650,000 in 1920. New low rents of course encouraged more cash crop production – and soon coffee. All the Ugandan peasantry had gained from colonialism were limited landholding rights, four acres, an 'iron hoe, a few yards of imported cloth and an occasional blanket'.

The other key development in the post World War One Ugandan economy was the switch in its cotton exports from the UK to India. By 1939, Uganda's cotton gins were controlled by an expatriate Indian bourgeoisie, with strong links to the local Indian traders and gin owners within Uganda. The colonial authorities were nothing if not good at recognizing realities. With the beginnings of a thriving Ugandan–Indian cotton trade, and the need for more to bolster colonial tax revenues, the last thing they needed was a restrictive aristocratic caste in Uganda further blocking their power. The Buganda chiefs were not pushing ahead with new areas under cotton – as in other provinces where no such favourable deal had been done. The colonial state no longer needed the excessively favourable terms which it had given in 1900 to the Bugandan chiefs, so by 1928, the independent power of the old chiefly aristocracy was destroyed by restricting the rents they could charge. Now all in Uganda were entirely dependent on the state's favour. On such has a century of Uganda 'corruption' been built. Whatever accumulation was going on in Uganda was mediated through the state, which became the only substantial way to accrue wealth, power or military might. The dictatorships of Africa learnt this lesson well from their colonial masters. As Mamdani comments, the missionaries had campaigned against slavery only to acquiesce in the enforcement of a new (tax and economic) slavery in the interests of a 'Christian' civilization.[28]

Ethiopia: appeasement and invasion

Apart from saving Christian civilization, one of the rationales given for the invasion of Iraq is that of the supposed lessons of the appeasement of the dictators of the 1930s. After the London bombings of 7/7, the spirit of the 1940s Blitz has been claimed too; we are told that as the people faced down our enemies then, we too must not let our 'terrorist' enemies win now. The cold war against communism is to be replaced by the intelligence, security and police war against terror. If Churchill could claim business as usual in 1914, London is asked to use the tube, turn up for work and continue business as usual – with just a better eye for dangerous baggage or for suspicious people, like the Brazilian electrician shot by the police. These analogies are all false and part of the myth-making exercise of justifying the elite's wars. It was hardly business as usual when ten million people were killed after August 1914; nor was the Blitz equally shared: the East End, by the Docks, was hit by far the hardest – Shoreditch losing 40 per cent of its long-term population.

Most misleading of all, is the comparison with appeasement. The last great test of the old 'United Nations' was Italy's invasion of Ethiopia in 1935. Once it had failed to stop Mussolini, the League of Nations was effectively dead, and it was shown to be so when Hitler marched into the Rhineland in 1936. Further pursuit of the historical parallels is rather more revealing than the usual analogy of 'appeasing Hitler', first used by Bush I in Gulf War I. Although Saddam was a peculiarly violent dictator, who had been a threat to his neighbours in Iran and Kuwait, the appropriate comparison is not with Hitler and Mussolini. For here is not a world colossus, but a client regime, a tinpot dictator who ruled a semi-feudal countryside and was only able to throw his weight around because of a calculated use of the Western powers, who had armed both Iraq and Iran and were happy to see the Iranian revolution attacked. Equally, a 'tinpot dictator' is a fairly apt description of Haile Selassie's Ethiopia in 1935: an imperial monarchy, which had used British empire-building in East Africa to build its own empire from the Abyssinian heartlands out into what became Ethiopia. This followed a tradition in Africa also used by the Bugandan kings to build what became the British 'protectorate' of Uganda; a term the British grew to like in Iraq. It was this dictator who Mussolini had invaded and tried to subdue. It is a commonplace to say that Ethiopia is the only country in Africa never conquered by the Europeans, but the colonial inheritance has scarred Ethiopia like the rest of Africa; much of the development impetus of last 30 years has been dominated and blocked by a war with Eritrea, partially created out of the Italian invasion. If the Italians had seen the potential of Ethiopia, so too had the British, who toyed with the notion of making Ethiopia yet another protectorate during the Great War.[29] The Ethiopian army may have defeated the Italians in 1896, but Eritrea succumbed to Italian rule from 1935 to 1941 and then to British rule until 1952. It is a further irony that when the USA, as ever, stepped into the British breech for Ethiopia to become its greatest ally in black Africa, the US policy debate after 1974 went through another of its 'How did we lose Ethiopia' phases (as with China in 1949). Thereafter US military training, which had been greater in Ethiopia than in any other African state, was taken on by the Soviet Union and Ethiopia became another pawn in the Cold War game. The defeat of the Derg in 1991 has now brought Ethiopia back into the US fold as a client regime enforcing the Washington consensus despite (or because of) a continuing ability to repress its own people.[30]

The consequences of imperial wars

Until the Derg's military coup of 1974, 80 per cent of the land of Ethiopia was owned by 2 per cent of the population: the provincial nobility, the state and the church dominated the social order,

115

as in Britain in 1350. From the regime's nineteenth-century base in the Amhara heartlands, the Galla/Oromo peoples, who had lost at least two thirds of their old land to the invaders from the north, were paying anything from 50 to 75 per cent of their harvest in tribute. A 'semi-feudal' landholding – north and south – had left the ordinary Ethiopian, 80 per cent of whom were subsistence agriculturalists or pastoralists, with virtually no surplus and no reserves and, like the Chinese peasant, vulnerable to regular famine if the harvest failed. It was no wonder that even in 1974 only 25 per cent of produce was marketed for cash; much of this the coffee from estates, which sometimes provided up to 80 per cent of exports. In 1974, 75 per cent of farms were half a day's walk from the nearest road and 40 per cent were two days away. When the 'revolution' arrived there was going to be no quick solution despite plenty of 'socialist manifestos' and 'national development plans'. The class and regional divides that had occasionally surfaced since Haile Selassie had taken the throne in 1930 now reached a new crescendo. In the northern heartlands, the old communal heritage with noble rights of tribute on between 25 and 40 per cent of the land came under pressure, especially as an increasing population meant land hunger. Peasants were being dispossessed here too as traditional tribute rights were converted into modern outright ownership. The Ethiopian state encouraged this process while sometimes trying to protect the peasants, which meant that the provincial nobility increasingly resisted the central government. This resulted in outright rebellion in the 1960s in the fertile cereal-producing province of Gojjam in Amhara. The crisis was illuminated by a famine that killed 400,000, between 1970 and 1973, just before the monarch's downfall.[31] In February 1974 when Haile Selassie was first overthrown, as in England and France, it was the old aristocracy that revolted first, resisting the state over tax changes. This was ten years before Live Aid followed the famines caused largely by the Derg's war against Eritrea. If Iraq follows the Ethiopian path, there will be two more generations of bloodbaths still to come. Maybe oil will be Iraq's saving grace.

So if Saddam is akin to Haile Selassie, who in this analogy is akin to Mussolini and Hitler? Who appears to harbour ambitions of a world empire, where control of Middle Eastern oil is central to the new 1,000-year Reich – the end of foreseeable history – this new world order of peace, liberal democracy and successful 'enterprise'? For once, the neoconservative label may be nearly correct: neo-fascist would be closer. Hitler may have been defined as on the 'right': here was no conservatism, neo- or otherwise. And Mr Blair? Here our labels break down even if our analogies do not. For what is a so-called Christian Socialist doing supporting the neo-fascists? And how could even a supine Labour Party stomach such an outcome? In fact, New Labour have been the appeasers and have let the Empire define the terms. The only imperial, unilateral regime being appeased in the invasion of Iraq was that of George W. Bush. Blair has performed an abject act of appeasement that would make Neville Chamberlain turn in his grave. At least Chamberlain tried to avoid a war that would kill many. When will Mr Blair ever travel on a tube again unescorted? Mr Blair walked straight into the imperial game with his eyes wide open. By all means remember the appeasers and remember Ethiopia 1935. But get your analogies straight.

Grand imperial strategy

Understanding the historical analogies also applies to slogans for activists. Having understood the colonial history of East Africa in this chapter in a little more detail, we can now return to the contemporary Make Poverty History Campaign with a better sense of history. Stuart Hodkinson has performed an invaluable service by showing the links between Oxfam, New Labour development advisers and the World Bank. It was Oxfam – by far the wealthiest of the UK charities working on development – which in late 2003 initiated the process leading to the launch of Make Poverty History in September 2004. This followed on from Oxfam's own strategic review in 1997–8, which decided to move away from a focus on famines and disasters. The present (2006) director of Oxfam – Barbara Stocking – worked in the NHS as a director of 'modernization' and has written on the need to build a 'broader' 'constituency'. While appearing to attack neo-liberalism, this mentality is riddled with the same managerial globalization speak, and likes to use celebrity heroes. Like New Labour, there is no semblance of an untidy and potentially divisive debate. Oxfam and friends decide the policy, the UK's largest advertising agency is rolled out and Richard Curtis does his bit in *The Vicar of Dibley* and *The girl in the café*. The activists are asked to turn out and demonstrate on policies designed by the same neo-liberals, whom they claim to be opposing. No wonder the trademark Make Poverty History is registered by Comic Relief. They must be joking if they think this will make poverty history. Most of all, this campaign has been anxious to keep the issues of poverty and Iraq apart: from page 1 this book has argued this is to totally misunderstand what Chomsky calls the 'grand imperial strategy' in the Empire of Global Capital.[32]

Global capital is always looking to expand. Deepen the market and in Africa's case it could always go a lot deeper and wider. As Lucy Michaels argues, the African Commission could hardly have offered big business a better deal if the latter had written the report itself, while Paul Cammack notes that the Africa Commission has used a web of African bankers and industrialists, embedded into the consensus of IMF, World Bank and UN Commission for Africa. Governments can sell the poor services; but make sure you dress it up as aid, even better if you can make it military or 'policing' aid, because then you can get rid of your own redundant hardware. Better still if you can sell them the idea of education. The Africa Commission seemed tailor-made for expansionist British universities – competing of course with those in the USA. Let's sell lots of global governance courses to the Africa elites: that should be a good money spinner for a while. Give them four years in Blighty and they will always turn to their alma mater for money and advice. As Michaels concludes, the agencies now telling us how they propose to make Africa rich are central to the reasons why Africa is poor.[33]

The political leaders who have manipulated this campaign in their interests would not mind making poverty history, but that is not their aim. It will certainly not be the result. President Blair would like to go down in history as the man who made his mark on Africa: he looks indeed like a true successor to Cecil Rhodes, for Rhodes too believed that Africa could be developed and lived in an age when one could be proud to be an imperialist. Now the imperialists hide under the cloak of good global governance. Let's have a security state here and an expansionist global capitalism there, for that will give peace, prosperity and security for all. The Devil never tempts you to campaign in favour of injustice.

Making poverty history

Before we can begin to Make Poverty History, then, we need to understand rather more of the history of how poverty has been made. It has been the aim of this brief chapter to reveal how poverty was made under colonial rule through some indicative historical examples. Today under the new neo-colonialism, superbly exemplified in the Africa Commission, the NGOs are to be used, like the military and intelligence agencies, to give a superficial cover to aims that are far less wholesome – not only by the George II regime but by Blair and Brown and by the African elites as well. There is nothing more insidious than claiming to operate against poverty and for justice, while actually operating on behalf of global capital. To manipulate goodwill and campaigning fervour for the cause of the expansion of empires leaves an extremely bad smell. But, of course, if you can take the average ordinary US soldier and send him to die or get maimed – 15,000 at the last count – for exactly this cause in Iraq, manipulating middle-class consciences about poverty is easy game.

Power to the African people

Sadly, Make Poverty History and its ilk obscure the fact that the only people who in the end are going to end their own poverty are not G8 leaders, but the ordinary people – in this case of Africa. It can hardly be a surprise that the African specialists rarely address what has gone on in Central and Latin America: rather than the 50 years of neo-colonial Africa, the South Americans have had nearly 200 years of nominal independence from which the Africans could learn. This is one reason why this book has emphasized the Latin American experience.

The African peoples face massive hurdles. They have to face the 'vampire' nation states imposed upon them by colonial and imperial powers, deliberately set up so that they could not rule themselves. If many Irish, Welsh and Scots feel that Britain does not represent them, or the Dutch may feel that the EU does not speak for them, how do you expect the average Dinka to believe that the Sudan means anything at all, other than governments that tax you, herd you around or kill you? And these are the kind of African client elite governments that the NGOs claim needs to be 'protected' from the West.

The African peoples will somehow have to take back the land that was stolen from them. The Zapatistas in Chiapas are still struggling to make sure that it doesn't get taken in the first place; listen to them not to Brown or Geldof. They have to develop their own agriculture where others don't control their surplus and market their produce. This doesn't just mean low prices for their commodities. If most African producers were allowed to keep their own marketable surplus and not have it taxed away by African elites and African government marketing boards, even before the Western multinationals get their hands on it, they would be much better off. In Ghana, for example, only 20 per cent of the (falling) final price – even of the raw cocoa – actually gets to the producer, once all the vampires have taken their cuts.[34]

This means that before confronting the North or the West they may be far better advised to confront their own client elites and rulers first. The revolution to Make Poverty History in Africa starts in Africa, and getting rid of their own elites would be a good start. Let's use the jargon: to make them democratically accountable. Since the present African nation states were created specifically not to do this, this is going to be a very tall order. It will not be done by G8 leaders, nor by debt relief, nor by trade rules, nor by conditional aid. It is about ordinary people banding together in discipleship groups and changing the immediate world around them. Leaders of empires make it their business to crucify such groups – usually today while pretending to do the opposite, holding out the hand of friendship and support at the same time.

Making the African elites accountable is not something Tom Mbeki is keen to do, because if he helps bring down Mugabe and his hangers-on perhaps we may have to look a little more closely at the ANC regime and whose interests it serves. Should we believe the African leaders all rally round Mugabe because they have been all carved out of the same material? When Saddam was brought down it took US and British troops to do it. When Idi Amin was brought down it took Tanzanian troops to do it. This unholy mess was the beginnings of a recovery in Uganda. To get rid of Mugabe, Zimababwe will probably need an internal revolution, which will mean many deaths, or an invasion from South Africa – which will mean many deaths. This is all a great deal less comforting. This is not at all appealing to middle-class campaigners. It is the hard and dirty stuff of today's global geopolitics.

Until the NGOs face up to some of these hard issues, all they will ever be doing is raising philanthropic money on the back of pricking people's consciences. This may prevent starvation, but it probably won't. It certainly won't Make Poverty History. Keep the masses in the dark about the real hard political and economic history. Tell them you're doing your best to Make Poverty History. And keep them in the dark about what's really going on. For darkness hates the light. And its best practice is to spin a lie that it can make bread out of the very stones that it created. For only the ordinary people of Africa will make their own bread. And our best efforts can be directed, not to campaigns with impossible slogans and time frames, but to spreading a little light about the lies that we are daily being told as truths.

5

Debt, Trade and Globalization

Imperial history for busy activists

The Jubilee, Trade Justice and Make Poverty History campaigns have radicalized many Christians on issues of globalization. Ed Mayo calls them emerging 'global citizens'. Yet it is notable how little most activist Christians know about similar past debates in church and society. For Christians and others have grappled with the issues of international capitalism and socialism, often in the wider context of imperialism and war, and with a global capitalism in both boom and bust. In the Christian debates on globalization, there has been little discussion on past 'socialist' and/or nationalist attempts to overcome the problems of poverty and social justice. In the nineteenth and twentieth centuries, the church has carried on these debates in the midst of a falling church attendance. As part of a search for a Christian political economy and theology that enables us to address the gospel afresh – with a theological and political language not trapped in religious categories – the aim in this chapter is to refresh our memory, expand our horizons and engage with the recent Christian critique of 'globalization'. What Mayo calls the 'fast growing maturity of the global justice movement' needs a broader-based political economy than the self-styled 'new economics' so often presented.[1]

The faith-based critique of the debt of the poorest countries has had considerable success in enlightening ordinary faith community members about global finance and economic issues. In Britain, it has both aided and persuaded New Labour (and

Gordon Brown, in particular) to make debt write-offs one of the keys to its development thinking. The relative lack of success in significantly reducing the debt of the poor can hardly be blamed on the Jubilee Campaign. It may be just one more sign of the sheer power of global capitalism – frequently violent – to resist change that affects profit. It is certainly welcome to see that the Jubilee Campaign has enabled many faith organizations to throw off the shackles of the conventional 'neo-liberal' ideology that has accompanied the increasing penetration of global capital. However, the analysis of history and global political economy contained within the Jubilee and Trade Justice campaigns is seriously flawed. As a result, the policy prescriptions of this gospel of discontent are frequently naive and the power of global capital, and the history of colonialism and imperialism are simply not sufficiently addressed or acknowledged.

A debt crisis?

The cause of global poverty – let us state it simply – is not debt, it is the inability of indebted people to control their production and income resources sufficiently to meet their needs – financial, economic, political and social. This may sound like splitting hairs, but it is an important economic point to understand. If we wish to fight global poverty, let us be clear that it is not debt, but the causes of debt, which we are fighting. It is the lack of productive development controlled by ordinary people that causes their poverty. When you can produce this sufficiency – and this is a historical, political and social question as much as a financial and economic one – you can then handle your debt. As Michael Northcott points out,[2] the USA in 1999 had a total debt of $3 trillion versus a sub-Saharan African debt of $200 billion – this does not make it poor. The USA as a whole, if not all the poor within it, has the sufficiency to finance the debt. So, unpayable debt is the symptom not the cause of poverty. To blame the problem of global poverty on debt is like blaming the famous Glasgow moneylenders (10 per cent interest a week) for the problems of Glasgow. Global banking and finance and Glasgow moneylenders both arise from the contradictions of wealth and poverty and add to it; they are not the prime cause of it.

The normal Jubilee 'beginners' history of the 'debt crisis' begins in the 1960s. It starts with what is virtually a monetarist explanation of the US budget deficit, forgetting that it was the anti-communist crusade of the Vietnam War that generated the deficit. Having already fallen into a monetarist explanation, OPEC's struggle to control their oil resources is reduced to an explanation of the problems caused by a falling dollar in the 1960s. This depoliticization of the issues runs through much of the Jubilee analysis. It then concentrates most on the oil price rises after 1973. All blame for the increase in borrowing in the 1970s is put on banks' lending; government budget and trade deficits arising from higher oil prices, or military spending, as in Argentina, are ignored.[3]

It is as if there had been no global political economy before 1973. Susan George reaches back to 1944 and the foundation of the IMF and World Bank. Understandably, she focuses on the World Bank since it has defined its mission since 1968 to be about 'significantly reducing' global poverty. She notes, unlike Jubilee, that McNamara – who gave the World Bank this mission statement – had cut his teeth on Vietnam. George is right to point out the World Bank's surrender to neo-liberalism, but ignores the IMF – the big ugly sister with far greater financial clout. Criticize the misguided idealism of the World Bank by all means, but as her later work comes to see, there was never much idealism in the IMF or in the global capitalist financial system. The implicit view is that somehow the global economy functioned better before 1945, or certainly before 1973. So, the hidden argument runs, let's abolish or reform the World Bank and abolish the debts laid on the poor in the last 50 years and all will be well.[4] Well, all may be better, but it is worth emphasizing the obvious hidden flaw in this analysis: all was not well in 1945. Two imperialist wars had just been fought in part at least because of the boundless competitive pressure of global capitalism – which in its turn had spawned colonialism and imperialism.

Taking liberties with history

In 2004, Christian Aid, produced two reports on trade justice as a part of its lobbying of government and international trade organizations. Trade justice, alongside debt relief and aid, has become the new theme that many of the 'Make Poverty History' campaigners of 2005 have appealed to. There are truths – especially in this critique of protectionist policies in the major powers – and certainly a moral and ethical concern in this work.[5] However, the lack of a sufficient historical and/or structural political and economic analysis is highly frustrating. Until in this instance Christian Aid, as a leader of British Christian opinion in these areas, can explicitly name the power of global capital – rather than just trade 'rules' – as the main source of global poverty and inequality, it will remain powerless to understand the forces at work in the twenty-first century's political economy. Until Christians can explicitly acknowledge the historic power of colonialism and imperialism, it will remain unrepentant too of the Church's own past and be unable to see continuities with today's Global Capitalist Empire.

The naive perception that giving the client state elites in the developing countries 'more power' will solve their problems is to misunderstand the problem entirely. At worst, it is, as Curtis puts it, a 'great deception', which we need to be rid of. For most of these client states are part of the problem whereby the mass of ordinary people are disempowered, not part of the solution. Until Christian Aid can see through its Christendom model, where an appeal is made to imperial power to be more benevolent for the sake of the common good, its practical politics degenerate into a weak liberal appeal to the conscience of the 'strong'.[6] This may be fine for morale and fund raising, but the Empire will bend a sympathetic ear and then proceed to accumulate profit and global capital as before. If NGOs persist in making simple one-issue campaigns their way into understanding global capital, they will always be focusing on outcomes and never understanding the causes. For neither debt, nor unequal exchange in trade get to the heart of the disempowering that lies at the heart of capitalism. Nor is it much use having a piece in 2004 on global justice that does not mention Iraq. If you understand what global capital is attempting in Iraq, you will come closer to seeing what the campaigns on global debt and justice really face. Iraq is the way in to seeing the Global Capitalist Empire at work.

Ironically by focusing on attempting to reform the world's trade, many of the campaigners for trade justice are still unconsciously borrowing the truisms of the neo-liberals. For both wish to 'bend' the trade system so that it delivers more for the poor. Many neo-liberals will argue that indeed the success of global capital in China, for example, has been to do precisely this. Ironically, the rule of the only remaining repressive Oriental despotism – named 'communism' by its rulers – is wonderfully suited to the rulers of global capital, who leave others to subdue the labour force and cope with the casualties. The reality of global capitalism, reaching back to colonial times, is that there have been huge costs in its creation – both in the North and the South. Colonialism, imperialism and global expansion have had the most violent roots and consequences. Make no mistake; it is this power we confront. And fight back the global elite will, when the whole global economy is at stake.

The British Empire: hub of the world economy 1846–73

From around 1846 to the Great Depression of the 1870s, the British Empire – the Workshop of the World – ruled through free trade. Profits could be maintained because increasingly Great British industry had a satellite world of formal or informal colonies, which made her the hub of international trade, lending, finance, insurance and settlements. A whole set of complementary trade relationships were established: cotton from the USA, wool from Australia, nitrates from Chile, rubber from Malaysia, wine from Portugal, gold from South Africa. Foodstuffs became particularly important as international trade and transport developed: wheat and beef from Argentina, dairy produce from Denmark and New Zealand. As Hobsbawm puts it, there is a real sense that many developing economies 'had no-one except Great Britain to sell to'.

Two areas had been of particular importance in the developing international trade and investment of the nineteenth century. The first was Latin America, which became the largest single market for British cotton exports, taking 35 per cent in 1840, mainly to Brazil. Trade with India, which was in massive surplus to Britain, financed up to 40 per cent of our potential trade deficit; truly the jewel in the crown. British manufacturing still possessed the 'natural' protection of a relatively large home market and the 'artificial' protection of the political control over a large empire. The greater the later manufacturing decline, the greater the desire to bolster imperial 'preference'. This was symbolized by Chamberlain's campaign for imperial preference after 1903 and was effectively set up after 1931 as Britain came off the Gold Standard. The cotton industry had 'escaped' competition by exporting to Asia and Africa, while its former markets now took textile machinery, which made up 25 per cent of all machinery exports. British coal went to the British merchant shipping fleet. By 1913, Argentina and India bought more British iron and steel exports then Europe; Australia alone more than twice as much as the USA.

Despite the early manufacturing domination, Britain never seemed to have had much of a surplus in the trade in goods (unlike Japan in the 1980s). In the nineteenth century, this did not matter much, for the 'invisible' surplus was enormous, covering the trade deficit after 1875. Britain had credits abroad of £250 million in the 1850s. By 1873, the accumulated balances had already reached £1 billion. In 1913, Britain owned £4 billion abroad, as against less than £5.5 billion for France, Germany, the USA, Holland and Belgium combined. Gross investment income had doubled from 4 to 5 per cent of national income in the 1870s to 9 per cent in 1910–13. It was never to attain this level again.[7]

Imperialism and the great deflation

Britain had become as dependent on her colonies for the external accumulation of surplus as Spain had on Latin America three centuries earlier. Initially, the global impact of British capitalism was the bombardment of other countries' domestic production, particularly textiles, with the 'heavy artillery' of low prices.[8] In the age after 1870, with increasing imperialist competition, this changed radically. As shipping and railways opened up the expanded world market, other national industrial capitalisms appeared to challenge the British and the rate of profit fell. The search for raw materials to fuel the expansion and for foodstuffs to feed the growing urban working classes was to run parallel to the need to search for higher profits. Britain still led the way in this new international phase: in 1880, she still accounted for 50 per cent of the world's meat imports and 55 per cent of all European imports of wool and cotton. In 1900, 30 per cent of the world trade in primary products depended on Britain. The production of raw materials by primitive pre-capitalist means – symbolized by the slave economy in the South of the USA – was being transformed. It was not just that the price of cotton rose during the American Civil War; there had been a general tendency for the price of all raw materials to rise in the middle of the nineteenth century. Primitive accumulation, which had previously occurred in the less developed countries, now became increasingly subject to the capitalist production of raw materials. The aim was to bring raw material costs and prices down.

There is every reason to be suspicious when the ideologists of global capitalism tell us that today we have a new world order. Hirst shows that there is sufficient evidence to debate whether the world economy today is actually more global than that under British hegemony before 1914.[9] In an age like ours, where we have been taught to fear the 'evil' of inflation, it is hard to imagine that the late nineteenth-century global economy was dominated by deflation – by falling prices. It is an era that we should bring back to mind more often as global productivity rises in both agriculture and manufacturing in the twenty-first century. It was an era too in which increasing imperial competition led to war. From the 1870s, new zones of global wheat production were opened up in the USA, Canada, Argentina and Australia. Even in Europe, Hungary, Romania and Russia appeared as much larger producers. By 1894, the price of wheat was only a third of that in 1867. The price shocks were naturally linked to an increasing national protectionism, particularly in the newly united nations (like Germany). Having fought a war of independence partly over tariffs, the USA was quick to protect its extensive wheat producing areas; the average US tariff rate was 60 per cent as late as 1897.

The year 1873 tends to be picked out as significant, for it was after this year that the price of most agricultural and raw material produce began to fall. The overall level of British prices, including both coal and textiles, dropped 40 per cent between 1873 and 1896. But this is to underestimate what was virtually a century-long trend of falling prices after the Napoleonic Wars. British wholesale prices had been rising slowly in the 1850s and

1860s and reached their previous 1839 peak in 1873. Prices then virtually halved to their lowest point in 1896; wholesale prices were now only a third of the level of the post-Napoleonic War price peak of 1818.[10] At the same time, world industrial output was rising dramatically. As iron output doubled in the five main producing nations, the price fell 50 per cent.[11] The British share of world manufactured exports fell from 41 per cent in 1880 to 30 per cent in 1913, while the German share rose from 19 per cent to 27 per cent and the US share from 3 per cent to 13 per cent.[12]

Monopoly, protection and the rise of the USA

The era of a perfectly competitive international capitalism – the era of so-called laissez faire so much beloved by neo-liberalism again today – did not last long in the nineteenth century. Its heyday was at best between 1848 and 1873. At a time when raw material prices were falling under the pressures of global deflation, it is perhaps not surprising that it was first and foremost in the sphere of raw material production that a new concentration of economic power was to be felt in the capitalist nations. By 1880, Standard Oil controlled 90 per cent of US oil refining; US Steel was responsible for 63 per cent of American steel output, while the Rhine-Westphalia coal syndicate controlled 90 per cent of coal output in the Ruhr. Although Britain remained with no tariffs, newly united Germany and Italy had started to protect their textile industries in the 1870s. The USA was to provide the best example of building up 'infant industries' behind protective tariff barriers. American commentators often conveniently forget this history when it comes to disputing the benefits of the same policy in Latin America from the 1920s. France first introduced tariffs in 1882, and the USA followed with the McKinley tariff in 1890, with more to follow in 1897. As monopoly and protection did their work, the world became divided up afresh in the 1890s. At the same time, international trade kept growing:

between 1880 and 1913, the international trade in primary products trebled and the world merchant fleet doubled in size. The more prosperous period leading up to 1914 had brought a 'belle époque' for the rising middle classes of the newly industrializing countries.[13]

The relative strength of sterling by 1914 reflected less and less the role of the British industrial economy, but more importantly the power of British overseas investment and finance at the hub of the world economy. After 1918, ascendancy was to pass to the USA. One easy way to see this is in the level of gold reserves. The USA now commanded 50 per cent of the world's total. The US gold reserve of $4.2 billion was six times the level of the British one.[14] It could be argued that the power elite in the USA was not fully aware of this until 1945; maybe not even until 1989. After a brief spell at Versailles redrawing the European map, it took until 1945 for the USA to take on 'world' responsibilities in an explicit manner, creating institutions like the IMF and World Bank to suit its own needs. Part of the inter-war impasse stemmed from this interregnum between empires.

The economic and political crisis in Europe that produced the potential revolutionary outbreaks of 1919–21 were not reflected in the US experience. In contrast to Britain and Germany particularly, the period between 1921 and 1929 saw a sustained boom in the USA. This was driven by new industrial development in what was becoming the world's largest economy. By the 1920s, the USA produced 40 per cent of the world's coal and over 50 per cent of the world's manufactures. It is understandable why the US government and business failed to pick up the international implications of what they were doing. US industrial production virtually doubled between 1921 and 1929. After the brief recession of 1920–1, unemployment remained below 4 per cent between 1923 and 1929 and was as low as 1.9 per cent in 1926; just as the British experienced the General Strike and German unemployment reached 22 per cent. The lead indicator of what became known as the Fordism of this new era of mass assembly line production was not surprisingly the car industry.[15]

The lessons of the 1920s: American protection

The impact of World War One on the global economy dominated the twentieth-century economic experience. Ramsay MacDonald described the world situation in the inter-war years as like 'searching for God's will in hell'. Between 1913 and 1921, world industrial production had fallen 20 per cent. It took until 1929 to get back to 1913 levels. One key to the economic hell often overlooked by a narrow emphasis on the US boom of the 1920s and crash of the 1930s is the renewed worldwide deflation that had been taking place. Forty per cent of world trade was in agricultural products, with a further 20 per cent in raw materials. World food prices had started to fall in 1923 and raw material prices from 1925. In cotton, new areas came into production in Brazil, Egypt, India and Peru and cotton prices were already 80 per cent lower in 1929 than they had been in 1920. Overproduction was endemic in coffee, rubber, silver, sugar and zinc. By 1929, agricultural prices generally were already 30 per cent lower. As boom in the USA turned to bust, food and raw material prices fell a further half to two thirds between 1929 and 1932. World trade in primary products was still 66 per cent below the 1913 level as late as 1938; a further fall of 33 per cent from the already depressed level of 1929.[16]

If this boom was not experienced in Europe, neither was it felt in the large US agricultural economy and, in 1930, 50 per cent of the population in the US was still rural. Direct agricultural employment still accounted for 25 per cent of the US labour force in 1929, while exports accounted for 28 per cent of farm income. Farm incomes as a whole fell 10 per cent between 1920 and 1929 and land values fell 50 per cent between 1920 and 1940. Many American farmers depended on debt to keep going, which had knock-on effects for the local and regional banks. US farm debt tripled between 1910 and 1925 from \$3.5 billion to \$9.4 billion. In some States, up to 85 per cent of farms were mortgaged. In the recession of 1920, 450,000 US farms had gone bust. Throughout the 1920s, the rate of bankruptcy in the agricultural sector was running at five times the rate of 1913–20. In some areas, the impact was devastating: in Montana, a third of the farms went bust between 1920 and 1923. The 1920s may have marked the start of the new American industrial boom and the new American Empire; they also marked the end of the old American rural dream. Despite the potential of its new international position, the domestic economic programme of the USA naturally reflected the voters suffering from this rural crisis and continued a Jeffersonian protection of the home farm. Despite increasing manufacturing production, the USA raised general tariffs to their highest ever in 1922. President Hoover's 1928 landslide election campaign majored on the theme of protecting farmers; a continuing policy of his six years as Secretary of Commerce. US Tariffs were to be raised again in 1930.[17]

The US boom continued in ignorance of the developing international crisis. The Federal Reserve Bank created in 1913 reflected US economic dominance in the 1920s, which, unlike Britain, was based on balance of trade and payment surpluses. Car production, the new leading sector, reached 5.4 million/year in 1929; it only just exceeded this in the post-World War Two boom. The boom was reflected and then exaggerated by the US stock market. In September 1929, this peaked five times higher than May 1924. Yet the car industry had reached a temporary saturation point. Already one in six of the population had a car. The number of cars registered rose from 8.2 million in 1920 to 21.6 million in 1928. But the demand for cars was highly price and income sensitive. It was also an industry where 68 per cent of demand was fuelled by credit – a level not reached again until 1968.[18]

Economic internationalism collapses: 1929

It was not only the American farmers who were suffering from the world's agricultural deflation; retaliatory tariffs, which had plagued the world economy since the 1870s, increased again. In Germany, a wheat tariff of $35 per tonne was imposed in 1925; it was $95 by 1930; the peasant farmers who were to vote for Hitler and the landed Junkers who helped him to power had the new American Empire to thank for higher world grain prices. In Japan, rice imports were banned in 1928. The French had a more agricultural economy and much lower unemployment (around one million) and the French economy had sucked in two million foreign workers in the 1920s. The French protection of their economy revolved around the reparation payments agreed in the Versailles Peace Treaty. After all, France had to pay reparations itself twice in the nineteenth century: to Britain after Napoleon's defeat in 1815 and to Germany after 1871. Keynes had first appeared as a major commentator in his *Economic Consequences of the Peace* of 1919 when he showed that the level of German payments made no sense. Germany could only pay by cutting down on her imports and indeed, when France reinvaded the Ruhr in 1923, it furthered the economic crisis in Germany without bringing much more in the way of reparation payments.

The pressures caused by deflation – as falling prices meant a coincident pressure on incomes and profits – were felt internationally. By 1929, world trade in manufactured goods had just regained its 1913 level, but by value, it had plummeted by half. It had still not recovered to 1913 levels in 1939. Boyce calls the governmental responses of the 1920s a 'collapse in economic internationalism'.[19] The international financial issues were dominated, as Keynes had predicted, by the twin issues of reparation payments and international debt. The US government was not prepared to cut the debt repayments due to them from the war as this would mean increased taxes (on impoverished farmers, as they saw it). The Dawes Plan of 1925 was one way out of the impasse. German reparation payments were to be cut and limited while US banks would lend to the German banks, which would enable Germany to continue to import both capital and manufactured goods (largely from the USA of course). Germany's continued recovery was made at least partially dependent on the flow of US capital to Germany. By the middle of 1928, the booming stock market was affecting the real world economy. High interest on 'call' money meant that most US bank loans stayed at home to fuel the boom, while corporate surpluses and overseas funds were also sucked in to sustain it. Six months before the US crash, capital inflows to Germany had virtually ceased.[20] The consequent crisis in international economic relations preceded the Wall Street Crash of 1929. With hindsight, the Great Crash turned out to be a belated US recognition of the new domestic and global reality, created more by the new dynamism of American capitalism and the weakness of European imperialism than anything else.

The continued US commitment to its farming lobby and the traditions of peasant protection in both France and Germany now began to make more sense in this light. It may be that neoliberal economists make too much of the benefits of free trade. However, the kind of protectionist policies now being advocated for the poor countries are precisely the kind of policies globally that were a disaster for the world economy in the 1920s and 1930s. This is not to argue in favour of today's US and EU protection; but with Polish peasants now adding to the EU's politics it is important to understand it. A Christian Aid analysis, for example, that forgets the lessons of the 1920s helps no one, least of all, the poor.

Crucified on a cross of gold

In the 1896 presidential campaign, Democrat William Bryant complained of the deflationary impact of the gold standard on US farmers, claiming they were being 'crucified on a cross of gold'.[21] This was never truer of the British economy that after its return to gold in 1925, as Churchill (then chancellor) gave in to the Bank of England, Treasury and City lobby in an attempt to reinstate London's leading role as the world financial centre. In Britain, this led to the long miners' strike and the brief and easily defeated General Strike of 1926. The British 'City' set in the middle of this web was still attempting to be financier to the world in the midst of a global recession, despite the continued weakness of its own domestic economy. International stock markets had seen the crisis coming before the USA. The German market peaked as US capital inflows dried up in mid 1928, the UK market peaked in January 1929, the French in February. By 1931, worldwide bust created massive unemployment in the USA (of at least 6.5 million), alongside falling consumption and falling investment. The other most noticeable feature of the crash was a banking crisis, driven particularly by a rural collapse in the West and far West. By October 1930, 522 small banks had gone in the USA. Hoover's answer was to raise tariffs again, especially on cotton. In Germany, unemployment stood at five million in January 1931 (as it does again today).

As in 1914 and 1929, global forces also precipitated a British political crisis in 1931. It is important to emphasize the important interrelatedness of the global economy even in the divided years of the 1930s. The British financial crisis that preceded the divisions of a Labour Cabinet over unemployment benefit and budget cuts started with a run on the German Mark, partly caused by a similar crisis in Germany the year before, precipitated by American imperial decision-making and French financial priorities. The Bank of England was warning an easily credulous Prime Minister MacDonald and Chancellor Snowden, who repeated the same lines to their Cabinet, of the virtual collapse of civilization as we know it, if Britain came off gold. In one sense, this was true. The laissez-faire global system, which had revolved around the British Empire, was ending. Symbolically, as if to signal the end of the British-led free trade and gold standard system, four countries had come off gold in 1929; four more in 1930. When Britain came off gold in September 1931, 19 more countries did so. The year 1931 in Britain was the outworking of the consequences of 1914. It was left to a minority Labour government – and the workers it represented – to pick up the bills for a global capitalist system they had always criticized but did not fully understand.[22]

Globalization: bankers and politicians

Pettifor's work, to which we now turn, correctly makes much of the similarity between the deflation of the 1920s and that of today. However, we are told that the 1920s were based on an 'orgy of speculation' as with today's 'global experiment'. This is only true of the USA, and is in any case only true of the US industrial and financial sectors; agriculture was already suffering. It is no description of Britain or Germany or anywhere else at all. Agrarian deflation, US isolationism, the new weakness of the British Empire, the weakness of the political base of the Weimar Republic, all these structural blocks in the inter-war political economy, can't all be laid at the door of financiers engaged in an orgy of speculation. Indeed, at its worst, this is just the kind of conspiracy theory that Hitler used so successfully in his populist appeal against the financiers (code-name, the Jews).

Yet, Pettifor is right to begin the economic and financial analysis with the USA. Why did the US power elite make the Vietnam War so important as to help create an economic and foreign policy crisis? A simple reading of Zinn's history will tell the story:

the US working class was successfully won over by US imperial and patriotic wars (in Cuba and the Philippines, for example) and its trade unions either smashed by violence or bought off. Fighting the 'communists' in Vietnam, like fighting the war on terror was the natural outcome of the brutal fighting the US power elite had engaged in from 1861 and before to spread the 'new' 'Yankee' capitalism; and this process began in the Southern States of the USA itself in the late 1860s. In other words, this cannot be understood without an assessment of the peculiarities of US capitalism and imperialism. This is where conventional economics is silent – or useless – but political economy is not. But to look for one major economic cause – the 'new' dominance of the financial system – oversimplifies. High finance and high politics has been fundamental since at least the sixteenth century; and often in control of the developing capitalist economy. But in Pettifor's piece, the problems of the 1930s are blamed only on finance. The analysis of the USA in this era consists of one long quote from Roosevelt's rhetoric against bankers. There is no proper analysis of the political coalition that built the New Deal.[23] Indeed, in the light of the desire to show capital liberalization and globalization as the source of all our problems, the analysis overreaches itself. It was not capital liberalization that was the problem of the 1930s but the opposite: autarchic and nationalistic solutions, which were part and parcel of the run up to 1939 in Europe. The new Bretton Woods order of 1944 was built not to restrict capital movements, as implied, but to build a better base for a capital flow to fund trade.[24]

The book opens up with an executive summary against a 'globalization' that was 'created by politicians and can be reversed by politicians'. This process, the theme runs, is not inevitable; it is created by people we have some power over – we elect them and therefore we can campaign to 'reverse' the trend. Even at this level, we have a problem since it was largely the result of US politicians, which disenfranchises most of the rest of us. Of course, most of today's power elite politicians have bought into globalization. But simply to understand these politicians as bought off, which most of them are, requires us to take one analytical step back. It is a commonplace to see a Reagan, or a George II as the front men for much bigger forces. This does not make globalization just 'corporate driven', or 'technology driven', or politician driven. The driving force of capital is far larger than any one politician, and quite impossible for any one politician to 'reverse'. A sociology of the interlinks within the US power elite make such 'politicians' not just the creatures of big business but so interlinked, by background, training and ideology, as to be the product of a particular US class structure. This enables them to embody the power and ideology of its ruling class and elite. This serves the interests of US, and today, of global capital. Without this perception, the analysis hangs on a complete misunderstanding of the sociology of contemporary capitalism. The simplistic notion that all we have to do is change the politicians is to rather underestimate the forces that we face.[25]

Globalization as propaganda

How does this propaganda tool – globalization – work? There are two major analytical ways in which the jargon word 'globalization', potentially distorts what is going on in the world today. First, it confuses cause and effect. Globalization is the result of global capitalism, it does not cause it. Second, it substitutes geography for necessary detailed political, economic and social analysis. The motive force of global capitalism – the same as it always was – is the private and corporate accumulation of profit, which is nowhere subject to democratic control. It is no more subject to the control of ordinary people in the United States than it is in Russia. Accumulate: that is the still law of our society today. It is this process which treats people as commodities and reduces social relations to the cash nexus which people of all faiths can and do oppose. It oppresses those in Brixton and those in Bangladesh; it impoverishes those in Harlem as it does those in Haiti. It is not enough to campaign about debt, one must understand the system that causes the debt. It is not globalization that is the dominant force in the world today, it is global capitalism. Globalization in the sense of linking the world together in new ways is to be welcomed; global capitalism, despite a number of positive features, is not neutral and has to be struggled with. What the clever ideologists of global capitalism do is make the one conflate into the other. So if you are against globalization, then you are not facing the realities of the modern world; you are a primitive, a reactionary and a fundamentalist. How can you be against bringing the peoples of the world closer together? By emphasizing geography as the major dividing point, the jargon of globalization potentially divides our common action. It is not the 'rich, North or First' world that exploits the poor 'South developing' countries. It is largely North-based global capital that exploits both workers in the East End and in the East. It is global capitalism that we need to struggle against, not globalization. The concept of globalization does not explain what is going on, and this is why the apologists of corporate and global power use the jargon.

The first use of the word 'globalization' was for 'capitalist' purposes. It was used by American Express as an advert for its credit card in the 1970s. It spread like wildfire in the financial and business press.[26] A new Pony Express was to link the refreshed financial empires for the 1970s and beyond. The propaganda was built as a necessary counterpart to the deregulation of exchange controls stemming from the USA coming off gold in 1971. Under the Reagan administration, globalization could justify the use of economic or political power – and, on the periphery, military power – 'radically' to transform the world's political economy to enable a convergence with the needs of capital in general, and of US capital in particular.[27] This seemingly 'radical' agenda was in fact deeply reactionary in terms of its impact on the defence mechanisms thrown up by the working class and the poor since the 1930s. By 1981, a general attack on 'New Deal' trade unionism and welfare-inspired regulation in the USA, could take place alongside a murderous offensive against the weakest nationalist and anti-American movements in Central and Latin America (so the pressure came on El Salvador, Nicaragua or Guatemala). This was ideologically justified as minimizing the role of the state's economic arm, while ignoring in Britain, the USA and Latin America, the re-enhanced role of the repressive state against strikes or against revolts at the periphery.

How new is globalization?

Thus, globalization is nothing like as new as its propagandists claim. However, there are two major elements that are new today. The first is the increasing internal spread of capitalist relations of production. Latin America, for example, is not only linked to the global economy through Spanish colonialism or American imperialism as it was; now exploitation of urban proletarianized labour is more common across the continent. In Brazil and Mexico especially, the national development efforts of the 1950s and 1960s built steel, car and chemical production for American capitalism in the 1990s better than the old peasant latifundia could ever do.[28] These industries are all environmental polluters the USA does not want now. When Frank in the 1960s reinstated a radical history of underdevelopment in Latin America, he emphasized capitalism as the root of the problems. Frank's work virtually marked the invention of 'development studies' as an academic discipline. It has been criticized by the left for reducing capitalism to colonialism and imperialism, while stressing internal social relationships less, thereby presenting a more sophisticated version of the simple-minded North/South clash. What Frank later came to see was the consequential development of internal class relationships within 'peripheral' capitalism. The power of domestic and/or 'client' ruling classes – using the army or parliamentary democracy as politics and levels of protest required – is vitally important: rich Brazilians exploit poor Brazilians far more than poor East Enders in London in the 'North' exploit poor Brazilians in the 'South'. So much of the 'Christian' analysis of global debt and justice ignores this: it is like taking the politics of Jesus with reference to the Romans but with no Herod, Pharisees or Sadducees.[29]

What has made the globalization propaganda appear correct is the second development: the reincorporation of large parts of the globe back into the control of international capital. The Cold War symbolized by the airlift and crossing point at Berlin was won when these continents were brought back. Global capital proclaims the triumph with the fall of the Berlin Wall in 1989. But see the politics and not just the geography. For all their huge failings, the greatest historic resistance to the power of global capitalism has come from the two largely peasant-dominated revolutions in Russia and China. To varying degrees, both South America and India between 1914 and 1985 also attempted to opt out of imperialist control while the 'great powers' were more preoccupied with each other. The reincorporation of two continents – Asia and South America – and the failed revolutions are the key historical political and economic histories we need to take on board before we even look further at a 'debt crisis'. The failures of the 'communist states' were political and military defeats, not just about economics. The forcible reintroduction and further penetration of Russia and Latin America into a 'new' capitalism bear unmistakable signs of the old imperialism. The re-emergence of primitive capitalist accumulation in Russia is also a reminder of the rules of the Roman Empire; you resist us, we obliterate you. Global capital's treatment of Russia from the 'Allied' intervention of 1918 (one British role being to secure the oil in Baku) has been almost as dismissive of the ordinary Russian as Stalin; yet all the new capitalist democracies of 1945–50 in Germany, Italy and Japan were gained largely by Russian blood. This implicit rule of empire is a far more powerful and dangerous one than so-called trade rules. Its logic has also been seen in the destruction of Fallujah at the end of 2004, whatever the rhetoric about putting down insurgents or making Iraq 'safe for democracy'.

The political in political economy: the East Asian models

In the midst of this Empire, Atherton is looking for 'egalitarian public policies' to generate 'successful, long term growth', as measured by something like a human development index. There is a major plank missing in the analysis here. Where do governments that implement such policies come from? In far too much of this 'Christian' work governments are analysed like exogenous variables. There is no understanding here of how different forms of government have come about – whether 'activist' or passive, whether corrupt or ethical – because the hard work on history, political economy, class and sociology, culture and ideology, or even the nature of local political alliances has simply not been done. Important political and practical consequences stem from such inadequate theory. Because it separates the political off to one side, neo-classical economics now works with an implicit acceptance of the liberal parliamentary order, which is normally set against 'corrupt governments', or today of 'rogue states'. But such an economics has no way of understanding how political forms relate and react with the economic, other than by bringing in 'government' as an outside variable.

Atherton also argues that 'justice is good for the economy' in relation, for example, to some of the 'Asian models', where we are dealing with the 'economic consequences of social reform'.[30] But where and why did these economic and social reforms come from? The lack of an in-depth structural view of history and politics is shown all too clearly by some of Sen's comments on Japan.

Hutton had the same problems in his analysis of Germany and Japan in *The State We're In*. With behavioural theory and utility analysis, the emphasis on duty and loyalty in the Japanese corporate model completely misses the point about the Japanese feudal structure – the revolution from above that created early Japanese capitalism.[31] This was the source of Japan's strength and is now the base of its weakness.

Asia was the object of massive inter-imperialist wars from 1894 to 1945 as the UK, USA, Russia, China and Japan fought for control. The true World War Two began in 1931 when Japan invaded Manchuria. The recent politics and history of the 'Asian models' stem from the Cold War. After the US conquests, and under US tutelage, Japan, Taiwan and South Korea (under imperial Japan after 1905) replaced their old rulers and made the vital land reforms, which have always been discussed and hardly ever made in Latin America. By beginning effectively in 1945, Hutton for example, misses the point that it was precisely because of Japan's feudal imperialism that US administrators took steps to destroy the old basis of rule in Japan. Land reform gave the peasants more control of their land. High domestic demand provided a popular basis for the consumer goods the Japanese were to produce with such expertise until the late 1980s. Taiwan and South Korea too were also products of the Cold War. They were consciously built up as client states – as was Western Europe after 1945 – and bulwarks against communism in China (which in the domino theory was assumed to be threatening Indonesia and Indo-China). Economically, US demand for military hardware provided the basis for what became the heavy industries of these three countries: from then, it was not such a big step from shipbuilding to electronics. This model from Japan is now that for China via Hong Kong, Guangdong and on to Shanghai. As against this, the 'threat' of a 'communist' Cuba in the US backyard meant handling Latin America in a brutal way. So, the East Asian economies are in a very different place from Latin

America: it is not possible to read across a protectionist model as the solution.[32]

Liberalization, capital flows and protection

The dissolution and dismembering of the Soviet Empire after 1991 – with Ukraine and Georgia as recent additions to the 'Western side'[33] – mark the middle rather than the beginning of the process of reincorporation. In China, there was a kind of Thatcherism before Thatcher: the reintroduction of China into the world market began quite quickly after Mao's death in 1976, with the Deng Xiaoping led reforms from 1978.[34] The key watchwords for China were similar to Thatcher too: political repression by the central state against local autonomy, particularly after 1989 and Tiananmen Square, accompanied by economic liberalization with consumer goods (and in Britain house ownership) to keep the masses happy and committed. Similar trends were under way in India (to a degree) after the failure of the 'self-reliance' economy and the import substitution of the 1950s, symbolized by the cotton loom on the middle of independent India's flag. From the Rajiv Gandhi regime onwards in 1984, India's move to 'liberalization' stemmed from internal contradictions as well as external pressure. The key turning point was a balance of payments crisis in 1991.

When this is understood, the rise of an assertive nationalism (complete with WMD) in both India and China can also be understood. For example, the Congress Party of India (on which the ANC in South Africa was originally modelled) – for long an all-class and all-region alliance – plays the national card to buy off 'Hindu' parties like the BJP.[35] This style of nationalistic 'third worldism' arose initially after World War One, but mainly after World War Two, as the middle classes of countries like Brazil (sometimes organized around the military[36]) or India denounced their peripheral status and claimed their national right to autonomy. There is a continuing ideological argument for nationalist protection within the 'developing world', which unthinking Christian analysis can slide into. For the nationalist movements, a lazy North/South analysis is no less of an 'obsolete' tool than it was in 1947; given the 'liberalization' of India since the 1980s, it is ever more needed by India's local business elite. If you are poor in India, don't blame us; blame the 'West' or the 'North' (or the Muslims).

Much of the Christian work on trade justice is based on the conventional anti-globalization critique that the free movement of capital is a major source of developing countries' problems. Again, this oversimplifies. Germany could just as easily argue (with unemployment in the East at 20 per cent plus) that it needs capital controls to stop money leaving! Speaking of 'liberalization' of capital flows as the issue is to let the neo-liberals define the debate. The answer has been to lock into a defensive – probably protectionist – stance. The key is not in the liberalization itself – but who is controlling it. 'Complete liberalization may damage long-term security' sounds like it could as easily come out of the USA. It was exactly the basis on which Senator Kerry, for example, attempted to build his economic case against George II in 2004. Keeping the US and European markets open – and opening them up much further – is probably a much better way to go for the developing countries. Protecting domestic markets, as in Argentina or Africa, builds in monopoly profits for corrupt elites or TNCs.[37] Talking about protection in India or Malaysia is merely likely to encourage more of it in the USA. Since the East Asian crisis of 1997–8, there has been much talk of the need for the developing world's 'financial recovery'.[38] Where is the need for this in China? More capital controls protection for China may play into the hands of the Chinese (Communist) elite and Coca Cola; not the folks we wish to support.

Stiglitz's structural adjustment

Northcott's work is still the best Christian introduction to the debt and justice debate with a layperson's guide to neo-liberalism and structural adjustment and the economic and political implications for the South. He has a better sense of colonial and post-colonial history, an effective critique and some alternative proposals. However, a major criticism would be his lack of desire to pull all the symptoms together and go to the heart of the power of global capitalism as their root cause. This means that the difficult and radical politics of an anti-capitalist movement is to a degree avoided; too much faith is placed in 'responsible' governments of the Western sort. Yet, colonial and imperial relationships have led to subordinate, and frequently vicious, capitalist or landowning classes, often linked to the military, which have usually prevented such enlightened governments in the South. Turning to Stiglitz's critique of the IMF, we see again someone with the most inadequate political analysis of how different types of governments come into being. We have no real political economy at the national level, only, in his case, at the level of 'global governance'. Like many government consultants, he takes the politics as given. This is fine if you are acting as an adviser, but it will not do if you are trying to give the 'success' of the East Asian models, for example, any explanatory power. Stiglitz does see through his own practical experience the actual politics of the Washington consensus, and shows how a government like Malaysia has resisted its pressures, but there is no understanding of why such East Asian policies have come into being and what structural, historical and political forces have led them this way. Like Pettifor and Hutton, it is a critique of neo-liberalism that does not escape its own analytical traps; not surprising, given that Stiglitz was first and foremost a mathematical economist. He ends where we need to begin. Hirst and Thompson do a far better job on the East Asian 'crisis' of 1997–8. They show that the major problem for Thailand was an overvalued fixed exchange rate and that of Korea of indented major conglomerates (the chaebols). For neither of these issues can the IMF or the World Bank be blamed, whatever their later policy responses.[39]

The trouble with the North/South analysis is that it ignores poverty within the 'rich' world. Are 'we' seriously asking those on social security or migrant workers to be the 'we' in the rich world who are often asked to 'consume less'? What is actually meant by the 'we' is the middle classes with a conscience, but the activists can't actually say this. This 'we' language breaks down, because it avoids talking about class and relative inequality both here and there. Even more, is the illusion that most developing country governments' are somehow paragons of democratic virtue, even outside of Africa. Protectionism by China, Malaysia, India or Brazil can just as easily work in favour of their rich (increasingly capitalist) elites at the cost of the North's poor. You cannot assume that by supporting Malaysian capital controls, you are necessarily supporting the Malaysian poor; all you may be doing is transferring wealth from one elite to another. If we allow either the globalization or the so-called anti-globalization propaganda to confuse us, the main result is to divide people around the world from seeing their common exploitation. It obscures rather than clarifies the real power that we all face. Rather than uniting the poor in the USA with the poor in Africa, it has the potential to set them against each other. Divide and rule is an old colonial and imperial trick. We should not be naive in our easy acceptance of this nonsense about rich 'countries' exploiting poor 'countries'. Can the poor of the North be persuaded to see that their problems do not stem from other poor people in the developing countries (or from migrant workers/asylum seekers), but from their own rich? It means taking on the rich elites in the South too, because they are usually ignored in the 'developing country' rhetoric.

The Jubilee

The debt and trade justice campaigns, then, for all their genuine moral fervour and practical achievements are seriously flawed in their political and economic analysis. Despite its propaganda successes, it has only partially thought through a weak historical critique of global capitalism. Let us take as a comparison with today's global capitalism, the model of the good society presented in the Old Testament. For here, after the kingly city states of Canaan had been overthrown, the alternative vision of Israel was of a peasant society. In Old Testament times, the Jubilee legislation was enshrined to reinforce Israel's beginnings in a revolutionary deliverance from slavery. Selby reminds us that the Hebrews' slavery in Egypt came not in the usual ancient manner via conquest but from the consequences of getting into debt. But in the hoped-for Israel, everyone could tend their own land, live under the shade of their fig tree and pursue a self-sufficient life in their 'tribal' communities. For Isaiah the people 'shall build houses and inhabit them; they shall plant vineyards and eat their fruit. They shall not build and another inhabit; they shall not plant and another eat.'[40] But after centuries of imperialism and colonialism and under today's global capital, these self-sufficient economies have been destroyed. The people are forced to trade even though in the vast majority of cases they have lost control of their own production. Even if some are still peasants – and own their own land – many are now landless rural sharecroppers or proletarians. In either case, the local economy is still subordinated to the global. In Africa particularly, local economies are dependent on the global for the production of one or two cash crops or minerals. So, even with a more equal exchange in trade these people would still be massively subordinate.

The Jubilee ideal not only meant having the debt written off but regaining the land, the loss of which had usually been the cause of the peasants' indebtedness. In those days, controlling the land was at the essence of controlling production; under capitalism, it is controlling capital. Therefore, we need to understand the historical experience of the common people when they have attempted to resist the loss of their own control of their own production and today's politics of what it means to be part of the global struggle to regain that control. Furthermore, if people are to control their debt, they need to regain control of their productive capacity. To give the common people economic and political control over their own land and resources means giving less not more power to the client states that masquerade as 'governments'.

Unfortunately, the Jubilee ideal was never implemented. Israel fell from its idealistic hopes and the problems for the Jewish peasants got worse from David's monarchy until Jesus. When Amos spoke not only of unequal exchange, but the accumulation of lands and wealth at others' cost, the court prophets told him to get out of Israel. The Lugano Report symbolizes the increasing recognition that we may be received like Jesus when it comes to announcing the desirability of a new Jubilee.[41] As we turn to look at the gospel message, Northcott points out that in Luke Jesus begins his ministry by announcing a Jubilee.[42] He omits to mention that Jesus is stoned out of the village. We too will be stoned for our pains and threatened with exclusion from the global village. In the process of anti-capitalist protest, Christians will find others at work. We would be wise to take note of their analysis and of their experience in the struggle against global capital and for justice.

Part 2

Theological Stories of Political Economy

6

Jesus and the Political Economy of Galilee

A new look at Mark?

The theme of this book is that the gospel is shot through with a much greater sense of Jesus' social, economic and political message than the normal consensus 'spiritual' exegesis.[1] The politics and economics are inextricably linked with the faith message and are an intrinsic part of the good news. The aim in this chapter is to look especially at the subtle mix of political economy and theology in Mark's Gospel in a number of the stories where conventional exegesis has either completely missed or not thought through the political and economic implications of Jesus' message and actions.[2] There are two reasons for focusing on Mark. First, Mark can lay claim to have invented the genre of a written 'Gospel' itself.[3] Second, as there has also been a continuing reformulation of Paul's political theology by the latest generation of theologians, the most radical political theology on the Gospels has used Mark as its starting base.[4] Given an increasing focus on the political and economic background that has aided this rethink, it is now possible to see Mark as a social theorist as well as a theologian.[5] In this sense, Mark's Gospel speaks to our 'post-modern' world of global capitalism with a political clarity that much purely religious exegesis hides, obscures or distorts. Yet, the gulf between what has been going on in radical academia, particularly in the USA, and in the pew has never been wider.

Despite many active Christians' concerns for the issues of global debt and justice, an ongoing synthesis of this contemporary political economy with a radical political theology is required, in Britain especially. This book and chapter are intended to start this new reformulation by beginning with the shortest Gospel.[6]

As with Tom Wright on Paul, the book that opened my eyes to this possibility was Ched Myers' book on a 'political reading' of Mark. His work *Binding the Strong Man* was hailed by the Catholic Press commentary when it appeared in 1988 in the USA as nothing short of path breaking – and it is. It is an interesting commentary on the weight of conventional ideological thinking that not only has Myers' work been ignored; outside radical circles, it is virtually unknown.[7] It comes from the series on the Bible and Liberation, which symbolizes the huge gap between what is going on in the 'universities and seminaries' that is not trickling down to the level of the ordinary church member at all.[8] Using Myers as a base for a 'new look' at Mark, I have developed a political and economic commentary on a few specific 'pericopes': on the protest context implied in the apocalyptic beginnings of the Gospel; on the healing miracles; on the concept of the crowd in Galilee; on the legion of demons swept into the sea; and on the history, politics and economics of Tyre and Galilee. I go on to look in more detail at Jesus' entry into Jerusalem and his action and discourse at the Temple to assess the historical and contemporary meanings of 'Mark's Apocalypse'. I aim to show that Mark's Gospel shows Jesus engaging in a sustained theological and ideological attack on the old order of the collaborationist Jewish Establishment and the Roman colonial Empire. Mark's Gospel is dominated by a political and theological message; a Gospel that is consistent too with the critique of empire in the Old Testament, with the other Gospels, with Paul's writings and with the Revelation of John.

A new 'gospel': for and from the common people

Mark's Gospel is subversive.[9] From its beginning, Mark's new concept of 'gospel' attempts to overturn what was the proclamation of a victory for the Empire. For the imperial good news was a Roman victory on the borders. The accession of a new emperor was likewise announced throughout the Empire. In the imperial struggle to capture hearts and minds, the gospel was one of its ideological tools.[10] Now Mark has subverted the imperial language to announce the opposite.[11] From the borders of the Empire comes the story of a new emperor – of and from the common people, who is executed by the Romans for his faith and for his politics. Instead of Kyrios Caesar, there is the Lord Jesus Christ – Kyrios Christos. The 'anointed one' has his calling and approval from God and from his own people.[12]

For Myers, Mark's Gospel is not only the first Gospel, it 'stands … among the literary achievements of antiquity' for one reason: it is a narrative for and about the common people, 'written from below'.[13] Horsley calls the New Testament history for those 'at the bottom of the heap' and calls Mark a 'submerged Peoples History'.[14] Myers argues that the narrative home of the Gospel lies where the first half of the stories and action is centred: in Galilee, where Jesus grew up and where by all Gospel accounts he began his effective ministry. So, whoever 'Mark' actually was or wherever it was finally written, Mark's Gospel should be understood as coming out of the culture and experience of the early disciples in Galilee in particular, and is best understood as a document of the early Palestinian church.[15] The traditional linkage to Peter, rather than linking it to Rome, makes Mark far more the expression of another eyewitness from Galilee: even telling us that the multitude sat down on 'green grass' to be fed (Mark 6.39).[16] The later use of the suggested link to Peter to enhance Rome's prestige in the early church gives an early indication of the people's gospel being turned back the 'right' way round. In too much of the conventional exegesis, the subversive and bottom-up perceptions of Mark have been twisted the 'right' way up. By making Mark only a Gospel about a new religion, there has always been the danger of pandering to the powers that be in the imperial centre.

When Richard Horsley followed up his work on the sociology of Jesus' time with his own assessment of the 'politics of plot' in Mark, he did this because something seemed missing in conventional New Testament courses. He writes of the need to hear the whole story, to see the message of the Gospel as a whole and in its historical context.[17] In one of the best British academic theological studies of the *Message of Mark*, Morna Hooker emphasizes the gospel's 'barbarous' Greek. Myers points out that this would imply that Greek was at best Mark's second language. Indeed, one commentator has argued that the Gospel was originally written in Aramaic. But Greek was the language the Palestinian people had been forced to know since occupation and colonization under Alexander the Great. Mark writes from what today would be called the periphery of empire. Not surprising then that its natural equivalence would be in the liberation theology of Latin America, and many of these biblical and theological commentators draw on the Latin American experience. In his later co-operative work, Myers writes of the need to 'liberate space for change' and that is part and parcel of this book and chapter's purpose.[18]

Mark's apocalyptic Gospel

For Myers: 'the ideology of the apocalyptic holds the key to an accurate political reading of Mark'. This is not about dramatic end of the ages battles, but about a protest tradition that attempts to remove the veil of political, economic and religious ideology that keeps the common people in particular trapped in the thinking of the dominant power system. Jesus uses Isaiah early on in

Mark's Parable of the Sower, as an explanation of the power of the present world system's ideological ability to veil reality – and religion itself has often been its major tool. Thereby the common people are 'ever seeing but never perceiving' (4.12a). This is not about the Jews' inability to recognize the 'messianic secret', but about ordinary people being unable to grasp and seize the potential for their own liberation – both in spiritual and economic terms. Myers quotes another part of Isaiah in his later work: in this case, God promises to destroy 'the net that is cast over all people and the veil that is spread over all nations' (Isa. 25.7).[19]

Myers goes on to argue that Mark's 'literary strategy' from the tradition of 'Jewish apocalyptic' influences Mark more than any other. The themes borrowed from Jewish apocalyptic are so dominant in Mark that if anything this may slightly underestimate its importance. This 'apocalyptic imagination' is more than just a 'literary tradition'; it comes out of a culture and discourse of 'social protest'. It was based on demystifying the practices and pretensions of the established order; 'emperors were not divine and high priests were not sacrosanct'. Myers argues that Daniel has an 'overwhelming influence' on Mark, which Kee calls a 'disproportionate interest'.[20] Mark quotes from every chapter of Daniel. He also alludes to or uses the other classic apocalyptic texts: Isaiah, Ezekiel, Joel, Zechariah and Malachi. The 'Son of Man', Jesus' favourite term for himself, is from Daniel and Ezekiel. Even the concept of a 'secret' revelation, which has dominated discussions of Mark's 'messianic secret',[21] is an 'apocalyptic device'. The importance of Mark's apocalyptic Gospel is little taught in conventional religious exegesis. Perhaps this is not surprising given the domination of church teaching by the established order, while apocalyptic has its roots in protest and revolt. Thereby, in contrast to commentators who see it as 'religious escapism', Jewish apocalyptic hoped to have a strengthening effect on endurance,[22] while also potentially motivating further revolt.[23]

Mark also contains what many exegetes call 'Latinisms'. The

influence of the Empire of Rome is never far away; indeed all the Latinisms are used in Mark when he is alluding to either military or economic matters. Myers writes that in coming to see Mark's Gospel as a political theology he is conscious of 'learning to do theology in Pharaoh's household'; from what he and other radicals have called 'Empire America'. He comments, 'Few have dared to translate apocalyptic theology into the present day.'[24] The liberation theologians who could most benefit from it have been worried by the traditional definition of its 'primitive' religious escapism; this has unfortunately left the field largely clear for the popular paperback profiteers. In Britain, only Chris Rowland has consistently attempted to see apocalyptic theology as a potentially radical theology. My argument here is that the whole Gospel of Mark should be read in the light of Jesus' political and apocalyptic message. Jesus' political and social stance is essential to Mark; the 'New Age' had arrived and a poor Galilean was bringing in the kingdom.

The beginning of the gospel of Jesus Christ

Mark's prologue (1.1–13) has traditionally been treated as somehow lacking in theological wisdom or 'spirituality' compared to John, for example. In contrast, Mark is in fact full of eschatological and apocalyptic language and references: often in opposition to the conventional 'religion' of the day. The Established Judaism of the first century saw the work of the Holy Spirit being a work of the past, in establishing Israel, and a work of the future when Israel's true chosen nature would be revealed, but the Holy Spirit was not active in the present. Mark's Gospel, on the other hand, is written in the historic present tense. As the battle comes to earth, it is as though Mark brings us close to the immediacy of the action. There is a breathlessness about Mark – immediately is used 30 times – and many sentences are linked by 'ands' that are removed from the present translations.[25]

Myers describes Mark's opening as 'minimalist theatre'. This is a new story (1.1) that replaces the old (1.2). It is a 'subversive story' where a leader describes himself as an 'outlaw' and replaces his fallen predecessor; where common folk are chosen to overthrow 'the rule of the powers'. Mark's narrative begins with the abrupt: 'it is written' (1.2a). In a largely oral culture, the power of the prophetic word was based on the passing down of a remembered tradition. Writing itself was a sacred act available only to the elite. So the Scriptures literally mean 'that which is written' and the Bible is 'the Book'.[26] Mark appeals to the tradition of 'it is written'; it is the only place in the Gospel where Mark himself directly quotes the Old Testament, mixing the imagery of both Isaiah and Malachi. By writing down the new story, Mark now 'normalizes' the new tradition; the story, Myers believes, of the Galilean church's coming to discipleship. Indeed, Jesus pokes fun at the arrogant elite of literary scribes: 'Have you not read?' is his way of showing that a common carpenter can speak with more authority for the people.[27]

Hooker emphasizes that the Gospel jumps straight into an 'eschatological setting' by taking the reader, with barely a pause for breath, immediately into John the Baptist's ministry in Judaea (1.2–9). John's allusion to the 'stronger' one (1.7) – repeated by Jesus in 3.27 in his first confrontation with Jerusalem-based teachers of the law (1.22) – is a deliberate reference, obscure to us, to the 'Mighty One'. Untying sandals (1.7) was the job of a slave; yet John the Baptist considered himself not even worthy of this for Jesus – the living Mighty One, who according to tradition came to rescue Israel in times of war, and was now to overthrow the world system. Hooker calls this a reference to 'the eschatological deliverer'.[28] This introduction is the strongest part of her analysis, but despite the search for an overall message from Mark, she then moves on and, like most traditional commentators, never comes back to apocalyptic as a unifying or persistent theme. Yet, as with Ezekiel and in Revelation, Mark sees 'Heaven being torn open' (1.10b): a traditional apocalyptic sign. Likewise, the descent of the Holy Spirit (1.10c) is an 'eschatological event': God is coming to assist his people. Mark presents Jesus' temptations as a 'cosmic' 'eschatological battle'; while Jesus is led by the Spirit into the battle (1.12), the angels and the wild animals symbolize the desire for the potential – and lost – harmony with nature at the beginning and end of time. If the prologue in Mark then turns out to be seeing Jesus and John 'from God's angle', from a heavenly, or divine perspective, the global battle is then to be fought out 'down' on earth, starting locally in Galilee.[29]

The miracles of Mark as concrete liberation

One of the problems presented by Mark's Gospel for a contemporary reader is its immediate emphasis on miracle stories. As soon as the disciples are called (1.16–20), we move to the centre of Jesus' work at Capernaum (v. 21a) and we are presented with an exorcism (1.23–7). For some Pentecostalists, this suits their message entirely, but for many others – even Christians outside fundamentalist circles – it serves only to make Jesus' story oddly out of touch with our world; pre-modern, 'mythical', an ancient religious fable from 'primitive' peasants. Myers speaks for many: 'there must be more to these stories than is immediately obvious to the modern reader'.

Those who present Jesus – then or now – as just a miracle worker or healer tragically misunderstand the socio-historical point being made. Miracle workers were common in the Palestine of Jesus' day. They were allowed to practice freely and did not arouse the ire shown to Jesus. The first key to note in the exorcism story of Mark 1, therefore, is that it is framed by a dispute over Jesus' authority to teach (vv. 21b, 27) and by his popular appeal to the common people over the whole of Galilee (2.28). The pressure on Jesus from the needs of the people is often conveyed by Mark after the exorcisms in this chapter (vv. 37, 39, 45c);

perhaps it is best put in verse 33, 'the whole town gathered at the door'. The exorcism focuses on the social alienation created by sickness. Illness would have been a disaster for a day labourer, as Joseph probably was. It would not have been difficult for Jesus to identify with people whose experience was akin to his own family. 'Mark's Jesus seeks always to restore the social wholeness denied to the sick.' Theissen sums this up superbly: the popular character of these stories centres on people whose 'economic and social position left them no other outlet to articulate their hopes ... a degree of class correlation in the primitive Christian miracle studies can hardly be denied'. This takes us back to the first part of the miracles' political message: the bringing of liberation. 'The miracles are part of [Jesus'] struggle to bring concrete liberation to the oppressed and marginal of Palestinian society.' Ironically, it is from just such dispossessed people – the black ex-slaves of the USA – that modern day Pentecostalism originally arose.

However, the first exorcism story reminds us of another part of the liberation struggle. It is a struggle because there has to be liberation from oppressive powers. It is worth remembering the response of the demon in verse 24. For Myers, the demon is pleading on behalf of the scribal authorities; 'Have you come to destroy us?' As Kee puts it: 'the struggle is not a momentary one but part of a wider conflict. [This is] wholly compatible with the picture of apocalyptic Judaism – of God's agent locked in ... struggle with the powers of evil.' The demon attempts to control Jesus by naming him (v. 24b). Jesus' identity, as the Son of Man, may be hidden, but the demons, the powers that be, know exactly who he is (v. 34c) and of his threat to their status quo. Here the exorcisms recall for Myers 'the miracle of the exodus story [which] lies not in the nature of epiphanies and plagues but in the liberation of the Hebrew people from slavery ... The miracle is to be seen [not] in Yahweh's parting of the Red Sea ... but in vanquishing ... the Egyptian military machine.'[30] Mark continues his critique of the military legions that possessed and bound Israel when we look at another healing miracle in his chapter 5.

Jesus declares ideological war on the ruling class

It is important to emphasize that, contrary to the non-political readings of Mark, 'in the course of (Mark's) story virtually every identifiable ruling faction in Jewish society will oppose Jesus'.[31] This first becomes obvious in Galilee where even the Pharisees and the Herodians – political enemies, but nevertheless, the Galilean political elite – combine to battle against him. The ideological war is also announced against the priests, the scribes and the teachers of the law – the entire literary Establishment – on behalf of the illiterate common masses.

Mark, like Luke, uses the disease of leprosy early in his story (1.40–5) not only to show how Jesus intends to combat social alienation of all kinds, but also to reveal early on his clash with the religious authorities. Our normal religious interpretations tend to play this down and use the subtleties of translation to do this. Myers argues that the emotionally charged atmosphere of Jesus healing the leper is distorted by the translations. Taken literally the leper does not 'beg' Jesus but 'dares' him (1.40). Jesus is not full of 'compassion' but 'angry' or 'indignant' (v. 41a). Since the latter translation does not fit with Jesus' presumed attitude, Mark is reinterpreted. The key lies in the fact that a priest was supposed to preside over such a cleansing. So to ask Jesus to perform it was a challenge – a dare – to take on the religious powers that be. Jesus, angry perhaps that he has been put unnecessarily on the spot, nevertheless 'is willing' (v. 41c) to do as he is asked (1.41). The extent of the challenge to the priestly order is emphasized by Jesus having to give the man a 'strong warning' (1.43), which the man ignores (1.44–5). Even more, the man is sent back to the priests not for cleansing – but literally as a witness against them; not as usually put, as a testimony to them (1.44).[32]

Twisted as it normally is, the story of the leper does not make sense. Why should Jesus 'no longer be able to enter a town openly' (v. 45c)? Jesus has performed an act of compassionate healing and the leper has been sent back formally to the priest to report his cleansing. *The Living Bible* gives a wonderful example in its non-literal way of what the conventional religious teachers want us to think, for in verse 45 its translators insert 'such throngs surrounded Jesus' that he could not enter the town. The more literal translators tell us that what Mark actually wrote is 'as a result' (v. 45b). As a result of what? Well presumably, as a result of the leper ignoring Jesus and telling everyone his good news (v. 45a). Why should this news be such a problem? Because this 'news', which our modern religionists have been busy obscuring, was a direct challenge to the priestly order. Jesus had done something only the priests were allowed to do. No wonder Jesus couldn't enter the town openly. As we have seen, the throngs were nothing new, but such a direct challenge, now was. Jesus retreated here, not to contain his popularity but because he had become a marked man. Jesus had just protested against the 'entire purity apparatus that the priests controlled'. He had confronted the religious ideology of his day. Mark is making a living commentary on another of his favourite apocalyptic works, in this instance Malachi. For on the day of the Lord the priests (the Levites) will be cleansed, like the leper, when they bring their offerings in true justice (Malachi 3.3–5). 'For Yahweh will appear as a witness against those who use the cultic apparatus to oppress the poor and the marginalised.'[33]

The crowd and the common people in Jesus' Palestine

We first come across the 'crowd' in Mark 2 as Jesus heals the paralytic man in Capernaum (2.4). The word *ochlos* in Greek is used by Mark 38 times; it is not the usual word for people, *laos*, from which our word laity comes. It is a word used for Roman soldiers, apart from their officers, and often meant their non-combat menial accompaniment. Historically, it could be used to mean the people left behind when the elite left for Babylon after the Assyrian conquest. They were the 'people of the land'; today we could use a number of words to convey the same meaning: the masses, the proles, best of all perhaps the 'common people'. It is the people without their leaders, without the elite or the ruling class. In Mark, they are poor and ever present, often sinners and outcasts; the people to whom Jesus and his disciples are called. When throughout history, the religious, and particularly the priests, have criticized them, Jesus does not do so; unlike the disciples, they are not given special instructions or conditions. They are at the same time alienated from the Jewish leaders, feared and manipulated by them, particularly as regards to Jesus. They share common features with what Luke described as the poor or the pious ones and clearly were the people, like Mary, who harboured the greatest messianic hopes. Strictly, what we call the laity in church today should be called the 'ochlaity', the people apart from their clerical leadership. Today, they are probably best represented by the common people outside of the church; the people which the European church has preached at, ordered about and lost.

Before his journey to Jerusalem, Capernaum is mentioned five times in Jesus' travels and would appear to have been the centre of his ministry in Galilee. Today, it would probably feel more like a big village with a population of around 5,000 people. Capernaum sat just across the Sea of Galilee from Tiberias, which Antipas planned as his new capital. Tiberias had been built on a cemetery and to placate an emperor who had just expelled 4,000 Jews from Rome. Capernaum was also a border town. Leaving Philip the Tetrach's territory to the west, Capernaum would have been the first town you entered in Antipas' kingdom. So, Capernaum was an alternative centre to that of the political authorities, on the edge of their territory. Recent archaeological digs have shown that its building structures in this period would have been unable to support a masonry ceiling; so wooden beams and branches would have been used. This is why the paralytic man could have been let down through an opening in the roof (2.4). The homes of the people from whom Jesus came and to whom Jesus ministered were poor and simple. Yet, Myers emphasizes that the houses of the common people become the 'alternative sites of resistance' unlike the symbolic 'house of Israel' that Jesus attacks and binds. Jesus attends to the crowd from Simon's (Peter's) house (1.29–34), he eats in the people's homes (2.15 – even with the hated tax collectors) and the home is often the place of healing (1.31; 5.38; 7.24). Later in his ministry, as Jesus attempts to teach the disciples about real uncleanness (7.17), or about leadership (9.33) or relationships (10.10), he does so in the home. Herzog points out that healing the paralytic man put Jesus 'in direct competition' with the Temple hierarchy: right at the beginning of his ministry, Jesus' new centre of resistance is at odds with authority. The Gospels are well aware that Jesus disciples' are to be taken to the boundaries of their experience, to the borders of their lives, to the marginalized and oppressed on the edge of our existence. Here, as Myers puts it: God breaks in at the margins, far from the centre.[34]

The Roman legions as demons

At the beginning of Mark 5, Jesus crosses the lake to 'the other side' from his base at Capernaum. This is the first of four cross-over journeys where Jesus brings the possibility of 'liberation to the other side'. Theissen points out the significance of this story being in the region of the 'Gerasenes' (5.1). This journey puts Jesus over the border from Antipas' Galilee and into Decapolis. These 'Ten Cities' were a Roman creation; Pompey had 'liberated' the Hellenistic cities from Hasmonean rule, when conquering Israel in 63 BCE. So at the beginning of this story, for those in the know, as Myers rather modestly put it: 'this calls to mind the Roman military occupation'. Mark gives deliberately anti-Roman undertones to what looks merely to be a miracle story about demon possession. If this were written just before 70 CE as Roman troops moved through Galilee, Mark would have even more reason to hide his message in crafty allusions.

First, as Horsley rightly emphasizes, the demonic man is a symbol of the whole of society: for was Israel not possessed by evil and 'chained hand and foot' (5.2, 4a)? Galilee's new capital built in the tombs symbolized Israel's binding to the ways of death, while crying out for release (vv. 3–6). For all their military might, after nearly 100 years the Romans had still not subdued it (v. 4b). Second, besides the obvious 'legion', Myers points out that the story is full of military imagery: the word *agele* used for the 'herd' of pigs (5.11) was also used for military recruits – pigs do not normally form herds. The pigs are literally 'dismissed' and then 'charge' into the sea (5.13). Pigs would only be located in a Gentile region like Decapolis, but there was a side allusion: the Roman legions stationed over the border in Syria had boars on their standards. Third, Myers also points out that the confrontation at Gerasa parallels those that Jesus had just experienced in Capernaum. Here we now have Roman as well as Jewish opposition, so the local religious elite and the Roman Empire are in this together. Mark also calls upon a well-remembered event in Herod the Great's campaign in Galilee against the terrorist Hezekiah, when some of Herod's Galilean gentry support had been drowned in the Sea of Galilee, as Herod went to aid the Romans in Syria. In the same way, the 'legion' of swine was swept into the same sea. There is also the sense here of the Beast from the Sea, a metaphor used later by John in Revelation: the Roman army was to be swept back into the Mediterranean Sea from which they came. The legion's fate was to be the same ultimately as that of Pharaoh's army of chariots thrown into the Reed Sea.[35]

Yet, unlike Nineham, who can only see in this story a message of Jesus' 'power'; the power that most feared in Israel was
the power of the Romans. It was so threatening, it could easily
seem superhuman and demonic, unleashing destructive forces
in which the people could be 'swamped' and 'drown': the kind
of fear that our government uses to justify 'anti-terrorist' measures. Horsley points out that in the storm (4.37–9) and in the
healing of the dumb boy (9.25), these evil spirits are 'rebuked'.
The Hebrew equivalent used in the Old Testament means to root
out, destroy, or vanquish – usually Israel's enemies. The threat of
potential destruction is seen clearly by the demons threatening
Israel (1.24; 5.10; 9.20, 26) if not by the people themselves. The
people of Decapolis did not want to throw legions into the sea
(5.17), and asked Jesus to leave, for he was spoiling their 'deli-
cately balanced compromise with the new world order'.[36]

A political Elijah threatens the king

In contrast the new world offered by Jesus sees the people like
the man in Gerasa 'in his right mind' (5.15) or like the healed
woman; Israel can now live in peace and be freed from suffering
(5.34). So, Mark returns to the links between Jesus and John the
Baptist and sets out afresh the hopes of a covenant renewal they
both preached. In the two stories in the second half of chapter 5,
the hope of Israel is stressed by a wordplay associated with the
number 12. The first woman healed has been suffering for 12
years (5.25); Jairus' daughter was 12 years old, just of childbear-
ing age (5.42). Elijah was expected to return and restore the 12
tribes. As Horsley emphasizes, these early chapters also play on
Jesus' repetition of Moses and Elijah's ministries – the testing of
40 days in the wilderness (for Elijah, see 1 Kings 19.8) and the
feeding of the hungry people during a famine (1 Kings 17.2–16),
the summoning of followers and a dead child raised and fed (in
1 Kings 17.17–24; in Mark, a girl – 5.35–44; in Luke, as with

Elijah, a widow's son – Luke 7.11–17) all led the disciples to con-
clude that Jesus was a new Elijah (Matt. 16.14; Mark 8.28). In
Mark, Jesus confirms that John has 'come again' as Elijah and repeated Elijah's ministry – this, to his close disciples at the Transfiguration, which also includes Moses (9.1–13); in Matthew, Jesus
preaches it to the crowd (11.14). The usual emphasis on the links
between John, Jesus and Elijah stresses their prophetic roles.
What Horsley stresses however is that Israel's renewal here is
bound up with an attack on her present leaders. John certainly
came from the desert and modelled himself on Elijah's 'primitive
tradition'; but Elijah was also specifically appointed to be a revolutionary – to overthrow oppressive kings and to anoint others
in their place (1 Kings 19.15–17). This reaches its fulfilment in
Elijah's disciple – Elisha – who presides over the replacement
of both the king of Damascus (the Aramaeans) and the king
of Israel (2 Kings 8—10).[37] In the latter case, the king of Israel
sees at his death that it was the injustice over the land – Naboth's
vineyard – that had caused this day of judgement to come on
him (1 Kings 21; 2 Kings 9.26). Not surprisingly, it is the 'king'
– Herod Antipas (who has most to fear) who first sees Jesus, not
only as John's disciple, like Elisha, but another John resurrected
from the dead (Mark 6.14–16). Matthew emphasizes the close
relationship between John and Jesus differently from Luke: not
only does he record their conversation at the baptism (3.14–15),
he is the only writer to note that on John's death, Jesus is the first
to be told (14.12b).

Theissen has an excellent account of the politics behind John
the Baptist's execution. Antipas had married his brother's wife
(called Herodias), both gaining a divorce to do so, his divorce
being from a daughter of the king of Nabataea, to the south of
Judaea. John had criticized this marriage; since John came out
of the southern desert, Antipas may even have assumed that he
was in league with the Nabataeans. Antipas' time of cunning
finally ran out. In 36 CE, a few years after Jesus' death, an army

from Nabataea, invaded and deposed him. Many later saw this as judgement for his execution of John. The 'reed shaking in the wind' (Matt. 11.7) is another critique of Antipas. His first coins bore the symbol of the reed – a symbol of authority – and yet here we are given the imagery of a ruler merely swaying with the pre-vailing winds of political fortune. Myers also shows how Mark models Jesus' story on the ministry and death of John the Baptist. For him, the story in chapter 6 is by no means apolitical: it is a savage and sarcastic social caricature of a king who kills for the sake of honour in a licentious party and banquet.[38]

Traditional exegesis

The wider historical, political and economic relationships between Galilee, Israel and Tyre, which lie behind the story of the Syro-Phoenician woman, shed some more light on our understanding of Jesus' economic and political message. This healing story has always been a problem for me, for taken at face value Jesus appears to be insulting to the women who simply asks for her daughter to be healed. Calling someone a 'dog' (Mark 7.27c) is usually an insult in any culture, and it certainly was in the Jewish one of Jesus' time. The word here could be translated as 'little dog' – a household pet or a stray – and this tones down the phrase, but the problem remains. Theissen, whose analysis is largely used here, suggests that subsequent traditional exegesis has had three ways round the problem. The first has been to make Jesus' statement a test of the woman's faith. The translators of the NIV entitle the piece the 'faith of a Syro-Phoenician woman' even though Mark never mentions her 'faith' at all; in the text, Jesus simply compliments her on her reply to him (7.29). Another traditional escape has been to slide into psychology; Jesus was tired of the needs of the crowd pressing in on him, when he was looking for peace and quiet. Doesn't Mark (in v. 24c) say that he wanted his 'presence' kept 'secret'? There is some justification for this interpretation as both ideas are found in Matthew's exegesis of Mark. Matthew in his introduction to the story says that Jesus 'withdrew' to Tyre and Sidon (Matt. 15.21) implying he wanted to get away; he has only just heard of John's death and his immediate reaction is to withdraw to a solitary place or to a mountain (14.12–13, 23). Unlike Mark, it is Matthew who stresses the woman's 'great faith' (15.28), perhaps surprising in what he calls a 'Canaanite' (15.22), a people who had been lambasted in the Old Testament for their idolatry and lack of faith.[39]

The third traditional approach is to interpret Jesus' initial rejection as a case of salvation history symbolism. Again, this appears to be part of Matthew's exegesis. At first, Jesus refuses to answer (15.23a) and the disciples even want to send her away (v. 23b). Jesus appears to confirm this 'I was sent only to the lost sheep of Israel' (v. 24). So, the story becomes for some a reflection on the debates in the early church in places like Antioch (a city that some theologians have regarded as Matthew or Mark's base) about the opening up of the gospel to the Gentiles. The children being referred to are the people of Israel; the dogs, their common term for the Gentiles. Set in the middle of the feeding miracles in Mark (6.30–44 and 8.1–13), the bread must symbolically be the gospel. So the 'children's bread' is the good news originally brought to the Jews, but now being shared with the Gentiles, like Canaanites or Syro-Phoenicians. This is the interpretation most evangelical Christians have normally heard. It is given added credence by Mark placing it next to a debate on unclean foods with the Pharisees (7.1–23). As early Christian exegesis did indeed make this a story of the problem of early Jewish Christians and Gentiles eating together, because of their different attitude to unclean foods, this also becomes a religious story about accepting each other's religious conventions. As Theissen points out, however, 'Why should anyone create a complex concealment … within a miracle story?' Why give an attitude of rejection to Jesus when the story is about acceptance? Our original problem still remains: 'How can one refuse a request for the healing of a child by saying that children are to be preferred to dogs?'[40] In fact, the long and largely hostile relationship between Israel and Tyre forms the context for Jesus' dialogue with the woman asking for healing for her daughter. Once we have understood this history better, we can assess the theological and economic implications.

Galilee: the circle of the peoples

The name Galilee is short for *galil ha-goyim*, the circle of the peoples. For like Israel itself, Galilee was encircled geographically and politically. The Galileans were a fiercely independent people who fought against successive potential overlords from the Canaanite city states, until in Jesus' time, the Roman Empire. The rocky mountainsides celebrated in the early Liberation Song of Deborah as the 'heights of the field' in Naphtali (Judg. 5.18b) reflected an early agricultural subsistence economy further from the threat of such potential rulers. The people of Zebulun meanwhile were known as the 'people who scorned death' (v. 18a). Gottwald argues that the reference to the tribe of Issachar (in Gen. 49.15b) bending to their burden and submitting to forced labour implies that an underclass of labourers in the valley of Jezreel may well have joined Israel as they threw off the yoke of city states and fortresses like Megiddo (from which our word Armageddon is derived).

This independence was reflected too in their attitudes to the Davidic kingdom centred on Jerusalem. The Philistine threat that had precipitated David to power perhaps meant less to them, as it was largely further south. There were two major rebellions against David; in the second, both the rebels and David's mercenaries stormed right through Naphtali in Galilee. The local people were even less likely than the areas further south to be loyal to David's successors. Solomon restored Megiddo to reassert his control over Lower Galilee and set up his new administrative control in the area by ignoring the old tribal distinctions. David had also set the trends both in the use of forced labour and in a treaty with Tyre to consolidate his northern frontier: 1 Kings 9.10–15 tells a story not only of the use of forced labour to fortify Megiddo (9.15), but the ceding of 20 towns in Galilee to the king of Tyre (Hiram) to pay for the cedar and pine required for the Temple, palace and fort buildings (9.11). As Bright comments, with his usual understatement, 'One wonders whether this could have been a popular transaction.'[41] Not only was a long resentment set up in Galilee against Tyre, the hostility between north (Samaria) and south (Judah) was to lead in Galilee to an 800-year separation – and divergence – from rule by Jerusalem.

If Israel as a whole suffered from a loss of independence for 600 years before Jesus, the tradition of being dominated and ruled by outsiders was even worse and lasted for longer in Galilee. When the northern kingdom broke away after Solomon, Galilee was often in the path of invading armies from north and south and frequently a pawn in their power plays. When Omri's dynasty was established in Samaria by the ninth century BCE, Omri married his son, Ahab, to Jezebel, daughter of the Sidon king, allowing her to follow the gods of Tyre, as part of the defensive alliance with Tyre and Sidon (1 Kings 16.3). Omri's empire was also based on a temporary end to the feud with Judah; the wealth accumulated was specifically linked to the new deal offered to Damascus and Tyre merchants in the northern cities (1 Kings 20.34). So, the resentment of Damascus and Tyre was now also linked to the poverty of the peasantry, who had been suffering from three years of drought (1 Kings 17.1; 18.1, 5). It was this political and dynastic marriage – with its religious overtones – and the consequent peasant poverty with which it was associated, that Elijah had opposed. In the generations after Elijah and Elisha, a nasty cycle of attack and counter-attack took place across Galilee until Samaria fell in 722 BCE. The north, therefore, always had a considerably more mixed population than Judah and this remained true until Jesus' time.

Galilee children and the breadbasket of the dogs of Tyre

For the last 100 years before Jesus, Galilee had been brought back into the fold by the Hasmonean dynasty, but the 1,000-year-old suspicion of both Tyre and central rule from Jerusalem resonates throughout Mark's story. Theissen's work is most concerned to show the historicity of the story in Mark and concludes that its 'historic core' is probably of Palestinian origin. He argues that to understand this passage the cultural context is the key: Jesus' 're-jection' of the woman expresses a bitterness that had built up in the border regions between Tyre and Galilee. The first tellers and hearers would have been familiar with the situation and would have seen it as 'true to life'. The story in Mark 7 begins with Jesus travelling to the 'vicinity' of Tyre (v. 24a); Matthew calls it the 'region' of Tyre (15.21). He does not appear to have travelled into the city itself. Theissen makes the point that since there was a later Christian church in Tyre (Acts 21.3–7), the story would have undoubtedly mentioned the city itself if Jesus had gone in. This restriction of Jesus to the rural hinterland probably corresponds to the actual 'pre-Easter situation'.[42]

Unlike Matthew, Mark stresses that the woman was Greek and born in Syrian Phoenicia (v. 26a). By Jesus' time, the result of years of planting Hellenistic cities in the north would have meant a great mixing of populations, as the cities sat in the midst of Jewish villages. Freyne points out there were no natural geographical borders between Galilee and the Tyre hinterland. Indeed, Tyre's restatement of its political influence in Upper Galilee had occurred as close to Jesus' time as 42 BCE, when the Tyrian tyrant (!) king invaded and garrisoned three Galilean forts. Being Greek-speaking implies that the woman was upper class, from the same aristocracy that only a generation before had invaded Jesus' homeland. The common people spoke only Aramaic; the elite were more likely to be bilingual. Theissen calls it the meeting of 'two different social worlds'.[43]

Ancient cities, like Tyre, were unlike medieval cities, which had autonomous guild industries, in that they lived off the country-side surrounding them. The landowners of the 'vicinity' perhaps like the woman in Mark would live in the city, not like a medi-eval lord who lived on the land. This dependence on the local produce of the dependent peasantry was even more the case for Tyre, which was on an island; as Ezekiel put it 'surrounded by the sea' (27.32). The coast nearby was also unsuitable for cultivation; a modern-day equivalent would perhaps be Hong Kong. The role of providing wheat and olive oil for Tyre was established 1,000 years before Jesus in King Solomon's time (1 Kings 5.11). As in Elijah's time, a drought in Palestine would mean a potential fam-ine in Tyre and Sidon (1 Kings 17.7–16). After Jesus' time, Tyre and Sidon petitioned Herod Agrippa I for food from Palestine (Acts 12.20). In short, Galilee was the breadbasket, that provided Tyre with its food.

So then at last we have explained why Mark places his Tyre story in the middle of feeding miracles, for bread lay at the heart of the relationship between Galilee and Tyre. We also come closer to seeing the resentment that Jesus expresses to the woman who comes for healing, for Galilee got the short end of this deal. At this point of her need, Jesus is pointing out that the normal power relationship has been reversed. 'She is sharply reminded of the normal situation' between country and town; his 'cynical words reflect a bitterness grounded in real relationships'.

The agrarian Jewish economy was largely a self-sufficient one not geared to the market economy; important to the peasants because it enabled them to keep their relative independence. However, the pressure of military extractions and of tax took its toll. To pay their debts, Galilean wheat would often be sold to Tyre while their own children would go hungry. So Jesus' apparent insult is based on the kingdom's new economics: let the poor people in the Jewish rural areas (the children of Galilee) be fed first; it is not good to take their food and toss it to the rich Gentiles – the dogs – in the cities. While stating the realities of the Galilean political economy and of the women's role in it, Jesus is nevertheless able to see beyond the power structures to the individuals involved. He compliments the woman for her reply and heals her daughter. There are two positive stories about little dogs in the Jewish apocrypha. The first is used to show how hard it is to separate ourselves from things that are close to us; it is used of parents saying farewell to their son. In the second, a royal queen throws her 'unclean' food out of her banquet where it is eaten by stray dogs.[44] In a mixed society like Galilee or Samaria, where Jews and Greeks were intermingled by history, it was impossible for the Jews (the children) to separate themselves from the heathen Gentiles (the dogs), who lived so close; but the little strays like this women were also able to benefit from the banquet which the new king was bringing. This was not just a religious gospel; although the political and economic realities were harsh – even insulting– she as a member of the ruling class would not just be lined up against a wall and shot, but offered the benefits, challenges and healing of the new kingdom.

But there is also a point for today's international economy hidden away in this powerful story. The key link between Tyre and Galilee was economic. Particularly from the Hellenistic period, Galilee's main trading links would have been with Tyre as well as Jerusalem. Ezekiel mentions the main exports from Israel and Judah to Tyre as wheat, honey and (olive) oil (27.17). Horsley adds figs and olives and goes on to point out that Tyre was not only the main trading centre, it was also the main money supplier and financial centre in the Levant. With this economic control – and the dependency of the rural areas so familiar in Central and Latin America today – Tyre was an early recipient of prophetic ire for its idolatry of money and the necessary political alliances that flowed from it, beginning with Amos (1.9–10). The conclusion here is that finance that does not serve ordinary people is to be condemned. Ezekiel 27, rather like Revelation 18 for Rome, lists the ways that Tyre is a huge merchant (v. 2) trading and shipping (vv. 4, 26) centre for goods and peoples. Although dating from 600 years before Christ, this is almost a piece of globalization analysis: wood from Lebanon (v. 5), linen from Egypt (v. 7), soldiers from Persia (v. 10), slaves from Greece (v. 13), sheep from Arabia (v. 21) – all are listed. Finance even in first-century Palestine was important. One of the principal mechanisms for transferring surplus from the countryside, for example, from the 'region' around Tyre would have been through the city, which would have taken the peasantry's payments of rent and debt interest. Because the Tyrian currency was stable, the Jerusalem temple money was kept in this currency so that it would not depreciate in value – hence the money changers in the Temple. This was despite the fact that the coins depicted the Tyrian god Baal Melkart. Financial control over the peasantry was given the added twist of idolatry, so that Matthew could assume that the peasantry would equate Tyre and Sidon with Sodom (Matthew 11.22–24). Despite sharing this judgement, Jesus offered healing to all. The major issue between Galilee and Tyre then rested on military and strategic ownership of the land and thereby the rights to the bread that it produced. From this stemmed the city of Tyre's exploitative role. The consequence – not the cause – was debt and a further consequence was the bitterness that Jesus reflects in his conversation with the Syro-Phoenician woman.

We can now link the critique of the Jubilee, debt and trade campaigners with one of the best known of Amos' oracles against Israel; this prophet was also one of the first to condemn Tyre. Amos is famously remembered for his poetic denunciation: 'They sell the righteous for silver and the needy for a pair of sandals' (Amos 2.6b; 8.6a). Like the trade justice campaigners,

Amos seems to be complaining about unequal exchange, using a metaphor. The poor, getting bad prices for their products, were by this process being 'trampled' underfoot (Amos 5.11). This wonderful phrase could be nothing more than literary licence meaning that the poor were sold into slavery even though the debts were trivial. But as Polley points out, sandals were placed in the hands of new owners to symbolize the transfer of land. The implication is of a potentially corrupt increase in land holdings and thereby of political and social, as well as economic inequality. Losing the land would usually mean losing the right to participate in the peasant assembly.[45] So, what may just appear to be about bad pricing and debt – an exchange issue reflecting the weak bargaining position of the poor – is much more fundamentally about who owns the resource and the political and economic power that flow from it.

What is vitally important in both the political and theological analysis of global capitalism today is that we take a recommendation of Negri and Hardt to heart. For borrowing from Marx, they emphasize that we must 'move from the noisy sphere of exchange and descend into the hidden abode of production'.[46] Tyre, Babylon and Rome are all symbolic biblical expressions, of economic, political, social – and indeed spiritual – power against all of us, the multitude of commoners. Today, this is largely the power that global capital occupies.

Proclaiming justice to the nations

Sandwiched around the stories of the woman from Tyre are the two feeding miracles in chapters 6 and 8 of Mark's Gospel. Myers argues that too much of a religious eucharistic and meaning has been read into these stories. For at heart, they are about the politics and economics of sharing – in this instance, of that most basic human need for food. In chapter 6, the opulence of the new kingdom is implicitly contrasted with John the Baptist, whose death earlier in the chapter reminds us of his message. Myers argues that there is a rejection of what he calls 'market economics'. But there can be little doubt that the most basic needs of the poor peasants of the area could not simply be bought (6.36). Bread is mentioned nine times in Mark, alongside frequent references to eating, loaves, fish, feasts and banquets; for impoverished share-croppers, on this present earth, this could only mean a more just society. This is a hope of justice for all: for the twelve baskets, remaining from the first feeding symbolized Israel (6.43) and the seven baskets from the second, the Gentiles. As Myers concludes: 'It is part of the tragedy of ... theology that the social dimensions of the primitive Christian struggle to reconcile Jew and Gentile have been so thoroughly suppressed despite the fact that it is central to the writings of Paul and his disciples.'

At the end of this analysis of sharing and of justice, it is important to remember the apocalyptic beginnings of Mark. I have always been taught and therefore have seen the calling of Jesus, as represented by his baptism, as a religious vocation and a 'proof' of his messianic identity as the Son of God, but as Myers points out, Mark's allusion here is to Isaiah 42 – and the key proclamation is that this servant of the Lord will bring justice to the nations (1.1b).[47] This justice is not the self-righteousness of the religious few, but a concrete political and economic justice for the apparently faithless many. For many Christians have the spirit to see that a just world is not the objective of the Washington consensus, which, I have argued, is driven ideologically by the aggressive expansionism of the Global Capitalist Empire. To make the breakthrough in our theology will hopefully help such Christians make a breakthrough in their thinking about society. For non-Christians, it can perhaps reveal afresh that the gospel is not just about religion, but is an alternative challenge to empire. For us to proclaim the good news afresh today, we need then to understand better the history and theology of the Gospels. We also need to reapply the economic, social and political message as we seek to understand far better the processes at work in global capitalism. Only then can the good news of a new kingdom of justice for the nations be truly proclaimed.

7

The Temple State:
Crucifixion and Resurrection

Popular culture and the female songs of liberation

The problem for many contemporary readers of Scripture is that many are unaware of Palestine's political and economic history. The Gospels are so often taught as conveying timeless truths taken out of their historical situation. This means that we can miss some of the deeper and broader meanings hidden in the text. With a greater understanding of the history and culture out of which Jesus came, it is possible to look at the Gospels in a different light. To understand this revolutionary protest culture, we shall move outside Mark briefly and look at the birth stories in the other Gospels. Before the 'new look at Mark', the political content of Luke – particularly in his coverage of feminine and social issues – meant that much of the work on the politics of Jesus looked to Luke as its first source. Ironically, Yoder argues that he chose to base his work on Luke because Luke had been accused of writing an apology for the Christians to the Roman authorities; something of which Mark has also been accused.[1] We shall see that this is not the case in Luke, at least in the infancy narratives and in the parables analysed here.

Horsley argues that the fundamental conflict in first-century Jewish society was

> not between Judaism and Hellenism, the Jews and the Romans, or Judaism and Christianity. Rather the fundamental conflict

was between the Roman, Herodian and high priestly *rulers* on the one hand and the Judean and Galilean villagers, whose produce supplied tribute for Caesar, taxes for the Herodian dynasty and tithes … for the priests and temple apparatus.[2]

It was in other words a conflict between 'the rulers and the ruled'. Jesus placed himself, and was rooted in, Israel's 'popular tradition' – a prophetic culture – out of which messianic, other revolutionary movements and banditry had flowed. It is a culture, not surprisingly, that he inherited partly from his mother, but also shared with his cousin, John. In Luke, the opening context of the Gospel resonates with a messianic expectation that must have been deeply embedded in Jewish peasant culture, if not in that of the rulers. The revolutionary expectation is best found in the Magnificat (Luke 1.39–55). Green notes that we often forget that Luke's story resounds with 'the thunder and tenor' of Mary's song, its 'revolutionary beat'. Yet, so often it is 'wrapped in antiseptic'. Mary clearly thinks and sings about the history of her people; 'from generation to generation' (v. 50); 'to Abraham and his posterity for ever (v. 54)'. Here is popular people's culture that nurtured the hope of liberation; so like the Palestine of today. This is a historical tradition that Mary knew; the birth of her son is linked in her mind both to the past and to the promises to Israel for the future. 'With a few words taken out, we would hardly have thought they were about the birth of a child.'[3] After the Annunciation and Mary's visit to Elizabeth finishes in Luke 1.45, the verse that most naturally follows on would appear to be v. 57. Luke appears to have inserted the liberation songs from pre-Lucan popular Palestinian material. They must have been of great importance to be preserved. Seven times the song uses the past tense, which emphasizes that Mary was probably singing from a historical liberation tradition; it is unlikely that she composed it. Given its nationalist and revolutionary overtones the people's popular culture certainly borrowed from the Maccabean Wars of the previous century and the liberation struggles of earlier days. It is noticeable that Mary's Song has strong connections with the songs of past liberations – with the Song of Miriam (Ex. 15) and Deborah (Judg. 5).

A holy war against empire fought by women

Today Gabriel is just a name for an angel. Given what has been, and will be, stressed about the apocalyptic potential of the Gospels, it is worth emphasizing that the name Gabriel means 'God is my warrior'. The 'Mighty One' is a frequent Old Testament image borrowed from the Canaanite view of God as a mighty warrior. In this militant 'holy war' God, the mighty one (Luke 1.49) fought for his people and performed 'mighty deeds with his arm' against their enemies (v. 51a and see Luke 2.71, 74). So, it would have been highly significant to Luke – and probably to Mary – that it was Gabriel who was the messenger who spoke to her. Gabriel makes his first appearance in the Old Testament in the book of Daniel. The key promise that Gabriel gave to Daniel is that the saints would eventually triumph despite the abomination of desolation represented by the overpowering Empire. The sign of deliverance, as in Isaiah's time, was now true for Mary; it was to be a child, which a heavenly army (host) proclaimed (Luke 2.13).[4] As for the Palestinian people today, this would be a very powerful political message for people living under Rome. By no means was it just a 'religious' message. Yet, as we shall see, unlike the fighters of today or the zealots of the first century, Jesus was not about a violent confrontation with empire; but there was a confrontation, and the consequences would pierce Mary's soul, as Simeon prophesied.

Gabriel's Annunciation to Mary has lost its ability to shock us with a revolutionary God who turns the world upside down. Gabriel's commissioning of Mary is modelled on Moses and Gideon who were called to be deliverers of the nation at a time of crisis. Moses like Mary (Luke 1.28) was told that in freeing the slaves God would be with him (Ex. 4.15). Gideon too had been called a mighty warrior (Judges 6.12b), continuing the fight once the people were in Palestine. Both were given signs to show God's presence, despite, like Mary (Luke 1.29, 34), their anxiety and doubt. Moses shows the same fear (Ex. 3.7) and questions (Ex. 3.11, 13); as does Gideon (Judg. 6.13, 15, 22–23). In all cases 'I will be with you' is the key promise (Ex. 3.12, Judg. 6.12, 16, Luke 1.28b). A sign dominates Gideon's story (Judg. 17, 36–40); for Mary it is a baby son (Luke 1.31), but the sign here is also announced to the people, the shepherds, the symbols of the popular culture as opposed to the actual leaders and so-called shepherds of the people (Luke 2.10–12). The Annunciation of Jesus' birth, in typical patriarchal fashion, is given to Joseph in Matthew's Gospel. Luke balances his account by sending Gabriel to Zechariah as well (and not to Elizabeth) (1.5–25), but nevertheless builds up a picture of a wider popular culture. Yet even Matthew has a further balancing factor: the genealogy including four renegade women – Tamar (Matt. 1.3), Rahab (v. 5), Ruth (v. 5) and Bathsheba (v. 6, who was so bad she had to be called Uriah's wife). Looking at the role of women in particular we discover that by placing their lives in the revolutionary history of Israel, they are not at all the pictures of feminine submissiveness we might expect. Deborah, Ruth and Rahab were strong independent women given vital roles in the deliverance of their people; so too with Mary, Jesus' mother. Horsley concludes: 'Women's actions provided the means by which the people were delivered ... Even the Matthew infancy narrative would appear to undermine as well as defend patriarchal structures.' In Luke, Simeon addresses Mary not Joseph and it is Anna, the prophetess who closes the infancy story with Mary as the female 'specially commissioned ... [and] principal agent of deliverance'. So the historical Mary is much closer in spirit to a peasant revolutionary or a Joan of Arc than to some mythical Mary, meek and mild.

The Magnificat as a Maccabean battle hymn

Mary's Magnificat is most likely to have been a Maccabean battle hymn. As Yoder puts it, we see 'the maiden Miriam as a Maccabean'. Mary's song follows in a tradition established by Isaiah and others. It is clearly focused on the importance of economics – the hungry are filled (Luke 1.53); and politics – the rulers are brought down from their thrones (v. 52). In the Magnificat, Mary is clearly shown to be in sympathy with the Old Testament revolutionary tradition. Being described as 'blessed are you among women' (1.42, 48b) links Mary to a now obscure revolutionary woman called Jael, who murdered one of the Canaanite kings, Sisera, in Rahab's time, with a tent peg (Judg. 4.17–22; 5.24–31). Such is the murderous nationalistic background and, with it, the conflict between the rulers and the ruled. Such is a background so many exegetes forget in their understanding of Mary, Jesus and the Gospels.

First Isaiah had also described his contemporary rulers of Israel as 'proud and lofty' (2.12); denouncing the 'arrogance of the haughty, the pride of the ruthless' (13.11). This links power and class to spirituality. In the true Israel, on the other hand, the world is turned upside down as God lifts up the humble (Luke 1.52b). The stress on the 'humble' and 'lowly' is as much about class and economics – 'low estate' (v. 48) or low 'degree' (v. 52b RSV) – as about spirituality. This is also brought out by a comparison between the Magnificat and the story of Hannah, the mother of Samuel, who had perhaps been Israel's greatest prophet and had anointed Israel's greatest king. Mary's song starts just like Hannah's with praise – like a psalm – so v. 47 reflects 1 Samuel 2.1 ('My heart rejoices'). Hannah means 'grace' or 'favoured one' so there is also a clear link with Mary, who is told twice by the angel that she is highly favoured by God (1.28,30). Jesus is also presented in the Temple (2.22–4) just like Samuel (1 Sam. 1.24–7). In 1 Samuel 2, the humble are directly linked to the hungry, the poor and the needy (vv. 5–8a) and as Hannah puts it: God 'seats them [the poor] with princes and has them inherit a throne of honour' (1 Sam. 2.8b). After the failures of the restoration of Israel after the exile, the theological view of the later disciples of Isaiah developed further. Only a remnant, sometimes known as the servants, would inherit the kingdom, the resurrected Israel. Linked to the 'pious ones' (who were often fighting militants), they were also known as the 'poor or lowly ones' (the Anawim) and they often took books like Daniel for their theology.

Mary's Song clearly comes from this old tradition. Yet, it is more explicitly political than anything in the book of Samuel. This is not too surprising: in Hannah's time, Israel was genuinely independent. Here, as in 1 Samuel 2.1–3a, the 'Proud' (Luke 1.51b) is a term of abuse for arrogant rulers; the opposite of the pious poor. Horsley argues that the Magnificat seems to endorse a different kind of politics: 'the overthrow of existing governmental authority'. The future Mary hoped for was 'no less specific and concrete than the previous great historical acts of deliverance … from bondage in Egypt … (and) from the Canaanite Kings'.[5] Mary has been made into the pious believer, pushing her concrete hopes to an undefined spiritual future. But the role of the Church today is to show in its common life – male and female – that the kingdom of God is near in concrete as well as spiritual realities; part of this is to fill 'the hungry with good things', but to send 'the rich empty away' (v. 53).

Zechariah, John the Baptist and popular politics

The prophetic culture sits alongside the protest. It can be seen in Zechariah's Song (Luke 1.69–77), in Simeon's statement to Mary (2.25–35) and in the prophetess, Anna (2.36–38). In the gospel stories, John the Baptist, the son of Zechariah, clearly represents the strongest links with this popular prophetic culture. For 200 years, a plethora of radical new sects on the fringe of Judaism had grown up with revolutionary expectations for the overthrow of the existing Jewish order, with the Maccabean revolt as its symbol. We know a little about these sects from the Dead Sea Scrolls and the community at Qumran. John and his disciples appear to share this revolutionary expectation. In coming to John for baptism, as is stressed in all four Gospels, Jesus has sanctioned and aligned himself with John's dangerous and political prophetic ministry and the call to return to the old covenant. The initial similarity of John's and Jesus' messages is particularly noticeable in Matthew's Gospel. John says 'Repent for the Kingdom of heaven is near' (3.1). The same opening comes from Jesus (4.17). Similarly, Mark makes it clear that Jesus' ministry consciously inherits John's political mantle for he starts preaching as John goes into prison (1.14).

Horsley argues that Zechariah's Song – traditionally known as the Benedictus – is not Christological. The tone of the Benedictus is more of relief than of triumph. Our principal difficulty thereby is to 'strip away the [later] Christological concepts … that are simply not in the biblical text … to cut through the peculiar modern assumption that biblical literature and its message are somehow primarily "religious" and not politico-economic as well'. It has suited the Church over the centuries to look at salvation as individual and spiritual and to have 'neglected the collective and concrete socio-political'.[6]

Likewise, if we now go back to Mark's Gospel, John preached a baptism of repentance for the forgiveness of sins (1.4). Jesus' first preaching also stresses repentance and the new kingdom being on hand (1.15). If we don't understand the popular fervour to re-create and restore the old concept of Israel, we do not fully grasp the significance of this announcement of the new kingdom. The comparison of both John and Jesus to Elijah also resounds in the synoptic narratives. If Myers reminds us that Mark's allusions to the prophet Malachi occur at crucial points in his Gospel, it can hardly be a surprise that it is Malachi's forecast of the return of Elijah (Mal. 4.5) that is linked both to the covenant laws of Moses (4.4) and to the coming justice against evil rulers (4.1–3, 7). Jesus picks up this prophetic understanding of the exodus and covenant hope for Israel in his preaching of the new kingdom. The old covenant was to be replaced by a new covenant initiated by Jesus himself.

Yoder argues that Luke's borrowing of Zechariah's hopes and of John the Baptist's themes are all the 'more politically conscious' if they were circulating in popular post-Maccabean circles. It is certainly not the case that John the Baptist had a 'political' message while Jesus only had a 'spiritual' one. If so, Luke would have found some way to hint that Mary and Zechariah and John's hopes were unrealistic. Even more, why would Jesus use John the Baptist's political terms – kingdom and gospel – if Jesus were not interested in politics?[7] In Jesus' life, like those of the prophets, 'politics and religion' were always mixed. Despite the fact that, as still in the Middle East, 'every religious breath has politics over it', these political tones have often been hugely overlooked by conventional exegesis.

The rule of the fox and the birds of the air

Jesus was constantly faced with a major political issue throughout his ministry: his attitude to the Jewish Establishment and their Roman masters. Jesus' ministry in Galilee would have been carried out under Herod's son, the Tetrarch Herod Antipas. His new puppet state was surrounded by hostile forces on all sides. Antipas, like his father, needed to be cunning to survive. Perowne suggests that he had stayed in Rome before the division of the kingdom, presuming that his father had not included him in the will and therefore conspiring against his brothers. Bailey, in his fascinating study looking at the parables of Luke 'through peasant eyes', suggests that the difficulties and dangers of oppression meant that Jesus had to speak in symbols or in parables, much clearer then than they are today. Many of Jesus' parables and statements had political connotations, which most ordinary New Testament readers could not be aware of today. Even so, they bit home then; as Dodd in his *Parables of the Kingdom* argues, no one would have crucified a Galilean itinerant preacher who told picturesque stories to enforce moral platitudes.

Jesus openly describes Antipas as 'that fox' even when the Pharisees warn him of the dangers (Luke 13.31–2). Take the wonderful verse, 'Foxes have holes and the birds of the air have their nests, but the Son of Man has nowhere to lay his head' (Luke 9.58). This appears to be a graphical way of putting the costs for an itinerant like Jesus and for his followers in discipleship. In the intertestamental period, however, the fox was a symbol for the Edomites, the people from whom Herod's mother came; the birds of the air were an apocalyptical sign for the Gentile nations, here probably the Romans. Bailey summarizes the politics and ethics of Jesus' statement: 'Everybody is at home in Israel except the true Israel.' The birds of the air – the Roman overlords – are good at feathering their nests; the foxes – the Herodian kingly interlopers – have made their position secure and like foxes have stalked their prey with cunning. 'They disinherit the true Israel: and if you cast your lot with me and mine, you join the ranks of the dispossessed and you must be prepared to serve God under these conditions.'[8]

Jesus' ministry from the start was among the common people whose lives were threatened by hostile forces. The common people's economy in Galilee would have been largely rural and poor. Like his father, Antipas started to levy heavy taxes for his rebuilding projects; just as Saddam spent on his palaces as the people starved. If Joseph originally came from Bethlehem, Horsley suggests that he was probably working as a migrant labourer on the rebuilding of Sepphoris, an old Hellenistic fortress city with a population of perhaps 10,000 to 15,000, destroyed in an uprising on Herod the Great's death. Nazareth is about three to four miles away. It must have been possible to see the fort for miles around as it towered 400 feet above the plain. There would hardly have been enough work for a carpenter in a small peasant village like Nazareth, with a population of perhaps 500. Refugees are common when debt and death are a normal form of imperial and semi-colonial policy. Joseph and Mary were not just homeless for the census at the time of Jesus' birth, but forced to be part of a migrant people, disrupted by the civil wars and unrest of the Herodian period. A call for a new revolutionary Jubilee (Luke 4.16–30) might be more of a threat than a relief for the people of Nazareth whose economy depended on Sepphoris and who knew locally of the vengeance of both Rome and its client kings.[9]

Archelaus and Pilate in Judaea: imperial governance

When Jesus' mission took him into Judaea, he knew he was likely to be killed. Indeed, it is worth stressing that if we only had the Synoptic Gospels to work from, Jesus only seems to go to Jerusalem once: as soon as he does, he is dead within the week. Ironically, if he had not stepped foot in Judaea he would not have come under imperial jurisdiction. In Judaea, it was another of Herod's sons, Archelaus, who first became ruler, aged only 18. He had the added disadvantage in Judaea of a Samaritan mother. Even the local aristocracy were involved in the protest against Archelaus, sending a delegation to Rome to request a Roman governor. In Jerusalem, when the common people came into town for Passover, their protests exploded with appeals for lower taxes, for prisoners to be released and for the replacement of the corrupt high priest. Archelaus' own troops killed 3,000, with many scattering to the hills. This was followed by a general uprising at Pentecost, in which Herod's old troops in some cases joined with the rebels. The uprising was eventually put down by the Syrian governor, with 2,000 later crucified. No wonder then that Matthew's Gospel reveals Joseph's shrewdness; he was afraid to go to Judaea with Archelaus in charge (2.22). Like Antipas, Archelaus also divorced and remarried another half-brother's wife. Both Jews and Samaritans denounced him to Caesar and he was removed in 6 CE to be replaced by governors direct from Rome. Truly, as Jesus remarked to the scribes from Jerusalem, this was a house – and a kingdom – divided against itself (Mark 3.25–6).

In 26 CE, Pontius Pilate was appointed governor of Judaea. The precedents for imperial governance of occupied countries are not good. After Pompey's conquest, the Romans became heirs to the imperialism of the Hellenistic civilizations of the Eastern Mediterranean. The New Testament is not about 'honouring such Caesars'. The biblical history is full of the stories of people suffering from the distorted promises of empire and its collaborationist local client kings. Contrary to the story of the Jewish Wars as they are often presented – as 'religious' risings – the Romans, according to Horsley, took some care to avoid unnecessarily offending Jewish religious scruples. Pilate certainly had an ambiguous record. Twice he gave in to popular protests against the presence in the Temple of standards used to honour Caesar. However, when it came to money, Pilate had fewer scruples. Besides its 'religious' role, the Temple was also the central bank and its treasury was frequently raided by the imperial and colonial rulers. Pilate's excuse was that he wanted the money to construct an aqueduct for Jerusalem. This time many were clubbed to death in the protests. There were also political power games at work. It was not only the Pharisees who wrote to Tiberias to complain, but four other sons of Herod, including Antipas and Philip.[10] So, Pilate's coming trial of Jesus in the Gospels has its historical antecedents. In both cases, the Herodians and the Pharisees could come together. The Jewish religious establishment had been more than willing to collude with the powers of the established authorities for generations. For his part, Pilate would not want another letter of protest to be dispatched to Caesar, and John's Gospel makes this threat explicit (19.12,

15). Knowing all this background, Jesus stayed true to his mission and message and set his face towards the centre of historic Israel; despite his own family thinking from early on that he was 'out of his mind' to risk himself (3.22).

Entering the den of thieves

When Jesus arrived in Jerusalem in the Synoptic Gospels, it was as if Robin Hood had walked into Nottingham Castle, denounced the sheriff, and celebrated the removal of Prince John by a more legitimate popular king: the Messiah. All the following stories in chapters 11 and 12 build up the rising political crescendo to this crisis, starting and ending with attacks on the Temple. The challenge to the compromises of colonial rule and imperial governance is well and truly laid down by the style of Jesus' 'triumphal' entry into Jerusalem (in chapter 11.1–10) and then his clearing of the temple precincts (11.5–17). Myers calls the entry a piece of 'messianic street theatre'. Simon Maccabaeus had entered Jerusalem in the same manner, with palm branches waving, during the victorious war against the Seleucid Empire in 166 BCE; the leaders of the revolt in 66 CE, which would have probably occurred before Mark was writing, did the same. The 'parade' starts on the Mount of Olives (v. 1), just as in Zechariah's vision of the final battle for Jerusalem. Belo even goes so far as to claim that the literal translation to Hosanna 'in the highest places' (11.10c) is a reference to 'save us' from the Romans; for did they not rule from on high?[11]

In Mark, Jesus' first act is to head for the Temple (v. 11). Horsley notes that the Temple was being magnificently rebuilt at this time to double its previous size; the work was only just completed before its destruction in 70. There was not only a 'religious' Temple rebuilding, the king's palace in Jerusalem and fortresses around the country were also being strengthened. To curry favour with Rome, the new temples and cities were dedicated to Caesar, as in Tiberias, for example. As Wright emphasizes, rebuilding the Temple was central to Herod's dynastic claims and ambition. To rebuild the Temple, as Herod and his son had been doing in an attempt to win a greater 'religious' legitimacy for their regime, the Jewish peasantry's tax burden had increased enormously. There were now three layers of tax on the peasantry: to Rome, to Herod's dynasty and to the Temple. Indebtedness, as reflected in the parables, fed off the increase in taxes, which even before loan repayments and interest took 40 per cent of the peasants' production. Tax take under the Romans had doubled. When Jesus entered Jerusalem, his statement 'you have made it a den of robbers' (11.17b) was politically loaded. As a recent BBC documentary brought out, and as is often preached, the money changers were fiddling the change, while also blocking the Gentiles' entrances for prayer. The extortion worked in the high priest's favour. But Jesus' allusion was double loaded politically. In the revolt of 166 BCE, the high priest's brother had been killed for extorting so much in temple tax; he was known as the 'temple robber'.[12] Jesus was deliberately identifying himself with the rationale, if not all the actions, of the past revolt. Jesus' statement was not just about the Temple, but also about Israel, and the history of Israel's betrayal of the covenant, particularly by its leaders. The covenant with God and his 'tabernacle' with his people, which the high priest in the Temple was supposed to represent, were now to be opened instead to all the nations.

Horsley calls 'driving' the money changers out of the temple a 'blatant revolutionary act'.[13] Certainly, Mark makes the temple clearing the final cause of the decision by the ruling class ('chief priests and teachers of the law' (v. 18) to kill Jesus. The Pharisees and Herodians, who had come up to Galilee, had already reached this conclusion (3.6) in light of Jesus' popularity there (2.22, 27–8, 45). Jesus was to be rejected as early in his ministry in Jerusalem by the ruling class there as he had been by the ruling class in Galilee.

Render unto Caesar

In Mark 12 each of the shepherds of the Jewish state is attacked in Jerusalem itself. Likewise, the authority of both the collaborationist Sadducees (12.18–27) and the Roman Empire (vv. 13–17) is called into question. For Jesus, judgement on the failed leadership of Israel is already on its way, as symbolized by the withered fig tree (11.20–1) and the parable of the vineyard (12.1–12). The Jewish ruling class were often absentee landlords, but regarded themselves as the owners – not tenants of Israel and of Yahweh. In what Myers calls the most revolutionary language of the Gospel, the true owner 'will come and kill these tenants and give the vineyard to others' (12.9).[14] The present ruling-class tenants, sufficiently threatened by this parable told against them (v. 12), try to trick Jesus with a loaded political question about paying taxes to Caesar. This is despite the fact that in normal Establishment politics they would have been opponents. Luke says they sent spies twice so they could get him arrested (20.20–1). If Jesus says, 'don't pay', the Herodians have got him for being a nationalist sympathizer – maybe a zealot; if he says 'yes', the Pharisees have got him to disown his popular connections. Jesus' answer was as clever as any politician's. By asking to see a coin, Jesus was making a political connection most of us today would be unaware of. At the time of the Maccabean revolt, Palestine was ruled by the Seleucid kings of Syria; in particular, the 'little horn' of the book of Daniel, Antiochus IV (175–163 BCE). Antiochus was known as 'Epiphanes' because like Alexander the Great he claimed to be God 'manifest' in a human. This was declared by coins that bore his image. The test of political loyalty was the age-old submission to the absolute authority of the god king. From Augustus on, the Roman Caesar demanded the same. Here again is the ancient equation of the divine with the ruling order. It was also Antiochus who had started the tradition of auctioning the high priest's office off to the highest bidder: the effective subordinate ruler of Palestine under the Seleucids was a bought man. Everyone who heard Jesus' words would know the disgust with which the Jewish people had regarded Antiochus' reign. By linking Caesar to Antiochus and the tradition of rebellion, Jesus was making his opposition to emperor or king worship quite clear without actually stating it. So, he had stumped the Pharisees. There is a scarcely veiled sarcasm in Jesus' reply 'render to Caesar'. For a Jew reared on the commandments, to worship an image was idolatry.

Wengst's work has a perceptive analysis of this dialogue. Normally, Jesus' answer is seen as 'essentially affirmative': honour Caesar in his realm by paying his tax, but honour God in your life. For Wengst, this misinterpreted comment from Jesus has usually been the basis either for an 'honouring Caesar' style of theology, used even in passing by New Labour Christian socialists, for example, or by Luther's older 'two kingdoms' approach – the political and the spiritual – which I have consistently criticized here. Wengst begins his analysis of the story with a simple but unusual linked pair of points. As Judaea was by this time ruled by a Roman governor, only this Israelite province paid the Roman imperial tax. Jesus – a Galilean – would not need to have paid it. It can be seen more clearly how false the trap posed by the 'spies' was, in the sense that neither Jesus himself, nor his Galilean disciples, would have faced this problem. He was only involved as an ethical adviser. There was no mileage for him to say anything other than the affirmative. Saying 'don't pay' would be dangerous; saying 'yes' would involve no danger.

You have taken the Empire's money

The story does not necessarily imply that Jesus did not have a coin – but by not taking one out of his pocket, Jesus shows that it was not his problem, Wengst suggests. The further – and major – implication often overlooked in conventional exegesis is that if Jesus did not have Caesar's money, he owed nothing back to Caesar. On the other hand, unlike the common people, many of the Pharisees and the Herodians, as the ruling elite, would have taken Caesar's money. Wengst paraphrases a cruder answer from Jesus and puts it in today's terms, 'You have taken the Empire's money, you deal in it.' For the Herodians in particular had long since given way to the reality appointed and controlled by Rome, and this Jesus was saying is shown by the coins in their pockets. So, Jesus was saying: if you have given way at this level, in money, the economic and political consequences follow. The answer that is so often presented as the solution – give to God what is due to God – is a serious indication of the problem that Jesus posed for the Pharisees and Herodians. They attempt to throw him a trick question and he throws it back to them as a serious problem. Since there is actually no separation of spheres in Jesus or in the ancient way of thinking, he challenged those who had made their peace with the existing system. By selling out to Empire the questioners may have sold out on God, rather than 'honouring' him. Be careful, Jesus is saying, that 'rendering to Caesar' does not mean such a compromise with imperial power that economic and political decisions not only leave one compromised, but also reveal nothing more than lip-service to God.[15] Our 'Christian Socialist' leaders taking us to war in Iraq in 2003–04 have been learning some of the consequences of this compromise ever since. Should we take their references to God as nothing more than lip-service? (cf. Mark 7.6)

The widow's story

The political and economic context for the widow's story is the gulf between the rich and the poor. While the Jewish rulers 'devour widows' houses' (12.40), the Temple treasury has become a den for the rich (11.17; 12.41). It was not that the money changing would have been at all surprising or abnormal, although

Myers suggests that some of the lawyers who were supposed to hold estates in trust from the deceased for their widows may have been embezzling the funds. The people not only paid for their own subjugation via taxes – to keep 'law and order' – but also for the very forces that were threatening their continuity as a people. It is the poor widows of Israel (12.42–44) whose wealth and well-being now depended on Jesus' new order.[16] There is more than a little irony in Jesus' statement about the widow; truly she and her kind had given 'more ... than all the others' (v. 43) and 'all she had to live on' (v. 44), just like the sick woman in the crowd (5.26). The widow, specially provided for by the gleanings in rural Israel, was the symbol of the ordinary people being devoured by the temple robbers. But the Temple state was defrauding the labourers of their wages, depriving the people of justice and oppressing the widows; no wonder Mark was reminded of the prophet Malachi, for here was a prophet who also looked to see the Lord suddenly come to his temple in judgement (Mal. 3.2–5).[17]

Every stone will be thrown down: Jesus and the Temple

The importance of the widow's story is the political and economic introduction it provides to Mark 13, sometimes known as 'Mark's Apocalypse'. Geddert argues that 'Mark's Temple theology' is of great significance in Mark and essential to the message of the Gospel. All the Synoptic Gospels contain versions of what is sometimes called Jesus' 'Olivet' or 'eschatological' discourse. It is the 'longest consecutive speech in the whole gospel'. For Dodd, it is a speech of 'warning' in the tradition of leaders like Moses in their farewell discourse. Nineham argues that since Mark 14—15 existed in some form before Mark, Mark 13 is the 'climax' of the Gospel that Mark himself was composing. Nineham concludes that 'the destruction of the temple is an integral part of the final drama'.[18] Mark 13's apocalypse begins then with

Jesus' prophecy that the Temple would be destroyed (v. 2). It is placed after a rather naive statement from one of the disciples about the Temple's magnificence (v. 1). Beasley Murray argues that nowhere else in Mark do we have one unnamed disciple addressing Jesus in this way; it is as if Mark wishes to distance Jesus from this disciple's lack of understanding. Myers notes the similarity between the unknown disciple's language and the story of the fig tree, a traditional symbol of the good life for Israel – there is the same 'look, master' from Peter (11.21); the awed status given to powerful social institutions is part of the ideological veil that blinds.

In Mark and Matthew, Jesus' sermon is set on the Mount of Olives (v. 3), opposite the Temple. The mount setting implies that this discourse is symbolically put on a par with Matthew's Sermon on the Mount and on other mountaintop experiences, like the Transfiguration (9.1–13). The position across from the Temple also implies that opposition is now going to mount against the Temple Establishment. As Beasley Murray stresses, Jesus' condemnation of the Temple is far more than a prediction: it is a judgement.[19] For both Luke and Matthew the condemnation of the Temple extends to the whole city. Jeremias calculates that in early Hellenistic times, 1,500 priests lived in Jerusalem out of 8,000 in the whole of Israel. The number of priests by Jesus' time in Israel had increased to 18,000 so, with the same ratio, over 3,000 priests would be based in the city. More of the priests in Jerusalem would be from the high priestly families; to keep them under his thumb, Herod had also brought in priests from Babylon and Egypt. Horsley argues that as the city of Jerusalem was dominated by its priests, therefore they had a continuing economic vested interest in the continuing use of the Temple.[20]

The key to understanding the threat posed to the established order by Jesus' temple stories is to realize that the Temple was far more the religious centre of Israel. After the return from exile, it lay at the heart of the Jewish Establishment and of its power.

Because the high priest was responsible for collecting taxes, the treasury of the Temple was our equivalent of the Bank of England; because he had been head of state (although he was now subject to the Romans), it was also akin to our Houses of Parliament. It also contained the Holy of Holies where God dwelt with Israel. This combination of Westminster, the Bank of England, the Stock Exchange and St Paul's – being magnificently rebuilt – is what Jesus is saying would not have one stone left on another. The equivalent in England would be to devastate the central and historic power symbols of the city. It is symbolically akin to what 9/11 attempted to do violently by attacking the US centres of power.

How long should we put up with this spiritualizing?

Keener, in his relatively recent commentary on Matthew, in a line also adopted in a recent BBC documentary on Jesus, sees the judgement on the Temple as an attack on 'the religious establishment', but the tone of all the Gospels makes it far more than this. So many commentaries also miss the political extent and the history of Jesus' point: he had already condemned the Temple state for its robbery of the people; now he was condemning it so far as to see its destruction. It is not Jewish 'religion' that is condemned, but the entire Jewish religious Establishment that is, in turn, completely intertwined with the existing political and economic order. Myers complains thereby that too many scholars have been 'oblivious to Mark's critique of the political economy of the Temple'. In Mark's Gospel, Jesus never enters the temple precincts again after his condemnation of its iniquity. It is as if a signal has been given that God has departed from his dwelling in Zion and so leaves it to its fate. Yet, Geddert stresses that it is a judgement on the Jewish leaders rather than the Jewish nation.[21] The Temple and the compromised Jewish Establishment in particular, are abandoned to their political enemies.

The Temple State: Crucifixion and Resurrection

As Jesus reinterprets Daniel's themes of the temple robber and of the Son of Man, the disciples' question in v. 4 also echoes Daniel. If under the Seleucids, the Jewish rebels asked 'how long' will we have to endure (Dan. 12.6), Jesus is asked the same by the disciples. Jesus' answer is bleak and comes later to refer to a similar 'abomination of desolation' as Daniel (v. 14). The theme of 'how long' is reiterated in the passage in Revelation (6.10–11). So, there is a constant repetition here of the saints' struggle against the abominations of empire. This takes place in our real history, in today's eschatological time, not in some dimly seen end of the world. If pushed out into the spiritual future, the real political critique and struggle against empire is pushed into some millennial otherworldliness, or into an inward spiritual struggle, shorn of its political content. It is not the Gospel text that does this, but the 'spiritual exegesis' of later generations often serving a conscious or unconscious subservient political purpose. Theissen steers round this issue without confronting it. But his analysis reveals enough for us to be wary of pushing the real political issues out of our analysis. Barclay shows the sleight of hand of this approach: Mark 13.3–8 and 24–7 are made to refer to the 'Second Coming' (with a sermon on heresy for v. 5 thrown in), while verses 14–20 and verse 30 are turned into actual history (correctly).[22]

There are two questions in verse 4: 'when will this happen?' and 'what will be the sign?' It is Matthew who provides the language that later editors have used to summarize the theme of 'Signs of the End of the Age' (v. 3b) sometimes used as the heading for this chapter. Today this is often made into end-of-the-world signs and of Jesus' 'Second Coming', but it is not at all clear from the text that this passage needs to be interpreted in this way. Mark 13.5–23 and 28–30, for example, can perfectly well be explained by events within the disciples' own lives. Indeed, this more historical (yet still eschatological) explanation fits much better with what becomes the very difficult verse 30 – 'this generation will not pass away until all these things have happened'. The kind of strained exegesis that Barclay represents serves to distort the political message of Mark. Instead, if Mark 13's apocalyptic message is located in concrete and actual historical experience then it will help us further understand our experience of today's Global Capitalist Empire – of wars, of persecutions, of famines.

The real history 34–41: wars, persecutions and Caligula

Theissen then provides some analysis of the real political and military issues, which Mark would have been aware of when he was writing chapter 13. He argues that the historical allusions from Mark 13 show that the apocalyptic themes were embedded in Mark's 'origins' as early as between 34 and 41. The war between Antipas and the Nabataeans over the divorced wife in 36–7 could then be the war of verse 7 and of nation rising against nation in verse 8. The way in which war also precedes the rumour of war (v. 7) in a strange reversal of normal logic – you would expect the rumours to start before the war breaks out – is also explained by the actual history. For with Antipas' defeat, there were rumours of Roman intervention in support of their client king. This period also fits with verse 8. Although earthquakes were quite common throughout the region, and more occurred in the 60s, there were also earthquakes in both Antioch and Syria in 37.

The persecution related in verse 9 onwards was clearly a regular feature of early Christian life. However, it is worth emphasizing that in the 30s the persecution of Christians often occurred in the context of Judaism's growing conflict with Empire. In 39, after conflicts between Greeks and Jews in Alexandria, a new imperial altar was erected in Jamnia, a mixed area of Jews and Greeks. This was on traditional Jewish land not in the usual Hellenistic settlements. This brought back memories of the Maccabean Wars, which were so central to Daniel, and the Jamnia altar was thrown down. The Maccabean revolt had started the same way with the altar at Modein only 35 kilometres away. The Emperor Caligula's retaliation was similar to that of Antiochus IV: the abomination of desolation for Mark (v. 14) could then have been Caligula's setting up of an imperial altar in the Temple. The year 40–1 was perhaps a Sabbath year so the answering threat was a Jewish resistance to sowing the land, which would have meant no payment of taxes. The governor of Syria was preparing to move on Judaea to crush any further revolt with two legions; though even in 66, when an actual Roman invasion began, only one legion was sent. A real threat now underlay the rumours of war. The crisis only abated when Caligula was murdered in 41. Thus Theissen concludes the events of 34–41 are thereby clearly visible in Mark 13.[23]

The importance of Mark's inclusion of this real history into Jesus' temple speech stems then from the Palestinian people's and church's experience of war and persecution after Jesus' death even given the hope provided by the resurrection. The judgement that Mark relates in the real history of Israel stems from political and economic oppression, as much as from the 'spiritual' nature of Israel's failings. For Mark, this sermon at the Temple is Jesus' Sermon on the Mount against the Temple state; it is on the politics and economics of faith in the midst of a hostile religiously sanctioned state. Myers makes the theme of his second book the idea that faith can move the mountains into the sea. His opening quote from Isaiah 25 stresses that it will be 'on this holy mountain' that the veil will be destroyed (v. 7). In Mark, the two structural powers of demonic oppression are being vanquished. In Galilee, the Roman legions, symbol of Empire, are thrown like a herd of pigs into the sea. Now in Jerusalem Jesus threatens the Jewish client state with the faith that can throw such mountains into the sea. The Temple Mount itself is to be discarded and destroyed by God himself.[24] The theological challenge against empire – and against its client rulers – is clearly laid out for us; not something seen in the Bible by the missionaries who took it around with the British Empire, or George Bush II's modern ideological equivalent.

The show trial

Yet to see Mark's story as proclaiming good news, we also need to understand the political meanings of Jesus' trial and death, and of his resurrection. Myers calls it a 'kangaroo court' and Herzog a 'show trial', and a piece of political theatre. The Jewish and Roman trials in Mark parallel each other and show that both authorities bear equal responsibility for Jesus' death – how could it be otherwise with an empire and its client state? Herzog argues that there is nothing specifically anti-Jewish in Mark's story. When Jesus appeared to announce that the revolution was at hand, the reaction of the Jewish elite was – and is – typical of such elites; nor does anyone hold twenty-first century Italians responsible for what the Romans did. Instead, Mark's portrayal reveals the 'casual brutality' of empire – as seen so recently in Iraq – and the extent of the terror used by the state to protect its power.[25] For those radical optimists who struggle for a more just and participative world, the Cross must still be at the heart of our politics. The lesson of Jesus' trial and crucifixion is not about some religious fate demanded in propitiation by God; it is about the political inevitability of the empire's reaction. At the heart of empire, there is always killing dressed up as peace.

When challenged, empires kill, often publicly and brutally, sometimes secretly and in a hurry, as Jesus' sentence was rushed through before the usual unrest of Passover week. The fear of the Jewish elite at the beginning of Mark 14 is that 'the people may riot' (v. 2b). Mark quickly moves to the other side of the story; here is a picture of something close to a revolutionary conspiracy, with Jesus and his disciples making contact through codes (he will be carrying a jar of water – v. 13) and staying under cover in the city in a safe house. The new leader is duly anointed and holds a simple banquet (vv. 3–9, 12–16) The constant fear of betrayal, of broken relationships and the tiredness induced by stress dominate the disciples' story until Jesus' arrest (vv. 17–42). The trial of Jesus was not a legal trial. Taking place after the kind of night arrest so beloved of Stalin and the Nazis, the night trial had no status in rabbinic law. Convicted of blasphemy, the Jewish elite could not sentence Jesus under Jewish law; besides they needed the approval of their masters at such a dangerous time. So as John the Baptist, the Galilean martyr, had been bound (6.17) and executed by a client king; now Jesus was to be 'handed over' by the Judaean ruling class, bound and sent to Pilate (15.1), the local representative of Empire, despite the fact that it was not normal to bind someone only accused of an offence. Those who were to free the weak from the oppression of the strong were to undergo the same binding experience themselves.[26]

Contrary to those theologians who have seen Mark as an apologia for the Roman Church, playing down Jesus' anti-Roman sentiments, Mark's portrayal of both Pilate and the battalion of Roman soldiers mocking Jesus hardly makes a good apology. Mark's interpretation shows Pilate as deeply cynical – he mocks Jesus, the Judaean elite and the crowd at the same time – giving the crowd the appearance of a choice (vv. 2–15), while having no intention of giving his power over events to them. The crowd is easily manipulated in this theatre. The release of Barabbas is the only time Mark explicitly uses the words of a potential revolutionary uprising (v. 7). The wearing of imperial purple, the crown (of thorns), the prostration are all taken from the rituals of the religious imperial cult that deified the emperor and mock at the same time Jesus' anti-imperial stance (vv. 16–20). As with John in Galilee, Pilate 'hands' Jesus over (v. 15) to the powers.[27]

Bandits in the garden and terrorists on the cross

Crucifying bandits had long been traditional under Roman rule. Banditry, before and after Herod's brutal rule, was endemic and Galilee remained a breeding ground for 'robbers'. Just before Jesus was born, Hezekiah's son, Judas, was at the centre of another rising. When the Romans recaptured Sepphoris from Judas it had been burnt down again. Banditry, as Hobsbawm pointed out, is often a form of pre-political rebellion. Horsley notes that *lestes*, often translated as robber in the Gospels, actually means bandit; the word for robber is *kleptes*. The difficulty for non-sociologically minded translators communicates well the difficult continuum between social banditry and political rebellion. In the NIV, in all three Synoptic Gospels, as he is arrested, Jesus asks 'Am I leading a rebellion that you have come with swords and clubs to capture me?' (Matt 26.55; Luke 22.52, Mark 14.48). In the RSV, it is translated 'Am I a robber?' (*lestes*) in all three verses. In the *Good News Bible*, we have 'outlaw', which takes us back to Robin Hood and our own traditions of social banditry! It was not by accident that Jesus was crucified not alongside two thieves as normally translated, but alongside two bandits; the 'lawless ones' (Mark 15.28). After the debate about positions of honour among the disciples, two bandits actually take the positions of honour to the right and left of Jesus (15.27–8). Nor was it by coincidence that a social bandit would be aware enough of Jesus' message to ask to be remembered when the new kingdom finally came (Luke 23.42).

Where banditry took an explicitly political – and sometimes violent – form, the New Testament sometimes calls the radicals 'zealots'.[28] Naturally, both Josephus and the Romans liked to play down the politics; they were simply cleansing the land of 'thieves'. Rowland, writing in 1988, 13 years before 9/11, suggests guerrillas or terrorists would be a more apt modern translation for *lestes*. Sadly, we have rather gone along with the Roman definition of the issue, as it has rather suited non-political exegesis. In Iraq or Palestine today, Jesus and his disciples would have a fair chance of being labelled terrorists – as, earlier in the century, bolsheviks or communists. The Judaean abuse label of the time, as brought out in John's Gospel, was to accuse Jesus of being a Samaritan (8.48).[29] With our proliferation of so-called anti-terrorist legislation, one wonders whether British Muslims today receive the same abuse as the Samaritans – for after all, didn't the Samaritans and the Jews also have a common father in Abraham?

Four more zealots?

It gets even more complicated. There is some evidence that Jesus was close to the revolutionary movement and that at least four more disciples had zealot connections. Do you remember James and John, the sons of Zebedee? They wanted to bring fire down from heaven on a Samaritan town that rejected Jesus (Luke 9.54); they had disputed with their mother about who should be Jesus' right-hand man. (Mark 10.37); they were even known as the sons of thunder. If they had zealot connections, this makes even more sense. From Matthew's Gospel, written later than Mark, and after the appearance of the Zealot party in the uprising of the late 60s, we have one known disciple, listed as a zealot. Then we have Peter, once known as Simon bar Jonah. No one knows what bar Jonah means; sometimes it is translated as son of John. But Cullman points out that in ancient Hebrew, in a word borrowed from an even more ancient language – Accadian – *barjonah* means terrorist. In Mark, it was Peter that Jesus rebuked as Satan, for having a different perception of what Jesus being the Messiah meant (8.32–3). In John, it is said twice that it was Peter who wielded the sword, even as late as Jesus' arrest, and was again rebuked (John 18.10–11, 26). Is this why – full of disillusion – he then denied Jesus?

Last of all, we have Judas. Now people in those days did not have our surnames. Iscariot is not like Judas Wilde. What does Iscariot mean? Some think it means *ish Kerioth*, the man from Kerioth. It is more likely that Iscariot is a Semitic translation of a Latin word. This word is *sicarii*, the word the Romans used for Zealots. Literally, it means cutthroat, assassin or bandit. Now we even have a clear reason for Judas' betrayal. This could have been an attempt to force Jesus' hand that went badly wrong. Even at that last minute, the subject of his anguished prayers a moment before, Jesus could have chosen the zealot option, the violent option. This takes us back to the temptations of Mark (1.12–14) and in Luke we are given more details right at the beginning of the story. Should Jesus allow himself to take the cup of non-violence or fight? We can suspect that this is what Judas, Peter (and maybe other disciples) wanted. So now, we have with Jesus – a known troublemaker – Simon the Zealot, Peter the Galilean terrorist, Judas the bandit and two Sons of Thunder: a bunch of ferocious highland peasants who stage a demo as they enter town. In this instance, Jesus Christ Superstar has a better feel for the politics than many of the 'spiritualized' modern commentators.

Wright notes that the argument consistently put forward here that Jesus was executed for rebellion is 'controversial in most orthodox circles'. He nevertheless argues that the search for an 'atonement theology' has ignored the actual story the evangelists were telling – with all its rough political edges –in favour of the theological schema the story was deemed to be inculcating! In answering the question why did Jesus die, Wright's conclusion certainly fits mine: 'here more than anywhere else it is worse than futile to separate theology from politics. The tired old split between the Jesus of history and the Christ of faith was never more misleading than at this point.'[30]

Jesus' refusal of the violent messianic route may have lost him popular political support, probably the betrayal of Judas and perhaps the short-term denial of Peter. Jesus' choice of non-violence and the precise differences with Barabbas, Peter, Judas and the Sons of Thunder over the right road for the new movement to tread was an irrelevance to Pilate. He was a potential threat. Their client elite wanted him out of the way. That was enough, whatever Pilate's personal uncertainties on the matter. The last thing he needed was to appear to be doing a bad job of governing Judaea. Civilian casualties were not being counted in this war either, especially if they could be called insurgents.

Crucifixion and resurrection

Jesus' final showdown with the Empire takes place 'in the Roman sphere' in the Roman Praetorium (15.16). 'Crucifixion was explicitly reserved in the provinces for enemies of the Imperial State.' It said, as Wright puts it, that the Romans are in charge and this (the cross) 'is what happens to rebel leaders'. Jesus' crucifixion means a 'political confrontation with, not the rehabilitation of, the Imperial State'. It also means for Mark, as for John, that Jesus being lifted up onto the Cross was a supreme 'apocalyptic moment' – a moment of God's revelation. At this moment of the creation of a new order, darkness covers the surface of the land (v. 33). Jesus gives a great gasp (15.37): the same sound as when evil is vanquished in Jesus' first healing in Galilee (1.26) and when the legions of demons shriek in the Roman cities (5.7). Again, both the Jewish and the Roman orders are symbolically challenged and defeated; the Temple curtain is 'torn in two from top to bottom' (v. 38) and it is the Roman centurion who recognizes the carpenter as the Son of God (v. 39) – a title normally reserved for kings and emperors, certainly not for terrorists on a cross.

If Mark's Gospel had ended here with the twin (client elite and imperial) collusion and with the potential defeat of the powers that be, as it often does with revolutionary stories, there would still be hope amidst all the appearance of betrayal and death. As

Myers points out, there is a sense in which the Roman centurion announces the climax of the Gospel.[31] Instead, the story moves on to the women watching Jesus' death from a distance (v. 40), his burial (vv. 42–7), and then being present much closer at his resurrection (16.1–7). Instead of the men of the inner circle, who have all fled, most radical of all for a patriarchal society, it is the women who are asked to go ahead and back to Galilee, to realize the overturning of the old world order. If the Cross is an apocalyptic representation of the power of the old world order, the resurrection represents the power of the new.

Mark still ends with ambiguity. The older manuscripts of Mark's Gospel end at 16.8 with the women afraid, trembling and bewildered, saying nothing to anyone. The idea of Mark writing in the late 60s with the Roman troops pounding at the door and breaking off his manuscript as a consequence has great poetic appeal: 'The clash of grounded spear buts in ... the courtyard, the harsh battering on the door, the hasty thrusting of the hurried last pages of the gospel into concealment – and the end.'[32]

Apocalyptic – and thereby political – imagery runs throughout the Gospels, not just in Mark. If Mark is ambiguous, Matthew's Gospel, for example, is not. Wengst points to Matthew's description of Jesus' crucifixion and resurrection. In Matthew 27, not only does darkness comes over the land (v. 45), but the curtain in the Temple is torn in two (v. 5a), there is an earthquake, the tombs break open and the 'holy' dead are resurrected and appear in Jerusalem where they are seen by many (vv. 51b–53). The centurion's comments are in Matthew's account partly brought on by the earthquake (v. 54).

Wengst describes the implications graphically: 'World history is opened ... The actual course of history is deprived of the triumph of being final and gives space and time to oppressed hopes.' As Paul developed this theme, what had seemed a victory to the powers that be was actually a major defeat. Likewise, as Myers elaborates in Mark's case, with the Roman legions stormtrooping

210

their way through Galilee after 67, burning and crucifying as they went, this is how it was possible to write a document about a crucified prophet of 35 years earlier and call it 'good news'.[33]

8

Apocalypse and Justice:
Mark and Central America

Oscar Romero: an execution for the oligarchies

On the evening of 24 March 1980, Archbishop Oscar Romero was shot and killed saying Mass. The day before he had preached in the cathedral asking the El Salvador National Guard not to kill their own people. He had been interrupted by applause five times.[1] Oscar Romero was executed, probably under the orders of a paramilitary leader later to become president, because he had become the symbol of opposition to the oligarchic dictatorship of El Salvador, putting the Church at the centre of her political life in the way she had perhaps never been. Graham Greene points out that Romero was the first archbishop to be murdered saying Mass since Thomas Beckett. Yet when he had been appointed in 1977 he had seemed the conservative choice and progressives in the Catholic Church were disappointed. For after all, Romero had links with Opus Dei – founded by a Spanish supporter of Franco. These apparently pro-catholic and anti- communist movements, so frequently linked to Latin American populism and fascism, had attracted many in the Latin American clergy. Romero was even reputed to have links to the El Salvador oligarchy. Three years later, attempting to be a faithful archbishop and to apply the gospel in El Salvador had changed Oscar Romero. His execution, so akin to that of his Lord, provides us with one experience of the role of political theology when faced with the power of empires like Rome or global capital and that of oligarchic client states like Judaea or El Salvador.

The story of El Salvador, as of Central America as a whole, is also a story of the USA's power over it. Central America is the only place in the world where the USA has truly – and fairly openly – operated as an imperial ruler, despite often waving the flag of anti-imperialism. Here the Monroe Doctrine, with twentieth-century amendments, has ruled supreme. The Central American experience of global capitalism has largely been via the local oligarchies aided, as LaFeber puts it, by the USA's military and industrial complex.[2] Although there has been nominal independence and sometimes the superficial appearance of parliamentary democracy, at its best in Costa Rica, Central America has never been allowed to step out of line in the USA's own strategic backyard. Even tiny Grenada got swept into the Reagan purge in the early 1980s, which came out of the symbolic threat of Nicaragua[3] and showed to the bigger Caribbean islands their limits, with Cuba as the only impoverished exception. The consequences for Central America have been devastating and show in brute form what the American Empire can do when it has unilateral rights to wield a big stick.[4] The ferocity of many in the 'Muslim world' – the clash of civilizations for some – to the impact of US 'imperialism' has been much commented on since 9/11. Latin Americans would have at least as much reason to hate the USA, given their own experience of killing.[5] Could it be that the Catholic Church has been an influence here? Or, more likely, is it that the peoples of Central America have experienced the ferocity of past US responses to the merest glimmer of real independence? They would know that 9/11 would actually do immense harm in Central America – as it has to many ordinary Iraqis – if carried out by say Nicaraguan 'terrorists'. After over 40 years of dictatorship under Somoza, wined and dined by US presidents, the attempt of the Nicaraguans to assert a form of national liberation, with a mixed economy and minimal 'socialism' was duly crushed, with

100,000 deaths between 1978 and 1984, with 100,000 more in Guatemala and at least 50,000 in El Salvador (equivalent to 13 million deaths, if carried out on the same scale in the USA).

Theology in dialogue with political economy

Atrocities like these have led radical theologians to develop their political theology. In Germany, Jürgen Moltmann's life has been driven by his own experience of a firestorm – that of the bombing of Hamburg in 1943. His theology, according to Bauckham, is driven by two thoughts: why have I survived and how can I live with this? When trapped behind barbed wire in a prisoner of war camp, Moltmann was still able to believe in freedom; in the midst of the experience of the cross, as he put it, Moltmann still emphasized a theology of hope.[6] In the USA, Walter Wink's three-volume piece on the 'Powers' – the important connection in New Testament thinking between spiritual and political power – began with his horror at the atrocities he found visited on the people of Latin America by his own government. Richard Horsley makes a detailed comparison of US rule in Central America and Roman rule in Palestine. In Britain, Chris Rowland makes extensive use of the gospel as seen by the poor in Nicaragua and elsewhere in Latin America.[7] The hope of Cuba (with the armed victory of 1959), Vatican II in 1962–5 and the Medellin Bishops' Conference in Colombia in 1968 inspired an earlier generation of Latin American 'liberation' theologians. Besides the 'warriors' like ex-priest Camillo Torres in Colombia who gave his life in 1965 fighting with the guerillas,[8] there are also the theologians like Jon Sobrino, himself largely based in El Salvador, who argues that Romero opposed the twin 'Gods' of 'unbridled capitalism' and of 'national security'. As Sobrino argues, the problem for Latin American theologians has not been a theology after Auschwitz; but a theology while still living through an Auschwitz.[9]

214

The spread of both empire and now capitalism to the Isthmus has been felt most by the 'Indian' population.[10] Dunkerley points out that the tradition of the 'disappeared' of Latin America appears in Guatemala in the 1960s well before the better known cases in Argentina, Brazil and Chile – and most of these were Indian.[11] In Central America, an agricultural economy dominated by cash crops for export is much closer economically and structurally to Africa than it is to post-1950 Mexico, Argentina or Brazil, which have large indigenous industrial markets and the potential for industrial as well as mineral resource exports. Central America shows a similar propensity to military dictatorships but with a far longer nominal independence than most of Africa; many of the policy recommendations argued by the trade justice lobby have been tried, especially since the 1930s. As with Africa we have to be careful not to blame all the problems on global capitalism or on debt or on unfair trade. The problems created by the landed oligarchies in Central America are paramount. Any simplistic notion that simply giving 'more power' to local governments via trade, exchange and capital controls will solve the problem is both naive and unhistorical. Instead, the economy is being restructured by internal capitalist relationships, with increasing numbers of rural landless, an impoverished rural proletariat and a squeezed peasantry. The experience of El Salvador where the common peoples movement suffered an early and massive defeat in 1932 – long before the troubles of the 1970s and 1980s – is perhaps the most instructive. What the Latin American experience as a whole has shown is that global capital can survive and prosper, justify and sustain a number of political styles from parliamentary dictatorship, to semi-fascist populism, to military dictatorship and old-fashioned oligarchic rule. Recommendations as to trade and debt policy cannot be sensibly done without this internal analysis; as we shall show with a brief look at both Honduras and El Salvador.

Honduras: still a banana republic ?

We shall start with Honduras – the poorest and most backward of the Central American economies. As with cotton in Kenya, Christian Aid introduces the problems of Honduras with the issue of cheap US rice being dumped on Honduran rice producers.[12] Again, with this focus on fair trade, the analysis gets nowhere near to the heart of the problems of Honduras; it severely underestimates the extent of the military, political and economic problems that Central America has faced in order to wrap up its ideas in simple slogans. In fact, Honduras was the classic banana republic. Until the 1960s, Honduras was dominated by two US 'fruit' corporations – given land to pay off foreign debt, exporting bananas and paying no tax. A political bloc of large landowners, supported and abetted with American military and foreign policy aid, has effectively occupied Honduras. This Honduran government has spent its whole life in 'Faustian' deals with the US elite. Furthermore, it is a client regime kept in place to aid the crushing of the lower orders in blood across Central America. The Christian Aid comment ignores the politics at work in the Isthmus since 1979. This is about a bit more than peasant-produced rice. To imply that all that Honduras needs is a debt write-off and fairer trade is to live in cloud cuckoo land.

The consistent domination of Honduras by the USA led to its pejorative title as a banana republic. Between 1913 and 1925, US troops intervened in Honduras six times. Like Iraq, Honduran villages were bombed by the US air force in 1927–31 as they tried to flush out the Nicaraguan rebel leader, Sandino. In 1954, the Honduran government allowed itself to be used as a starting point for a CIA-inspired guerilla band that helped overthrow the reformist government of Guatemala.[13] The occupation of Honduras as Washington's military base for US and Contra troops putting down the 'revolutionary' regime in Nicaragua was central to the 1980s. Even since the transfer to civilian rule in 1981, it had been dubbed a 'state for sale', a 'republic for rent', the 'Pentagon republic', the 'captive nation' or as a 'US aircraft carrier', the USS Honduras. Honduras has proved incapable of resisting virtual colony status. One Honduran politician argued that seven different armies had occupied Honduras in the 1980s: its own army, that of the USA, that of El Salvador (still holding some disputed territory), the Contras set up to fight against Nicaragua, British and Belizean forces (holding the Zapotillo Keys claimed by Honduras) and the unemployed. As one Honduran general commented: 'You can't destabilize Nicaragua any more from Honduras without also destabilizing Honduras.' George II's 2005 appointment of John Negroponte, as US ambassador to Iraq provides another symbolic re-enactment of the American Empire at work. For it was Negroponte, as career ambassador to Honduras, who was busy with what Dunkerley claims were the disingenuous disclaimers that the USA had no role in the fighting, while implicitly supporting the imposition of the draconian Decree 33 that imposed 20 years' gaol for 'subversion', meaning factory occupations or 'disorderly' demonstrations.[14] For the US ruling elite from Reagan onwards, Honduran and Central American destabilization remained an acceptable cost – more 'collateral damage' – for the successes scored against the 'left' in El Salvador and Nicaragua. By fighting shy of the dirty politics of class and violence in their fair trade analysis, the NGOs do not help as much as could be the case in the propaganda wars that will be unleashed against the 'communists and terrorists'. The government that has given up its powers to the USA is in the Christian Aid economic analysis, to be vainly given 'more power'; yet we have no accompanying historical, geopolitical or military analysis of why this has proved so difficult in Honduras. Rather more than fairer trade is going to be required for the kingdom to come and for justice to be established in Honduras.

El Salvador: coffee oligarchy and rural proletariat

In El Salvador, much the most densely populated country in the Isthmus, there has been over 100 years of rural proletarian protests that have been far harder to control than the larger and more peasant-dominated Honduras. This provides the essential backdrop to understanding the murder of Archbishop Romero. The brutality of much Central American political violence – stretching down from Mexico to Peru – has very deep and bitter roots. The records of Indian risings in nineteenth-century Central America have a resonance with those in Africa. They were driven by resentments against tax – up to 80 to 90 per cent of Indian income would be taken as tribute – and the expansion of the invaders' plantations into indigenous peoples' lands, as in Chiapas today. In El Salvador, for example, this was an era of indigo, used as a dye for the British textile industry. As in Africa, and as today, the young men were pressed into the military and self-sufficiency broken so that the Indians were forced to participate in the 'modern' imperial economy. Resistance was frequent, with extraordinary violence in 1833. In El Salvador the pressure to take Indian common lands became intense after the increasing replacement of indigo by coffee from the 1870s onwards. Outbreaks of violence are recorded in 1872, 1875, 1880, 1885 and 1889. The last resulted in the creation of a National Guard, often billeted and taking orders from the local landlord. Such paramilitaries 'policed' the Indian areas through into the 1980s. Within two generations, self-sufficiency was destroyed and a few made fortunes at the expense of the many.[15]

By 1904, coffee already accounted for 80 per cent of El Salvador's exports; by 1929 this had risen to 93 per cent. The 1930 census counted 309,000 agricultural wage labourers out of a population of only 1.5 million. As those peasants who had kept some land still performed seasonal picking in the coffee plantations, every labouring family was in effect linked seasonally to the coffee industry. This extensive rural proletariat also followed from the highly unequal land ownership: in the 1920s, 350 families (around 0.1 per cent of the population) owned more than 1,000 acres each. Even today, large farms of more than 200 acres account for nearly 40 per cent of the land cultivated, the bottom 90 per cent, with less than two hectares each, share only 20 per cent of the land. The biggest planters had gone on to own banks and the most dominant of these controlled the export trade. After 1871, every El Salvadorean president came from the planter class. In short, a tight-knit oligarchy owned much of El Salvador and controlled it politically. By 1920, 'defence' and 'security' were already taking 20 per cent of the government budget. In 1923, crowds gathering to protest against fraud in the election (which was to become a common accusation) were fired on by the military.[16]

The El Salvadorean economy was a classic case for dependency theory and 1929 hit El Salvador very hard. So much is said now about the unfair trade enshrined by the 'trade rules' of the WTO, yet falling commodity prices are nothing new in the global economy: the average price of coffee fell to a third of its previous level (from US 25 cents/pound to 9 cents/pound between 1929 and 1935). In 1931, a popularly elected government under Arturo Aranjo took power. Aranjo had lived for a time in Liverpool and modelled his party on the British Labour Party. The appearance of a sympathetic government promising land reform stirred a rural uprising, sometimes described as a peasant revolt, sometimes a communist revolt. US reports called Aranjo an anarchist. An army of peasants was stopped just short of the capital. The Communist Party, led by Farabundo Marti,[17] also played a small but significant role.

El Salvador: the slaughter and the economics

When Christians discuss the role of violence in these revolts it is worth remembering the number killed in this uprising – around 80 (around 30 civilians and 50 military). The USA quickly dispatched three warships; the Canadians, two. Aranjo was overthrown by the military in December. Then began a counter-revolution of such ferocity that Dunkerley describes the demographic impact as a 'trauma'. At least 10,000 peasants were killed in the reprisals, some estimates run to 40,000 in two months in January and February 1932.[18] The basis for 40 years of military rule was set, and even under civilian rule, the oligarchy via the military were given a permanent veto on economic policy. This revolt was put down by the national guard and militia, not by the USA (which made the intervention of the 1980s different), but the extent of 'communist' involvement may account for the ferocity of the response of El Salvador's military and landed oligarchy. From then on, being a communist – especially for a priest in El Salvador – was always seen in the context of 1932. The death toll would be equivalent to roughly six million in the USA today. No wonder that in El Salvador the year is known as the Matanza – the slaughter.

The story of this killing in Central America is sadly nothing new. The economic policies of the new military regime do not usually rate a mention. Here however are all the classic nostrums advocated by many in today's trade justice movement. Within a week, the military suspended all debt repayments. To control capital movements, it established its own central bank, and in 1935, exchange controls. To protect its 'artisan' industry, tariffs were first imposed in 1939. Despite having aided the coup in the best traditions of gunboat diplomacy, the USA was so annoyed by the regime's nationalism that it withheld recognition of the regime for four years. It was the first regime to recognize Franco and to endorse the puppet Japanese government in Manchuria. General Martinez stayed in power until 1944.[19]

After the massacre, El Salvador's oligarchy had more relative autonomy from the USA and less of the upheavals that afflicted others in Latin America in the late 1940s and 1950s. Not only the very rich gained: as government revenues increased fivefold because of higher coffee prices in the 1950s, the gains accrued probably to a rich peasantry and an urban petty bourgeois; the top 5–20 per cent of the population had an income share that rose from 17 per cent to 28 per cent. With diversification into agro-industrial processing, industrial employment increased from 52 to 85,000 between 1951 and 1961. In the era before the debt-induced problems overemphasized by the Jubilee Campaign, the rich in El Salvador still got richer and the poor got poorer. In 1946, the bottom 60 per cent of the population took 32 per cent of income; by 1961, it was down to 21 per cent. In the 1960s, the CIA held El Salvador up as its model of stability and progress, and the Alliance for Progress had given it more funds than anywhere else in the Isthmus. The new burst of US enthusiasm also covered an unusual burst in US investment in the mid 1960s. El Salvador's GDP grew by 12 per cent in 1964–5 and by 5.6 per cent overall in the 1960s. The diversification of the local oligarchy often into banking, real estate and insurance on the one hand and car parts, beer and sugar processing on the other, also ran alongside the increasing penetration of US agro-business.[20]

A looming hegemonic crisis: El Salvador 1960–72

All this 'modernization' had a huge downside, as the pressure on the peasants' landholdings grew steadily. Only 12 per cent of the population was landless in 1961, but this had increased to 29 per cent in 1971 and to 41 per cent in 1975. Even for those who had land, 96 per cent had less than five hectares – seven hectares was supposedly the minimum for self-sufficiency. Yet 50 per cent of the large farms lay fallow. Sixty per cent of the population lived on what was calculated to be the minimum income and most had a diet of corn, beans and rice. As Lafeber puts it, the average US cat had a better diet than the average Central American.[21]

The mini success of the 1950s enabled the military to slacken their repressive grip, at least until 1972 – with votes from both the groups in coffee and industry who could live with 'reforms under repression'. The US involvement in El Salvador had traditionally been a lot less than in Honduras or Nicaragua; in the 1960s, this began to change as military aid was doubled. As a part of this new optimism, the Christian Democrat Party was founded in 1960. The Christian Democrat philosophy in El Salvador was driven by the anti-communism of the USA and the ruling bloc; it looked for land reforms within the prevailing Catholic order and private property holdings. If the military party ran the government, Napoleon Duarte's Christian Democrats could run the capital city, San Salvador, and it looked as if reform could continue. One of the other safety valves after the counter-revolution had been the ability of El Salvadorean peasants to flee to Honduras, where there was much more vacant land. Formed in 1958, the Central American Common Market meant that El Salvador's small manufacturing sector was undercutting that in Honduras; by 1969, this aided in the so-called 'football war' when Honduras expelled peasant settlers back to El Salvador. Although the latter's army 'won' the subsequent battles, it raised the pressure. As Duarte looked set to win the 1972 election, with the promise of limited land reforms, he was beaten up and exiled by a coup. In 1971, 36 landlords still controlled 66 per cent of the capital of the largest 1,400 firms in El Salvador. When reforms went any step ahead of what they deemed acceptable, coups and violence were the inevitable result.[22]

The key problem for El Salvador by 1970, as with Argentina 40 years before, was the continuing viability of the agro export economy. This caused a division within the El Salvadorean ruling class. Those diversifying into industry wanted a free trade zone, akin to what Mexico developed in the 1990s. Even a military reared on repression had a reformist wing, which saw land reform as a long-term life insurance. This clashed, however, with the rest of the oligarchy who were being asked to pay tax for reforms that would take away some of their lands. Into this crisis of how to maintain the oligarchy's hegemony, came increasing US economic and military involvement. The US companies paid a minimum wage of $1 a day; the traditional oligarchy in desperation called the demand for better wages 'communist inspired'.[23] This hegemonic crisis lies at the heart of the violence of the 1970s, increased enormously by the US determination to make sure that the Nicaraguan revolution did not spread to El Salvador. This in turn led to a fractured military and a divided church hierarchy, while in the hegemonic gap arrived a better educated and more self aware popular bloc struggling to get the majority's needs and views heard. In the centre stood Oscar Romero.

The religious roots of rebellion in El Salvador

As the 1970s progressed, El Salvador began to look again more and more like a dictatorship along Guatemalan lines. In Guatemala, the largest country on the Isthmus, the collusion of the Eisenhower administration ensured that a land reform, so modest that its principal tenets were adopted by the US-inspired Alliance for Progress in the early 1960s, was put down quickly in 1954. The '10 years of spring in a land of tyranny' from 1944 to 1954 in Guatemala has since been replaced by the title: the 'Garrison State'.[24] The El Salvadorean oligarchy should have suspected that an honest archbishop would run foul of their policies. Archbishop Chavez y Gonzalez, the incumbent from 1939 until 1977 had sheltered opponents to the military regime of General Martinez and thereby had already been accused of being a communist. By 1970, as the church in El Salvador organized its own basic Christian communities, it was unable to anticipate the fury of the attacks that would be unleashed against it. Peasants began to be jailed for possessing 'subversive literature', which turned out to be the Pope's encyclical *Pacem in Terris*, distributed indeed by the Christian Democrats. Even as early as 1969, parishes that had taken part in demonstrations were occupied by Orden – a paramilitary organization set up to counter 'insurgency'. Churches where grass-roots work had gone the best were later to become the battlegrounds of the 1970s. Orden's leader, Major D'Aubuisson, was later accused of ordering Romero's murder. The theological work had been led by another bishop – Rivera y Damas – and, even in Latin American terms, was not revolutionary: looking to revisit and rethink the Catholic traditions. Far from being a revolutionary, Bishop Damas was friendly with the founders of the Christian Democrats, who in the early 1980s were to have the misfortune of carrying the political cloak, which the military used to hide behind and shoot around. Nevertheless, Damas was seen as the 'progressive'. In 1970, after a pastoral week for priests and laity in such parishes, Oscar Romero – then Bishop of Santiago de Maria –was brought in by the Catholic hierarchy to 'correct' the final conclusions into more moderate language. Romero was not only considered conservative, but seen as timid and in poor health.[25]

In 1974, the Christian Democrats may have again won the local elections. The army radio was taped instructing soldiers on how to rig the ballot boxes. No results were posted. In 1975, as the popular movements gained strength, death squads began to appear killing both rural leaders and clergy on the slogan: 'Be patriotic, kill a priest'. In 1976, even the generals tried a land reform: announced in June, it was cancelled by oligarchy opposition in October. Martin-Baro and Sobrino consider that the turning point for Archbishop Romero came with the murder of Father Rutilo Grande, the parish priest of Aguilares, only two weeks after the archbishop had been inaugurated in February 1977. Father Grande was a friend of Romero, heavily involved in the base communities work, and like many of the leading

Latin American priests and theologians, well educated in Catholic seminaries in Spain and Belgium. Nor was Father Grande a Torres; as Berryman puts it, he had his own 'Galilean crisis', he was wary of being aligned to any political group. Berryman argues, however, that Romero had been warned earlier when still a bishop: he had seen the hounding of a priest – David Rodriguez – as a 'communist', when all Romero saw was a priest applying the gospel to El Salvador.[26]

Institutional terror

Father Grande's parish of Aguilares is 27 miles north of San Salvador. It had 35 large haciendas, but the best land was given over to three sugar cane estates. The radical priest started work in the parish in 1972 and within a short while peasants educated by Father Grande became leaders of the popular organizations: one became a leader of the Peasants Union (Feccas) (which was illegal at this point) and another, Juan Chacon, a leader of the 'popular bloc'. These parish activists were soon to be hounded as 'protestants' (rather akin to calling Jesus a Samaritan), politicals or, worst of all, communists. There were struggles as the government requisitioned land for a new dam. Other peasants had wanted to rent uncultivated land, even depositing cash with a judge to show their good intent. When this got no response, they occupied it. Here, as in Aguilares in May 1977, the army was then sent in, killing 70 and arresting 300. One peasant was quoted to the effect that it was 'better to die of a bullet than of hunger'. Romero then made a point of holding a Mass there himself. The church itself was badly divided between those who saw the popular organizations as Marxists or terrorists, and others who saw them as virtually synonymous with the church. At least five of Romero's bishops supported the army: one bishop was even a colonel. On the other hand, Feccas had the word 'Christian' in its own title and was recognized as the popular front and base for the guerrilla movement, the FMLN (the Farabundo Marti National Liberation Front, named after the communist leader of 1932).[27]

Romero became archbishop only two days after an election that brought a less reformist General Humberto Romero (no relation) to power. In the wake of 1972, this election was again regarded by the opposition as fixed, and a week later the huge protest was fired on in the main square of the capital, killing probably 200, wounding many more. From then on, Romero's outspoken appeals for justice, including a public letter to President Carter in February 1980 and a pastoral letter criticizing, in Medellin language, the 'institutional violence' of El Salvador led to an increasing stand-off between the military and the archbishop. Some British MPs nominated him for the Nobel Peace Prize in 1978, while against him ranged a mounting terror. The killing campaign was legitimized by new anti-terror legislation in November 1977, which legalized arbitrary arrest and prison, systematic torture and the end of the right to hold public meetings. Deaths mounted from the 4,000 of 1978 to perhaps 14,000 others in 1980, alongside Oscar Romero. The paramilitaries opened fire on the huge march, involving up to as many as 250,000 in January for the anniversary of 1932, even firing into the churches. They did so again among the crowds of perhaps 80,000 at Romero's funeral (killing 40). By late 1980 all the legal opposition leaders had been killed, including Chacon, and three US nuns were also raped and killed. D'Aubisson labelled the Christian Democrat Attorney General a communist on TV and the judge was later assassinated. Ex-President (and ex-General) Molina, whose weak attempt at land reform had failed, was called a 'communist in uniform'. This was all tailor-made for Ronald Reagan's use: as US military aid rose, in 1981 17,000 more were killed – in two years alone, this was ten times the death rate of 9/11. In all the Reagan years of escalating aid not a single member of the El Salvadorean military – responsible for most of the 60,000 deaths – was ever charged.[28]

The coup of 1979

What killed the possibilities for El Salvador was ironically the successful uprising in Nicaragua, with the Sandinistas in power there by October 1979. Within 12 hours of the news of the victory in Nicaragua, junior army officers, with eventually civilian and Christian Democrat support, overthrew Humberto Romero's government. For Dunkerley this time, unlike 1932, it was US intervention, particularly under Reagan, that stopped the El Salvador 'revolution'. The internal forces against a popular revolution were also powerful and can be seen, in Berryman's analysis, through the role of the army in the 1979 coup. He identifies three groups within the army: the reformers, who made the coup; the hardliners with strong links to the oligarchy; and those with the best links to the Pentagon. He argues that the last two groups allowed the reform to proceed while they consolidated their position. On the one hand, as one guerrilla group – the ERP – started an insurrection, occupying the suburbs of San Salvador and some factories, they made sure that this was put down using helicopters to machine-gun the people; on the other, by November they allowed Duarte back from exile and appeared to embark on yet another land reform.

By December 1979, the other civilians in government were complaining that the coup was a 'manouver against the people'.[29] As Romero never tired of pointing out, no killers had been brought to justice. Dunkerley suggested that the land reforms, finally unveiled in March 1980 and modelled on the US efforts in South Vietnam a generation earlier, were easily circumvented and like Molina's four years before were designed more to outflank the Christian Democrats. As Berryman points out, the actual outcome was an army occupation of the troubled villages. The army often demanded protection money and most of the killing took place where the demand for reform was the greatest. The example of Nicaragua's land reforms in particular was

227

something the oligarchy were determined to defeat, and pushed them into open participation in politics for the first time in 50 years. D'Aubuisson became a perfect front. Berryman sees Romero's killing as a calculated risk by the elite, rather like Caiaphas one might think. Although some of the guerillas saw it as an attempt to create a further insurrection and provoke an excuse for a bloodbath, the thinking seems to have been that if the head was cut off, the bloodbath would have no global mouth piece. When some land was redistributed, supporters of D'Aubuisson's Orden got it. Fewer than 10 per cent of the peasantry received land. None did so in the most impoverished north and east. The patronage that had always been used by the State to keep some peasants on side was to be re-employed to good effect. As Berryman concludes 'the oligarchy found a way round the reforms it so bitterly oppose[d]'.

Two days after Romero's funeral, the US agreed military aid for 'non lethal hardware'. When Carter had gone, Reagan and Haig (his Secretary of State) decided to market the struggle in El Salvador as part of the global fight against the Cuban and Soviet threat. Lafeber argues that the FMLN was dying before Reagan made it a cause célèbre. Ten per cent of El Salvador's army then went for training in the USA. Struggling to get military aid through Congress, Reagan could always blame the 'liberals' if it failed, while being determined to remove any revolutionary regimes in Nicaragua, El Salvador or Guatemala.[30]

US aid, arena and the Christian Democrats: 1979–89

As the Contras continued to be secretly funded, the US Congress struggled to uncover what was going on from the labyrinth of CIA documents. Thirteen thousand of El Salvador's asylum seekers in the US were told in 1984 that it was safe to return home.[31]

The Pope also did his bit to help the new crusade against global communism and insurgency. Damas was made only an interim archbishop on Romero's death and the appointment was not confirmed for three years. Damas had been made a hostage to the Pope's definition of his good behaviour and, with his past closeness to the Christian Democrats, seemed more frightened of Marxism than of Orden. After fifty priests left their parishes, a third of the parishes were without priests.[32]

The landlords did rather well out of the land reform, as indeed did their political party named Arena. Some who got inflated prices for their land moved to Miami; others subdivided the big estates within the family; others hired Orden to kill peasants who tried to move onto the land. Arena was now amply funded and in recognition of US pressure more than anything internally, won the 1982 election that the left, whose candidates feared assassination, had boycotted. Thirteen thousand still 'disappeared' in 1982. As Dunkerley puts it, the 1982 election was between the right and the extreme right, with Arena in traditional style describing the Christian Democrats as 'crypto communists'. Arena's ability to continue waging war was now funded by US purse strings. US military aid rose from just short of $6 million in 1980 to a peak of $197 million in 1984. It was still running at over $80 million a year in the early 1990s. Despite US economic aid, which rose from $58 million in 1980 to $433 million in 1985, the El Salvadorean economy was in deep recession, in common with the rest of Central America. By comparison, Nicaraguan aid also running at $60 million in 1981 had fallen to nothing by 1983, while Costa Rican US aid peaked at $220 million in 1985 and Guatemalan at $147 million in 1989. El Salvador's GDP fell by 25 per cent between 1978 and 1984, while real wages fell 40 per cent and basic grain production by 15 per cent.[33]

Dunkerley argues that it took the USA five years from Romero's death to help 'orchestrate' the Christian Democrat government it wanted. Although Duarte's long exile had left him only in charge of a rump of his party, he was an acceptable face for the military particularly because of his good relations with the

USA. Duarte won the presidential election of 1984 and the benefit of US support for him meant that El Salvador's US aid kept on rising, peaking at $509 million in 1987. By the late 1980s, with US aid still running at between $200 million and $300 million a year, it covered virtually the entire government budget. This was especially good news for the oligarchy which did not like paying taxes. The land reform actually meant that many of them got richer as peasants unable to gain credit for their lands went bust; the oligarchy bought back the land at knock-down prices. Wealth thereby was even more unevenly distributed in 1987 than it had been in 1979.[34]

Pacification and re-composition of the ruling bloc: 1989–2004

By 1989, with yet another FMLN offensive, it was clear that the guerilla army could not be defeated militarily. The army could not win the war partly because of its own inefficiencies; money for phantom conscripts tended to end up in the pockets of the commanders. The desertion rate of the peasant conscript army and deaths ran as high as 20 per cent combined. Unlike the military in Argentina or Chile, in El Salvador there was stalemate. The FMLN commanded allegiance right across the El Salvador spectrum, except in the oligarchy. This was partly a reflection of US politics too: Reagan would not let the FMLN win and the US Congress would not condone Arena. Duarte had tried negotiations after 1987, but presumably with US pressure would not lift the FMLN's surrender as a pre-condition.[35]

The key ironically again was Nicaragua; the US war on Nicaragua had finally destroyed the Sandinista regime and a Nicaraguan people tired of war voted in their opposition in 1990.[36] In El Salvador, the FMLN having held out for its troops to be incorporated into the army, accepted their inclusion into a new police force in September 1991 and an accord was signed in January,

1992. The new elections of 1994 and 1999 were won by Calderon Sol of Arena. The FMLN is now an ordinary political party. This sounds so much like Northern Ireland at times, one thinks the history of the two would make an interesting parallel (the major difference being the Unionist working class, the equivalent in El Salvador being peasants given land by Orden and voting for a continued union with the oligarchy's Arena). Representing a new mobile lower middle class, the FMLN's old commanders are now in business and parliament. The FMLN, according to Petras, now pursues a social democratic model with a stress on technology and entrepreneurship. Land occupations are again deemed illegal.[37] One thinks of Morris again, ideas that others fought for may have to be fought for again under another name.[38]

To use Dunkerley's terms, in a generation, El Salvador had been 'pacified' with methods akin to that of the subjugation of the original indigenous peoples. If there had been a crisis for the dominant bloc by 1972, it had been 're-composed' within a new party system, including Arena and the FMLN. The 'radical reformers' had won – at what a cost. Tariff barriers were reduced in 2003 and the new role is best symbolized by the textile exports from the 'maquiladora' free trade zones established in El Salvador, on Mexican-style lines. Thirty years on, the economic reforms that a minority within the oligarchy and army had always wanted had been enacted. Remittances from immigrants to the USA in 2004 of around $2 billion a year, accounted for 17 per cent of GDP. El Salvador is still close to the bottom of the value added chain, but its subordinate role behind Mexico is clear.

This is the kind of time frame and purpose that the US elite will use for Iraq (with oil and Middle East politics making an important difference to the link). The strategy of imperial control is however clear and similar. It may take the US elite a generation, but the plan is to reincorporate Iraq within the Global Empire of Capital. To prevent the 'revolutions' in Nicaragua and El Salvador, which as time has shown were barely more than those for a genuine national independence and liberation from oligarchic and imperial rule, the USA ended up supporting two of the most squalid dictatorships in the world – in Guatemala and El Salvador. Nothing new here then. As Duarte remarked, 'the North Americans preach democracy to us, while everywhere they support dictatorships'.[39] When the rule of the US global elite (not all North Americans, please note) is attacked by a single man with a whip, driving the money changers out of their temples, the reversion to oligarchy (Caiaphas) and to false governance (Pilate) leads to early executions.

Mark and apocalypse

It is important to see the political economy here and not just the Roman Catholic Church and its newly won Vatican II theology, nor even the crucified people and priests of El Salvador, as in the Christology of Sobrino. Theologians philosophizing about social theory or liberation do not make a revolution, without the other side of the dialectic being in place. In the critique of the debt and trade justice campaigns, I have emphasized the need for a less simplistic political economy, which more thoroughly understands the role of class and of empire, with policy alternatives against global capitalism, in my case focused on Britain. To understand and critique these developments theologically requires doing the hard work on the political economy. On El Salvador therefore, I have attempted briefly to show how this set of dialectical relationships are intertwined. Berryman's work is an excellent example of what can be done and is required globally on many different countries.

Returning to Mark's gospel with Romero's example and the El Salvador experience in mind, the aim of the final one and a half chapters is twofold: first to pursue some alternative economic and political policy proposals that do not depend on a heavy-handed State; second, to build on other theological strands in

Mark – specifically those to do with an apocalyptic vision and with a movement based on a more open and libertarian concept of leadership.

If we are to proclaim a liberating and radical gospel, which cuts through the obfuscation of much religious debate, and which amounts to more than a reflection of discontent with the present world order, we will need a more realistic assessment of the likely opposition of the ruling powers within our present global elites. If we wish to develop another world based on economic and political justice, for many Christians and others, we are still in need of an apocalyptic vision to see through the superficial presentations of ideology and spin to the underlying realities lying behind. We will need to cross this river of fire.

In Chapters 6 and 7, we saw how Jesus called upon historical memories and upon the tradition of apocalyptic protest, prevalent in the popular culture around him. Mark's Gospel stresses that the first step in the process of building a new kingdom is the 'challenge to see and hear'. Not by accident are the feeding stories, to do essentially with community and global economics, surrounded by four healing stories – two of the deaf and mute (7.31–7 and 9.14–32) and two of the blind (8.22–6 and 10.46–52). For against the power of today's media, seemingly so open and democratic with text messages and phone lines, many are either blinded or made mute as the Global Capitalist Empire expands its might and reach. Geddert points out that far too much of the emphasis on the secrecy of the king has focused historically on doctrinal Christology – on whether Jesus saw himself as the messiah, or the Son of God – and not enough on the secrets of the kingdom. Sobrino argues in his attempt at a 'Latin American Christology' that there is a collective cross on which the poor peoples of the 'third world' hang. As Romero said to the common people of El Salvador: 'you are the image of the pierced saviour'.[40] For too many of today's Christians, it is the kingdom seen outside of a purely religious definition, that is hard to visualize. Seeing that another world is possible in practical terms, as attempted here, is as hard today against the weight of ideological propaganda to the contrary – there is no alternative to capitalism – that makes an apocalyptic vision and hope so important.

Watch out for your rulers

Geddert makes the Greek *blepete* – 'watch out' – the key 'watchword' to his interpretation of Mark's Gospel and places this at the heart of the Gospel context leading to his analysis of Mark's 'apocalyptic' chapter 13. Myers argues that sight and deafness are 'central metaphors' in Mark. But he develops this point more politically in a chapter entitled 'revolutionary patience'. Watch out is applied here to the rulers, specifically the rulers that were to kill Jesus. For Jesus' warning about this reality is interspersed, not just with Peter's messianic acknowledgement (in 8.31–8) as traditional commentators tend to emphasize, but throughout his miracles – opening the eyes of the blind and enabling the deaf to hear and the mute to have a voice (9.30–2; 10.32–4, 45). So, for Myers, we are told to watch out for 'imperial collaborators' (the Herodians) and for the 'nationalists' (the Pharisees and Sadducees); the rulers who will lie to us and mislead us, whether it be over the execution of a carpenter, an archbishop, or the reasons for going to war – whether over Belgium, WMD or security in London.[41]

This critique of the lordly leadership of the 'gentiles' becomes sharper when the disciples move back to their home base at Capernaum. Now the home site of resistance is explicitly positioned against the lordly style of the 'gentiles' (9.30–33). Myers comments that on their way to Jerusalem, the disciples' journey was degenerating into a power struggle (10.35–41). For Wengst, in his critique of the Pax Romana, Jesus shows himself to be a realist when it comes to the realities of power, as with the realities of economics in debate with the Syro-Phoenician woman. Wengst notes that the common translation of the Gentiles who are 'regarded as rulers'(10.42b, NIV) hints at Jesus' emphasis that such leaders only 'seem' to rule. Myers captures this in his contemporary translation: 'you know how it is among the so-called ruling class, their practice of domination, the tyranny of the great ones'. As we learn daily in Iraq: 'the existing order of peace' is based on the oppressive use of force. As Myers notes, Jesus' sarcasm is sometimes lost, 'this is not happening among you' (10.43) is his comment on their leadership squabble. To take up the cross is not about religious self-denial, it is a political act of resistance to such powers and to the existing models of political leadership.[42]

Sadly, in their accommodation to empire, New Labour and its leaders have fallen into this ancient trap. Writing a theological conclusion to this book in July 2005, just two days after the London bombings, I am seething with anger, fear, and impotent rage. Strangely, this is not directed at the young bombers who had performed the atrocity, but with 'our' own government. It was a feeling we suspect that the average Iraqi must have had for most days for a long time. It is notable how keen the government has been to play down the links between Iraq and the bombing. Yet it had always been blindingly obvious that the plan to go to war with Iraq to give us 'security' from the threat of a WMD terror attack was going to make Britain far more exposed: a front line in their war against terror. Their war in Iraq has achieved for ordinary Britons the absolute opposite of what it was supposed to do. The appeal to such global leaders has been increasingly shown to demand all the best sycophancy of Herod and sons before Rome.

The Parable of the Sower

When we looked at Jesus' ministry in Galilee in Chapter 6, we rather glossed over Mark's teaching chapter, that is the parables of chapter 4, which begins with the Parable of the Sower. As Hooker points out,[43] this is Mark's first major presentation of Jesus' teaching since his initial message of 1.15. We can now return with a greater political awareness of where this teaching led Jesus. Normally for the average churchgoer, this is taught as a parable about mission: the seed is the gospel, the farmer is the missionary and the degrees of receptivity define the individual psychological response to the preaching of repentance and forgiveness. Given this standard interpretation, Myers notes that the academic theologians have been dominated by a form critical theme, looking in the midst of this churchy definition for Jesus' original voice. Myers gives 12 pages to his commentary on the parables in this chapter, which it is impossible to fully reflect here. He brings out three main issues that relate to this book's themes: the extent of the parable's use of apocalyptic motifs; the intense political conflict that is reflected in the use of parables; and the degree to which Jesus and Mark draw upon prophetic imagery from Isaiah, Jeremiah, Ezekiel and Daniel. There is an emphasis on listening (4.3), the secrets of the kingdom only given to insiders (4.9–13), on the division between light and dark (4.22), on watching carefully (4.24) and on a final 'eschatalogical' harvest (4.29).

Much conventional exegesis reflects on the Jewish tradition: God is seen as the sower and the soils, the different peoples. But Barclay comments that Jesus' story also reflects the common agricultural practice of Israel in his time; the sowing was done before the ploughing, so that the seed that fell on the path would later have been ploughed in. So this story is not about the receptivity of the soil. For Myers, the Parable of the Sower is not about religious issues, but starts with the most basic economic issue in Jesus' time, the land.[44] We have already noted Galilee's role as the breadbasket for Tyre. Where the spiritual commentators see the growth of the Church, the Parable of the Sower is an affirmation of the possibilities for the economics of the ordinary people of the land. As Myers puts it the parable 'envisions the abolition of opposite relations of production that determined the horizons of the peasant's farmer's social world'.[44] Even more, where the land is operated for the common good, the productivity growth is remarkable and way beyond the usual parameters. The peasant sharecroppers are challenged to think of the possibilities for them all, if they control the surplus.

Herzog's piece on this parable is perhaps the most radical in his entire book on justice. He argues that the apocalyptic theme emerges in the parable's 'hidden transcript'. Herzog's greatest insight is to see most clearly the hidden politics of this parable. He stresses that the words used to describe the failure of the seed to grow are violent and lost in some translations: the birds did not come and eat, they 'devoured' (4.4); some plants are 'scorched' (4.6) while others are 'choked' (4.7). The hidden story leaves us to work out the participants, but the story's original hearers would have known them. The problem does not relate to the soil – the people of the land, if you will – but its enemies. As Herzog puts it well: who was it that had swooped down on the seed sown in Galilee, whose scorched earth policy had it been and who chokes the plants with tithes, rent and taxes?[45]

The birds of the air and the mustard seed alternative?

At the end of Mark 4, Jesus tells another parable, that of the mustard seed: 'The kingdom of God is like a mustard seed, which is the smallest seed … yet when it grows and becomes the largest of all, with such big branches that the birds of the air can perch in its shade'(Mark 4.30–2). One of the keys here is the role of the birds of the air. For we know from even conventional commentators like Barclay that the birds of the air in Ezekiel represented the Gentile powers – foreign empires – in Ezekiel's case Egypt. In Mark's case, Myers argues clearly it is Rome. For in the next chapter do we not meet the legion of demons doing Satan's work (4.15) in Israel? Now we do not have a story just about a spiritual gospel, but an economic and political one too. If the Romans and the Jewish Establishment were not swooping, choking and scorching the life-blood of the productivity of the people, then there would be plenty for all.

And today, what does this mean for our gospel? As the Roman Empire represented the birds of the air in Jesus' parable, so global capitalism's birds have crowed in triumph all over the world. Does it not mean that today the power of the Global Capitalist Empire and its compliant client elites swoops, chokes and scorches? Does this not describe the lot of the rural poor in El Salvador as clearly today as it did in Galilee? The common people starved 'to death on rich land, while they farm it'. As Archbishop Romero put it: 'a land stained with blood will not bear fruit'. One reason for Romero's murder was the growing pressure on the El Salvadorean military in the first three months of 1980, rather like Jesus' pressure on the Jewish Establishment in that last passion week in Jerusalem. For radical optimists who struggle for a more just and participative world, the Cross must still be at the heart of our politics. Most of all, as Sobrino puts it, the powers that be do not like the genuine self-liberation of the people; the hope that Romero began to symbolize,[46] must be defeated above all else.

And yet, there is still a hope. In the next four chapters of Mark, as Jesus feeds both Israel and the Gentiles, the utopian hope of the plentiful banquet to come is repeated. When the power of the Washington consensus and the prevailing ruling-class neoliberal ideology seems all-pervasive, so that the multitude of people are blind and or mute, there is the small mustard seed. In Jewish parables, a mustard seed represented the smallest thing possible. We may like to think, with Negri and Hardt, that the multitudes will oppose the reign of the birds of the air, but – at present – they do not. The chance of a little mustard seed growing in this threatened garden appears hopeless; there appear to be few alternatives. On the global scale, the socialist movement and the other alternative movements are again relatively small and powerless. If we were truly powerful, we would not need to hang on fine words and promises out of Gleneagles. The idea that 'another world is possible', capable of overshadowing even the largest of empires is still a long distant future hope; but this hope is also a key part of the gospel and of the hopes and dreams of humankind. In the next chapter we shall look at one idea that can start the re-sowing of the smallest alternative seeds.

Ever seeing, never perceiving

Watching the CNN coverage of the Argentine crisis in late 2001 (because the British coverage was virtually non-existent, as with the recent troubles in Bolivia and Venezuela), one could watch for hours and learn something of the killing and rioting and nothing that would give any perspective at all on how historically Argentina had come to this. My own all too brief account is in Chapter 2. Both Gottwald and Gorringe, as theologians, make it clear in their work that, following Marx, in any age the ruling ideas are those of the ruling class. It is Jesus' words at the end of the Parable of the Sower that come back to haunt me alongside those of Karl Marx. For truly watching the unfolding of the carnage and injustice in Iraq or Argentina or El Salvador, our postmodern culture screams at us: may they be ever seeing, but never perceiving, and ever hearing but never understanding (Mark 4.12). Usually, Jesus' words are seen religiously, for does not the next verse talk about repentance and forgiveness? The major effort of this book has been to begin to show that Jesus' message cannot be put into a 'religious box' like this. All the 'religions' were out in force on Sunday 10 July 2005 to unite in their abhorrence of the London bombing. On the same day, the 'Veterans Agency' in the British Ministry of Defence called on us to remember our glorious dead of the two world wars.[47] Can they not see that here is religion rolled out again to give heroic moral sanction to the government's wars, while condemning the wars of their enemies? How brave did the Archbishop need to be to say in plain English that the chances that these people died in London were massively increased by Blair's decision to support an illegal war in Iraq to pursue the age long cause of Empire?

At the end of the second banquet of hope, Jesus tells the disciples to 'beware of the leaven' of both the Pharisees and Herod (Mark 8.14–15) – both the nationalists and the client kings. Jesus repeats his frustration at their failure to understand the significance of the feast (8.16–21). The role of leaven is to make the bread rise and easier to eat. The role of political and economic leaven is to be the ideological justification that makes the stuff of ordinary exploitation more palatable and acceptable for and to the common people. So, Jesus does not speak just a theological truth, but a political and economic one too – it suits them to keep us ever seeing but never perceiving.

When one day, an archbishop does speak so direct a truth about the politics and economics – and the theology – of empire, then it is more likely that he will come closer to the fate of his Lord and of Oscar Romero. When one day, this mustard seed is sown, the alternative kingdom has a better chance of becoming the biggest plant in the garden. When the ideological veil is lifted – apocalypse – from our theology, politics and economics the people will have a better chance of seeing. Even so, the disciples must beware that the propaganda that makes the system viable to their minds will continue. For a long time, we may all still remain unable to do much better than the blind man at Bethsaida and only be able to see men like trees walking (8.22–26).

9

Crossing the River of Fire

An alternative to global capital

The capitalist-led Industrial Revolution of Britain transformed our lives. Our capitalist revolution constantly destroys old ways of living 'without automatically substituting anything else'.[1] When we talk of the 'traditional worlds' being destroyed by capitalism today in Africa, Asia or Latin America, we must remember that we are only a few generations away from the same ongoing transformation for ourselves. The Industrial Revolution was not just a take-off or acceleration in the growth of manufacturing output; it was a complete economic and social transformation. It had its ideological counterparts in political economy and in theological thinking. My aim in this brief last chapter is to point to one alternative way of looking at controlling global capital, using a democratic vote not at the level of the nation state, but in the control and running of the capitalist corporation itself. This will concentrate only on its application to Britain. Why in a piece on global capitalism – and on the global implications for a thoroughgoing reformulation of our theological and political thinking – is the focus on British solutions? On a practical level, this is because I am British. Rather than worrying about institutions we cannot control – US presidents, the G8 or the IMF – British Christians can at least engage here. It is not for me to call the strategy for the liberation of Africa, or of Argentina and El Salvador: what I can do is help others understand what is really going on in the

241

moving and shaking of global capital. The right place to start with alternatives to global capital is in our own nation.

The laboratory of British history

Some may ask, why in the context of a critique of global capitalism is there so much history in this book – and that of a century or more ago? To put it simply, as in Africa – and without the detail, it is also the case in India, China and Russia – the roots of today's problems go back at least 150 years. When Gramsci, imprisoned by the Italian Fascist regime, set out to understand the ability of the Italian ruling class to maintain its hegemony over workers and peasants, for example, it led him into a specific study of Italy's history, particularly after its reunification in the 'risorgimento' of 1870. Building on his insights British Marxist historians, like Perry Anderson, have stressed the importance of the 'reconnaissance' of each individual country to understand both capitalism and thereby any 'socialist' alternatives. This in turn goes back to Engels and Marx's work on England and Germany mentioned in Chapter 3. What makes the analysis more difficult than many histories is that both in the past but even more today, these histories need to be seen not in isolation but in the context of international interdependence. In Anderson's first pathbreaking work on the origins of 'The British Crisis' in 1964, he emphasized that it was vital to understand the past, not just as an academic historical exercise, but to better interpret the present and therefore to be more able to see the possible transformations for the future. As Elliott puts it, a theoretical history is a 'necessary condition' for an adequate socialist practice.[2]

Anderson argued in 1964 that the Labour Party had dominated the arena in England for the old working classes. This is even more a truism for Scotland and Wales historically – although the opening provided by devolution leaves an important space for the socialist parties now emerging there. For Anderson, this was akin to a hegemonic domination of the socialist movement in Britain, which New Labour has presently captured for the nation state with a clever blend of economic neo-liberalism (Blair/Brown), social democratic statism (Brown) and repressive reaction on home affairs (Blair/Blunkett). Anderson went on to argue that this hegemony made it 'equally impossible to formulate' a 'socialist strategy from inside or outside of it'. The old heartlands of the working class were strong on 'them and us'. Having a separate identity did not save them from being subordinate, unconsciously adopting many of the hegemonic views of their rulers. Anderson compared the 1960s in Britain to the 1840s in Germany where intellectual theory – the philosophers like Feuerbach – was divorced from the actual political struggles. In the 1850s Engels could see that the working classes, which had struggled since the 1790s, were 'exhausted after successive defeats' – the final defeat being that of Chartism by 1848. Anderson saw the defeats from 1921 to 1952 in the same way. Socialists will look back on the Blair/Brown regime in another ten years' time and see it as the biggest sell out and subordination to global capital of all. In 1964 Anderson saw a 'historic regression'.[3] In 2006, the New Labour Party has regressed further: it is today's equivalent of the Gladstonian Liberal Party, which kept the old radicals and trade unions as a left-wing rump at its fringes. From this view, Keir Hardie knew that it was time to give up on the Liberals. Similarly New Labour does not look saveable.

Christian socialist histories

In the context of a rapidly transforming global material environment, the usual Christian socialist histories are instead based around an idealist concept of history. We are presented with the ideals of those who wanted to change the poverty they saw around them. We are normally introduced to this history via a series of great men and occasionally, for the politically correct, women. We are then left to derive an ideological understanding of their importance to the forward march of socialism, which often culminates in New Labour or with the prosaic utterances of a Tony Blair or Stephen Timms. Rather like old-style theology, the history provides a context for these apostles of the labour movement; rarely is the political economy of these eras analysed in depth.[4] Even worse, when not rocking the electoral boat becomes all-consuming in the lust for power, any internal debate is seen as a reversal to the dark days of a powerless Michael Foot in the 1980s. 'Left' activists are marginalized from the people they need to 'convert' and are left hanging on to the old ideas of the faithful. In a minority for 100 years, today's left takes for its policies the old nationalizations and bureaucratic inheritance of Labourism. For all the highly creditable mobilization as a part of the opposition to the war, we have the impossible 'stop the war' slogan when it was clear to all with eyes to see that George II was going to war. Equally, we have the Christian Aid style NGOs, with less history to learn from, indulging in the equally impossible: to make poverty history in 2005. Angry with the spin from the top, the 'left' opposition indulges in the same ridiculous spinning. This is a re-run of the Gramscian perception of despair: 'pessimism of the intellect, optimism of the will' still going for another generation.

Morris and Christian socialism

Ironically, the attempt to create new ideas from the Christian constituency, and in the NGOs, is a remarkable reversion to the nationalist and protectionist, Little Britain style ideas of the Labour Party of the 1980s – now applied to Africa and Asia – quite unaware of their long history, especially in Latin America. All they have for a new economics is a cobbled together neo-Keynesianism with a social democrat glue.[5] We need to do far more than simply rehash the old ideas. We need to go back to rebuild, but taking on board the lessons of the last 100 years. Why then should William Morris have such a prominent place in this book? Morris was not a theologian, although he did have a puritanical evangelical upbringing and was originally intended for the Church. His moral sense links the English romantics of the late eighteenth century with the materially based political economy of Marxism in the late nineteenth century. This link between the ethical and the political, the moral and the material is what many are striving for today and the combination is vital to the critique of this book. As Part 2 tried to show, the left alternative needs to recognize the spirituality of power as well as its economics. This is why Morris is important as one ideological building block in looking back to look ahead. Being marginalized while looking for alternatives was a situation that Marx in the 1850s and Morris in the 1880s knew well. For both Christian socialists and Marxists can share what is ultimately a prophetic belief in the importance of applying lessons from history to the present and the future.

And utopias

Morris felt that his own critique of capital had led him to cross the river over to what appeared to be a 'Hades', where the anarchists, the socialists and the working classes struggled for a better life in the squalor of much of late-Victorian Britain. His time in politics was brief and a failure. Although many Labour leaders in particular from Lansbury to Attlee and Blair have claimed his influence, his 'utopianism' has not found favour in practical politics. As New Labour regresses even further historically to a position of complete accommodation to global capital, the argument in this book is that we need to call back the debates of the founding moments of what I have called British libertarian socialism. These traditions, which I hope to pursue in a forthcoming book, ultimately go all the way back to 1381, and through the Levellers in the seventeenth century, but we can find them highlighted again in the first 'modern' British socialist debates from the 1820s. I have chosen to use William Morris's libertarian or anarchist socialism as a focus through which to see these debates. For in them, we can see new insights for struggling against capital, against wage labour and against the state, which are not based on the corporate 'statist', mainstream routes of 1914 to 2005.

Meier begins his study of the influences on Morris by looking at 'God and the demons'. Morris, like Keir Hardie in his later life, took no part in religious observances, bar his daughter's baptism and a Marx memorial gathering, yet described his becoming a communist as a 'conversion' and as being 'born again'. His critique of the sterile conformity produced by the upper-class evangelical religion of his time, in which he had been reared, made it impossible to continue his vision in a theological vein. Religious conformity was one demon he had to resist. As he concluded, 'if there be a God, he or it, is a very different thing from what these religionists imagine'. He also saw very clearly the use of evangelical religion as the guardian of established order, the integral part it played in the state machine of Victorian Britain and its defence of the rights of capital in the name of private property. Despite his love of Catholic medievalism, he also eventually saw Catholicism had kept itself alive either by alliance with absolutist bureaucracy, as on the Continent, or in Britain, by its uneasy alliance with evangelicalism within the Church of England. But Morris also thought that 'if Christianity is a revelation addressed to all times it can not be neutral as to political and social institutions'. If he still loved the medieval heretics, he could champion men like John Ball, despite the fact that there is no religion and no clergy in *News From Nowhere*. As some conformist evangelicals rejected the Christian socialism of Maurice as not being Christian, Morris welcomed the Christian socialists into the broad fraternity of his socialist fellowship.[6] My 'utopianism' is however built upon a different strand, that of theological apocalyptic, which is both protest and vision; a protest against the global injustices of the present and a vision of a new heaven and a new earth that brings both healing for the individual and the nations.

Critic of imperialism: from Afghanistan to 1914

Morris, more eloquently than any other British socialist of his time, warned of the dangers of imperialism. His first involvement was in foreign affairs as a moral Gladstonian and he started with a critique of the Afghan War and of Disraeli who had 'an empty heart and a shifty head'.[7] By 1890, as Thompson describes it, Morris was already seeing imperialism as a 'major disaster bearing down on the European socialist movement'.[8] He was also warning of a 'regular epoch of war' to come. This was at a time when the Hyndman-led 'Marxist' Social Democratic Federation (SDF) were 'contradictory' on the subject of imperialism, the ILP 'evasive' (although Hardy, Mann and McDonald were not), and the Fabians were unambiguously pro-imperialist. Morris thereby clashed with the chauvinism, imperialism and dogmatism of Hyndman's appropriation of Marxism for his own ego in the early SDF of 1883–4.[9] Morris joined the SDF in January 1883, but was wary of Hyndman's imperialist views from the beginning and had resigned from it by December 1884. Morris's work on 'Socialism or Barbarism' pre-dates Rosa Luxemburg. He was concerned that the transformation to socialism could take place in an environment even more terrible and confused than the fall of Rome. He saw the collapse of the great powers 'pulling the roof of the world down upon its head'.[10] There has been no better prophet of both 1914 and the chaos of civil war in Russia in 1917 than Morris.

Critic of bureaucratic state socialism

If Morris certainly influenced later anarchist thinkers like Kropotkin, he was in turn able to gain from their critique of 'statism' and imperialism. Russian émigrés would be more aware of the dangers of the twentieth-century absolutist state, as against the liberal Empire of Victorian Britain. The dominance of 'statist' solutions, geared to an early centralized English state, has bedevilled British 'socialism' both from the right and even more from a left reared on the neutral state fantasies of the Fabians and ILP. (All 'we' have to do is seize the state via parliamentary elections preferably and all will be well.) For Morris, no number of merely administrative changes would bring about a genuine socialism, until ordinary people were in possession of power. Likewise, Morris's early critique of the Fabians and Labourism runs true to our experience over the last 100 years. Well before Hardie's public disillusion with radical Liberalism, never mind his later disillusion with the Labour Party, Morris was arguing against state socialism ('Quasi Socialist' machinery) that would make concessions to the working class while leaving the present system in operation. He concluded that 'any partial scheme ... is doomed to fail. It will be sucked into the tremendous stream of commercial production and vanish into it having played its part as a red herring to spoil the scent of revolution.'[11] Written in 1884, here is a reasonably accurate description of the British nationalized industries in 1985 before privatization finally killed them off. A 'socialism' that transformed capitalism only via 'quasi state machinery' would continue to be a 'tyranny'. His preferred solution for the twenty-first century was for the Houses of Westminster to be transformed into a place for storing 'dung'.[12]

Morris speaks of the 'Whig muddle of laissez faire' as 'backed up by coercion and smoothed by abundant corruption'; not a bad description of George Bush II's regime. Morris argued that if we failed to educate the people in real democratic socialism, we would end up with them being bought off in coalitions where 'Intelligent Tories and benevolent Whigs ... govern us kindly and wisely ... and rob us in moderation only'.[13] No better or more succinct description of New Labour could be found. Here is Blair, the intelligent Tory, and Brown, the temple robber, sitting in No 11 and for eight years running the country from the Treasury. In these words Morris also anticipated the British coalitions of 1917–21, 1931–45 and the Butskellite consensus of the 1950s.

We have previously discussed the Communist Manifesto as an analysis of 'globalization'. It is also important to look at its politics: in today's jargon, the policy options for 'governance'. The Manifesto was written as the Chartists were being defeated in England, and the 'liberal' parliamentary 'revolutions' failing on the Continent. For the Communist Manifesto, winning political power through the 'battle of democracy' was the best place to start; yet there was nowhere in the Europe of 1848 where universal suffrage existed. The Manifesto then looked for reforms which Marx and Engels knew exceeded the possibility of the existing regimes to deliver. Yet, some of the reforms – as apart from the revolutionary theoretical analysis – would make a huge practical difference. Such reforms, while being a benefit to ordinary people, are most unlikely to be delivered fully under capitalism. The aim is not only the reforms themselves, but is also to point out the limitations of today's global capital.

A revolutionary reform for Britain?

For now, I shall concentrate on only one of my major proposals, concerning capital. The other two on wage labour and the state will be pursued in later work. To challenge capital's control over our social production, I propose a reform of the voting structure of our capitalist corporations. The proposal on capital is to create in a capitalist corporation the same principle as in parliamentary democracy, that is of one person/one vote. I call it: one beneficial owner/one vote; or one share/one vote, a million shares/one vote. In effect, it would reverse the trend of the last 20 years and turn every joint stock company potentially into a mutually owned social co-operative.

The proposal on capital may not sound much of a reform but it is designed to attack and subvert the legitimacy of capital and capitalist thinking. To fully implement it would destroy the concepts lying behind capital's power over us. Under feudalism, after the Civil War and right up until the 1880s in Britain, the idea of one person/one vote appeared silly. Surely those with more property – with a greater stake in society – should have more say. This was the argument used by the barons for their role in Magna Carta. It was the argument used against the Levellers by Cromwell and also by Gladstone against votes for working men with no assets.[14] Most of the working class and all women were still disenfranchised in Britain until 1918. So, what appears an obvious principle to us now was revolutionary until 1918, and it took a 'total' war to bring it about. Capitalism – in terms of ownership and control – works on the same principle as the old parliaments prior to the 1832 Reform Act. Those who have the largest stakes get the biggest say. The old 'socialist' answer was of course to use the 'nation's' stake to nationalize the corporation with the idea that somehow the state would take on a mediating role and operate for all the people. We now know that partly because of the limitation of these nationalizations and the clear intention of not giving the workers any control, they did not work.[15] They could not possibly work today. You cannot take a globally owned and operating corporation like Royal Dutch Shell and run it for one nation.[16]

The key question remains: who owns and controls capital? Well, ironically, via other corporations with similarly differential access structures, 'we' all do. But as in 1880 and 1649, some have far larger stakes than others. (The Prudential used to own about

2 per cent of the entire British stock market.) My proposal would revolutionize the ownership of all publicly owned corporations at a parliamentary stroke. A trade union could buy a share and have as much power as the Prudential, any individual could have had a share in Manchester United and have as much say as Malcolm Glazer. The proposal is in effect to turn every public corporation into a voting co-operative, a mutual. We can't reform enough by creating 'our' own islands of mutuality (like, say, credit unions or the old co-op and 'mutual' friendly societies), while ignoring the power structure that dominates capitalist decision-making. The problem for so many failing mutuals has been that they have had to build up their capital base from scratch while still competing with joint stock companies, without any of their access to past capital accumulation. Now all would have access to the capital past generations have produced. This legislative change would be far more revolutionary than the parliamentary franchise. What I am also trying to avoid is a cumbersome structure, as to who has rights to sit on a board, as with the Bullock Committee Report of 1976. This would be like the worst of civil service government with endless committees and complicated bureaucracy. One intermediate step would be to establish the new voting principle and use it for electing subsidiary boards at global and national level in every country in which the company operates. The subsidiary board could learn from the German model and be given real responsibility for environmental issues, working conditions, pay and opportunities – eventually leading to the selection of the management and board. It would not be workers' control, but workers could have a vote each (if they bought a share each) and they could have a substantial say. It is a step close to workers' control, without an unnecessary bureaucracy, while recognizing that there are many other interests involved – local governments and consumer associations, for example.

The fight to control the surplus

Such a change would of course be resisted. At the very least, many companies will claim they already have subsidiary boards in some countries. Well, if so, they will just have to get used to new voting structures that the board cannot control so easily. I would expect most companies to fight these proposals to the death; we would certainly see the limits of existing politics. For the key is not about controlling 'markets', it is about who controls the accumulation of surplus and the uses to which it is put.

A major objection from the left would be that this reform leaves the capitalist and imperialist nature of global accumulation untouched. Without a huge further theoretical discussion, I would make one point here. There is nothing wrong in itself in any society with the process of surplus accumulation: all societies create a surplus, even if it is only food that it is consumed tomorrow rather than today. The key is that under capitalism, the joint stock company today largely controls and determines both the generation and allocation process, with governments blundering around in the middle. All I have suggested here is one method of showing how this dreadnought can be holed conceptually amidships. This would be a form of socialization and would keep the advantages of working in the 'market' economy. This is not to say that monopoly is not an issue, but that by attempting to control the corporation 'in the market' or through the state is to misunderstand the location of the problem.

Without a terrible bureaucratic structure to reflect the wider interests, a mutual structure of one vote per shareholder would be in place. This proposal would have the central government legislate a framework – across the European Union would be even better – but the state thereafter would not be in control. We have would started the process of taking the power away not only from the capitalist corporation, but also crucially from the capitalist state – by starting to give it back to civil society. Giving real power to ordinary people will mean being unable to predict the outcomes. It would be the first glimmer of an emancipation within the capitalist corporation. Of course, in this model, the medium term *financial* ownership would be unchanged. The Prudential would still have their 2 per cent with which to pay our insurances and endowment mortgages.

The crafty nature of this socialization is that it would not cost anything like the billions needed for nationalization with compensation. It is argued on the left that because of the nature of past accumulation no compensation should be paid. Theoretically, I agree no compensation is morally due. But what about the Dutch owners of Royal Dutch or the US owners of BP? Simply getting hold of the British affiliate would leave us with far less of the company and the foreign compensation issue would remain. My suggestion attempts to subvert this whole debate by focusing on voting power, which is what under the present system you are paying for. To 'nationalize', which of course is what Winston Churchill did first in BP's case, is actually playing the game by the capitalist – indeed, imperialist – rules.[17] The mutual corporation would be to re-create a new social and democratic control form within civil society with no compensation. You haven't nationalized, or changed the financial rules under which the companies operate, simply started to make them democratically accountable to ordinary people, without pretending that the state can do it.

It should not be surprising that New Labour has shown no interest whatsoever in revisiting the debates about worker directors. Instead, we have lots of bland PR about 'governance'. The attempt to introduce a stakeholder concept for corporate responsibility was first championed by Hutton: yet, the election of a Labour government had done little, as he puts it, to 'stem the tide' (of 'free market' thinking). The idea was picked up by Blair before the 1997 elections and then 'swiftly buried' like other bad news from 'fright, lack of intellectual support and the absence of open political pressure' – and from corporate opposition. Hutton writes correctly that most corporate annual general meetings have voting fixed in advance (largely via absentee institutional owners). Rather than have a proper debate with the 'left' on stakeholding in say health and education, policy has been pushed 'by stealth'.

A European context

Hutton is right to point to the lack of proper debate there has been about this on the 'left'. The pursuit of power has become so desperate after 18 years that creative attacks on capital were way off the agenda. Most importantly of all, Hutton is right to stress 'ownership matters', but is struggling to think this through given a totally inadequate analysis of the history of economic thinking; not helpful in one who claims a 'new economics is "struggling to be born"'.[18] The danger with 'stakeholder' reforms is that they become so meshed with the bureaucracies that their example will subvert and discredit the more revolutionary reform. In Yugoslavia, for example, where such ideas were tried under 'self management'; no one would join the board, because it was known, as with my own experience of local education, it was all responsibility and no real power.[19] It should be possible to learn the lessons of German experience of 'supervisory boards'; most of the big British companies with subsidiaries in Germany must have worked within their system. If it is impossible to convert the voting procedures in the short term, let's look at a 'stakeholder' route for appointing non-executive directors. As another intermediate step, I suggest lower tax rates for those companies setting up their own share ownership schemes, and new taxes on their UK revenues (not profits, for these get round transfer pricing) for those companies who resist or incorporate elsewhere.

Such 'revolutionary reforms' in Britain make even more sense in a European context. In terms of the pressures on the global corporations, my suggestions on mutualization, in particular, make most sense on a trans-European basis. It is possible that a BP would withdraw from incorporation and the British market to escape a more democratic voting structure, it would find it even harder to do so across all European markets. For much as Brown claims to the contrary, it is a joke to believe that any one chancellor, outside perhaps of the USA, controls the prospects for global bust and boom. Low interest rates and low inflation are largely the functions of the long-term global economy and have increasingly less to do with any country's control of its own exchange rate, monetary and fiscal policies. With massively increasing global manufacturing and agricultural production, it has taken the best efforts of European and US protectionism to keep a low rate of inflation, rather than the deflation we would have otherwise (as in Japan). Westminster can debate as much as it likes but the real power in economics, global trade, defence and foreign policy has shifted to the European level. Only the small states like Ireland, Scotland and Wales can admit that it makes more sense to see these powers move upwards (as they used to do to London) and get on with what they can influence locally. Watching devolving governments in Scotland and Wales here will be instructive: for it has given scope at the margins for socialist alternatives to New Labour. At the same time it has already left many Scots cynical about yet another layer of Scots mafia spending money with gay abandon on the new Scottish Parliament (and thereby appears to have weakened – maybe intentionally by New Labour – the nationalist position). Only England can pretend to operate like a great power and the great Iraq delusion was a part of this false sense of power.

Subverting empire

In a twenty-first century dominated at present by the ruling elite of a hegemonic superpower, masquerading under the labels of neoconservatism, or even worse of 'evangelical Christianity', transnational corporate capital rules supreme globally. Under what I have called the Global Capitalist Empire, it is vitally important that we relearn the lessons from Morris and the socialists who learnt the harsh truths about the global economy between 1850 and 1914. In 1911, Rosa Luxemburg argued that the peace 'utopias' of the ultra-imperialists like Kautsky would founder on the militarism of the Great Powers. Luxemburg linked militarism and imperialism to trade and tariff policies in a way that many global justice campaigners today have not yet been able to do so clearly: '[If governments] want to call a halt to the arms race they must begin to dismantle their trade policies and to give up their colonial raiding expeditions ... [and] their spheres of influence ... in short, in both foreign and domestic policies they must begin to do the exact opposite of what is now the very essence of capitalist class state politics.'[20]

In the biblical picture of the utopian life, on the other hand, people can enjoy the ownership and fruit of their own labour. The Old Testament picture of an ideal peasant society is thereby in favour of private property. This is why making the 'market' or private property, or even money, the evil is to quite misunderstand how capitalism works.

A Chilean economist (Mario Zanartu) put this well many years before the 'anti-globalization' critics tended to dominate the field, for such critics:

tend to leave capitalism un-defined [so they] include such elements [in their critique] like the market and price system,

... incentives, [and] competition to provide best productivity. They reject these elements with the same fervour as they reject capitalism without realising that they are independent of capitalism and are to be found, in different forms in every economic system.[21]

It is the private ownership of social production – capital – that is wrong, because to use a Blairist phrase positively for once, it gives power to the few and not the many. New Labour has admired this power, not done a thing to change it, and indeed has pursued policies largely to aid global capital. If we wish to build a new alternative vision of socialism, we will need to return to the roots and traditions of visionaries like Morris, against the ravages of an imperialist prime minister and his spin-doctor Iron Chancellor. The fight for a new co-operation, for better incomes and for a governance that does not lord it over the people is intimately linked to the fight against empire. Understanding the war in Iraq is a vital part of continuing the resistance to global capital. This is not a matter of understanding 'foreign policy' alone. What is done 'there', nakedly, to aid the penetration of capital is part and parcel of policies being pursued 'here'. We cannot 'move on' from empire and pretend that SATS results and hip operations are all that matter to ordinary people. Negri and Hardt put it like this: 'The passage to Empire and ... globalization offer new possibilities of liberation; our political task is not simply to resist but to re-organize ... Our struggle is to counter and subvert Empire – as well as to construct a real alternative.'[22] As a consequence, as the prophet Micah hoped: 'Nation will not take up sword against nation, nor will they train for war anymore. Every man will sit under his own vine and under his own fig tree and no one will make them afraid' (Mic. 4.3–4).

Under the Empire's fire

God may see my coming into being differently, but as far as I can humanly see, I am around today because my dad disobeyed orders: in May 1944, at the third battle of Casino, my dad stripped off his equipment, including bren gun and grenades, and told two younger Yorkshire lads to do the same. They were crossing the River Rapido at night in assault boats, under German shell and machine-gun fire. My dad's memory was hazy, but seconds or minutes later, the boat they were in was thrown on its side by an explosion and they were hurled into the fast-moving river. Everyone else loyally drowned at the bottom with all their equipment. Coming to a bank some way downstream, they were trapped by German fire in a gully for the rest of the day and another night. When the advance enabled them to raise their heads, my dad found one of his friends dead nearby, from whom he took his gun, so as to appear that he had not discarded his. On a human level, my father's instincts were good; having fought his way through North Africa and up Italy, he had a good sense of how to survive a war, which he was powerless to do anything about. He participated in a victory that in this phase of the battle of Casino he had done little to bring about; others died for him.[23] My grandad and dad fought for eight years between them in British imperial wars for 'democracy' and 'peace' in which they had been the poor bloody infantry, as outlined here in Chapter 3. Now my son heads off to do a Masters at LSE as the 'war on terror' is fought all around him. As I observe the consequences of the London bombings, I return again to lines in the introductory chapter to this book, first penned back in late 2002: 'No more than the Roman Empire, will the age of Bush and Blair and its fight against "global terrorism" bring peace and security. Today's Global Capitalist Empire will not bring peace or prosperity for all.' Both sentences stand equally true after the Gleneagles G8 and the London bombings of its opening day.

My critique of the Christian and NGO understanding of global capital has led me to suggest that the campaigners on debt and trade justice are also going to have some difficult rivers of understanding to cross, where the political and economic powers that be have to be seen for the ideological and spiritual power they wield. The political and economic critique of global capital surely leads us to the theology of the Cross, for empires crucify those who oppose their rule. Oscar Romero was shot because he asked the soldiers to obey 'God's law' not that of their officers. This threat to military discipline and the chain of command had to be faced down. Likewise, an empire will always remove an unwilling client king if it can, whether it be Herod Archelaus in Judaea or Saddam Hussein in Iraq. Fourteen months after Romero's death, on 14 May 1981, up to 600 peasants trying to escape El Salvador were drowned, bayoneted or shot by both Honduran and El Salvadorean anti-insurgency forces as they were attempting to cross the River Sumpal, the boundary between the two nations, under fire.[24] On the evening the Archbishop was killed, he preached on John's Gospel: 'Unless a grain of wheat falls to the earth and dies, it remains only a grain. But if it dies it bears much fruit' (12.23–6). Earlier he had said: 'if they kill me, I will rise again in the people of El Salvador. A Bishop will die, but the church of God – the people – will never die.'[25] Reflecting on Exodus, in his assessment of the state of liberation theology at the start of a new century, Sobrino concludes with a need for a stronger global economic vision. The cries of the people's oppression are still rising to heaven.[26] If we wish to proclaim the gospel and build a more just world, we will need an apocalyptic vision to see through the ideology of empire. When it comes to theology and political economy, we need to do more hard thinking to go with our action, if we are to help others avoid the fate of the young soldiers of May 1944 or of the peasants of El Salvador in May 1981. This is the hard river we have to cross.

Notes

Chapter 1

1. The first quote is from K. Wellesley, *The Long Year AD 69*, London, Elek, 1975, pp. 1–2. The second is from C. Tacitus, *The Histories*, London, Penguin, 1995, p. 16.

2. Details from descriptions of the firestorms in Dresden and Tokyo, at www.spartacus.schoolnet.co.uk.

3. www.towerstories.org. Put together by Damon DiMarco.

4. For Jesus' use of Daniel, see Chapter 6. The phrase 'devil's tinder-box' is from A. McKee, *Dresden 1945*, London, Souvenir Press, 1982.

5. See R. A. Horsley, *The Liberation of Christmas*, New York, Crossroad, 1989, pp. 40–2 and S. Perowne, *The Later Herods: The Political Background to the New Testament*, London, Hodder & Stoughton, 1958, p. 4. R. A. Horsley, *Archaeology, History and Society in Galilee*, Harrisburg, Trinity Press, 1996, p. 176.

6. See W. Barclay (ed.), *The Bible and History*, London, 1968, pp. 210–13, 226–7. K. Wengst, *Pax Romana and the Peace of Jesus Christ*, Fortress, 1987, p. 25 points out that both paid bribes to the Empire, off the peasants' labour.

7. B. W. Anderson, *The Living World of the Old Testament* (1958), London, Longman, 1993, p. 618 calls Daniel the 'theology of the Maccabean revolution'.

8. Barclay, *The Bible and History*, pp. 210–11.

9. N. T. Wright, *The New Testament and the People Of God*, London, SPCK, 1992, p. 160; R. A. Horsley, *Bandits, Prophets and Messiahs – Popular Movements in the Time of Jesus*, Harrisburg, Trinity Press International, 1985, pp. 46–7 and Barclay, *The Bible and History*, pp. 223–6.

10. G. Simons, *Iraq from Sumer to Saddam*, London, Macmillan, 1994, pp. 35–6.

11. Horsley, *Archaeology, History and Society*, pp. 21–9, 182. M. Hengel, *The Zealots: Investigations into the Jewish Freedom Movement from Herod*

Until 70 AD (1969), Edinburgh, T. & T. Clark, 1989, pp. 316–17.

12. Horsley, *Bandits, Prophets and Messiahs*, pp. 63–73; *The Liberation Of Christmas*, pp. 40–2; *Archaeology, History And Society*, pp. 27–30. Perowne, *The Later Herods*, p. 11.

13. On the division of Herod's kingdom, see Perowne, *The Later Herods*, pp. 8, 15–16. The effective division of Iraq into three regions by the no-fly zones roughly reflected the three separate Ottoman provinces prior to British rule: Basra (with a majority Shia community); the Baghdad region; and Mosul (where the Kurds are the majority). Committee Against Repression and For Democratic Rights in Iraq, *Saddam's Iraq: Revolution or Reaction*, London, Zed Press, 1986, p. 1.

14. Gore Vidal, *Permanent War for Permanent Peace*, Forest Row, Clairview Books, 2002, p. 20, quoting from the Princeton historian Charles Beard.

15. P. Schumpeter, *Imperialism and Social Classes*, New York, Kelley, 1989, p. 66. I first came across Schumpeter's work in this area through the editor's article 'US Imperial Ambitions and Iraq' in the *Monthly Review* (December 2002).

16. Wengst, *Pax Romana*, p. 2.

17. The Romans described the Empire and the emperor in what we would see today as religious language. Horace claimed that Augustus had 'wiped away our sins'. Horsley, *The Liberation of Christmas*, p. 26 and W. Howard-Brook and A. Gwyther, *Unveiling Empire: Reading Revelation Then And Now*, Maryknoll, Orbis, 1999 first introduced me to thinking about the 'theology of empire'. See also Horsley, *The Liberation of Christmas*, pp. 24–8 and particularly p. 27.

18. See N. T. Wright, *What St. Paul Really Said*, Oxford, Lion, 1997, pp. 46–7, 55–7, 88.

19. A. Negri and M. Hardt, *Empire*, Cambridge MA, Harvard University Press, 2000, p. xv.

20. N. Elliott, *Liberating Paul: The Justice of God and the Politics of the Apostle* (1994), Sheffield Academic Press, 1995, pp. ix–22, 188–215. The quote is from p. 195. 'Honouring Caesar' is taken from Stephen Timms' (Labour MP for East Ham) speech on the Christian Socialism archive at Sarum College, 26 April 2003.

21. See Negri and Hardt, *Empire*, pp. xi–xiv. On the Monroe Doctrine, see p. 177.

22. V. I. Lenin, *Imperialism: The Highest Stage of Capitalism* (1917), Moscow, Progress Publishers, 1982, particularly pp. 4–16. See also A. Brewer, *Marxist Theories of Imperialism: A Critical Study*, London, Routledge & Kegan Paul, 1980 pp. 2–7, 27.

23. R. Hilferding, *Finance Capital: A Study of the Latest Phase of Capitalist Development* (1910), London, Routledge & Kegan Paul, 1985, p. 331.

24. M. Curtis, *The Great Deception: Anglo American Power and World Order*, London, Pluto Press, 1998, pp. 35–41, 177–22.

25. Negri and Hardt, *Empire*, p. 225. See K. Marx and F. Engels, 'In bourgeois society, capital is independent', *The Communist Manifesto* (1848), London, Penguin, 1973, p. 81.

26. See J. Atherton, 'Religion and the Transcendence of Capitalism', unpublished paper, 2004.

27. J. Ruskin, *Unto This Last: Four Essays on the Principles of Political Economy* (1862).

28. See the thoughtful new look at the *Communist Manifesto* in Part 2 of D. Harvey, *Spaces of Hope*, Edinburgh University Press, 2000, p. 18.

29. Howard-Brook and Gwyther, *Unveiling Empire* opened my eyes to the book of Revelation as a sustained political, economic and spiritual critique of empire, as symbolized by Rome. On *apokalupto*, see p. 122.

30. See D. Jenkins, *Market Whys and Human Wherefores; Thinking again about Markets, Politics and People*, London, Cassell, 2000.

31. John Atherton has made an eloquent case for a reformulation of Christian political economy. See J. Atherton, *Marginalisation*, London, SCM Press, 2003, 'Reconnecting Economics, Ethics and Religion: Reflections on a Reformulated Tradition of Christian Political Economy', pp. 142f.

32. The first quote is from P. Meier, *William Morris: The Marxist Dreamer* (1972), Brighton, Harvester, 1978, p. viii, using R. Page Arnot's work *Morris: The Man and the Myth*, London, Lawrence & Wishart, 1964. It was in a speech entitled 'Appeal to Working-men'. The second quote is from Arnot, *Morris*, pp. 112–13.

33. K. Marx and F. Engels, *On Colonialism*, London, Lawrence & Wishart, 1976, p. 86.

34. See A. Rawnsley, *Servants of the People: The Inside Story of New Labour*, London, Penguin, 2000, p. xiii.

35. See E. P. Thompson, *Morris: Romantic to Revolutionary* (1955), London, Lawrence & Wishart, 1976 on crossing the river of fire pp. 244–5, 271–3. The quote is p. 244.

Chapter 2

1. W. W. Rostow, *Stages of Growth: A Non Communist Manifesto*, London, Cambridge University Press, 1960. Rostow stressed the multiple

causes of the stages of growth leading to an industrial and economic 'takeoff'.

2. On the Roman Empire, see R. Bauckham, *The Climax of Prophecy*, Edinburgh, T. & T. Clark, 1993, p. 362; on Athens, Anderson, *The Living World of the Old Testament*, p. 68; on Medieval Europe, M. Dobb, *Studies in the Development of Capitalism* (1946), London, Routledge & Kegan Paul, 1978, p. 72. On China, J. M. Roberts, *The Penguin History of the World* (1976), London, Penguin, 1995 pp. 440–1.

3. Achcar in Tariq Ali, *Masters of the Universe. Nato's Balkan Crusade?* London, Verso, 2000 argues that US military expenditures and planning post 1989 only make sense if the US worst case is a simultaneous Orwellian-style war against both Russia and China (p. 100). The importance of the statistical improvement in the Chinese standard of living for the falling numbers of those in global poverty in the last ten years was stressed by Clive Crook, deputy editor of the *Economist*, in debate with Ulrich Duchrow, at St Mary le Bow Church (Just Share Debate, February 2004).

4. This key difference between West and East Europe is central to Anderson's work in both his books. P. Anderson, *Passages from Antiquity to Feudalism* (1974), London, Verso, 1978, pp. 15–17, 234–7, 261–4 and *Lineages of the Absolutist State* (1974), London, Verso, 1980, pp. 430–1.

5. Barrington Moore Jr, *Social Origins of Dictatorship and Democracy. Lord and Peasant in the Modern World* (1966) London, Penguin, 1973. This work uses a historically based class analysis to understand political developments. It includes chapters on Japan, China and India; also see Anderson, *Lineages*, pp. 413–27.

6. See Chapter 4 for a critique of Ann Pettifor (ed.), *Real World Economic Outlook: The Legacy of Globalization – Debt and Deflation*, London, Palgrave, 2003; Christian Aid, *Trade Justice: A Christian Response to Global Poverty* (2004) and Christian Aid, *Taking Liberties: Poor People, Free Trade and Trade Justice* (2004).

7. Anderson, *Passages*, pp. 64–102; also see Roberts, *Penguin History of the World*, pp. 148, 510–12.

8. Marx and Engels, *On Colonialism*, pp. 46–53 was the first to point this out.

9. Marx argued that China still had a trade surplus until 1830, before the build up of the opium trade (Marx and Engels, *On Colonialism*, p. 20).

10. N. Chomsky, *Latin America. From Colonization to Globalization*, New Jersey, Ocean Press, p. 12 and H. Zinn, *A People's History of the United States. From 1492 to the Present* (1980), Harlow, Pearson Education, 1999 both date the capitalist world market from 1500 to roughly coincide

with the European colonial expansion in the Americas. I. Wallerstein, *The Capitalist World Economy*, Cambridge University Press, 1979, pp. 6–14 makes the capitalist agriculture of the sixteenth century the key and critiques Rostow's thesis.

11. This simplifies a huge debate on mercantile capitalism using E. Mandel, *Late Capitalism* (1975), London, Verso, 1980, pp. 48–9.

12. The two quotes are from D. Harvey, *Spaces of Hope*, Edinburgh University Press, 2000, pp. 7, 8 (see also pp. 3–17) and T. J. Gorringe, *Capital and the Kingdom: Theological Ethics and Economic Order*, London, SPCK, 1993, p. xi.

13. Atherton, *Marginalisation*, pp. 146–63 uses Sen in particular to advance his own dialogue with an ethical conventional economics. On Stiglitz, see Chapter 5.

14. On Hobson, see Chapter 1. G. Arrighi, *The Geometry of Imperialism: The Limits of Hobson's Paradigm*, London, Verso, 1978 goes back to Hobson to understand Lenin better (see pp. 23–4). Duchrow uses Arrighi's work in both of his major pieces on global capitalism, see U. Duchrow and F. J. Hinkelammert, *Property For People Not Profit: Alternatives to the Global Tyranny of Capital*, London CIIR, Zed Press, 2004, p. 29 and U. Duchrow, *Alternatives to Global Capitalism. Drawn from Biblical History, Designed for Political Action*, Kairos Europe, 1995, pp. 23–6.

15. Marx and Engels, *Communist Manifesto*, pp. 68, 71. I have substituted the word 'capital' where Marx and Engels used the word 'bourgeoisie'. Although both stressed the class nature of 'capital', I have used the more impersonal word to allow for the nature of the modern corporation rather more and the individual bourgeois owner rather less.

16. P. Heslam, *Unravelling the New Capitalism*, London, Grove Booklet, E125, 2002, p. 4 stresses that he is looking at 'technological' and 'economic' factors in globalization.

17. D. Harvey, *Limits to Capital*, Oxford, Blackwell, 1982, pp. xiv, 413.

18. Marx and Engels, *On Colonialism*, p. 303.

19. Duchrow and Hinkelammert, *Property For People Not Profit* discuss 'rebuilding the ownership system from below' pp. 166–72 and see the appendix pp. 225–7. This is discussed more fully in Chapter 9.

20. On Chile, see Duchrow and Hinkelammert, *Property For People Not Profit*, pp. x, 140. J. Diamond, *Guns, Germs and Steel. A Short History of Everybody for the Last 13,000 Years*, London, Vintage, 1998, pp. 68–81.

21. Quotes are from E. Williamson, *The Penguin History of Latin America*, London, Penguin, 1992 pp. 55 and 57.

22. On the silver trade, Williamson, *Penguin History of Latin America*, pp. 106–7.

23. Williamson, *Penguin History of Latin America*, pp. 38–42, 86–7, on the Brazilian population loss, p. 172.

24. A. G. Frank, *Capitalism and Underdevelopment in Latin America: Historical Studies in Chile and Brazil* (1967), London, Penguin, 1971, pp. 180–5; Williamson, *Penguin History of Latin America*, pp. 73, 182–3.

25. Williamson, *Penguin History of Latin America*, quotes pp. 69, 107, 195 and analysis pp. 69–115.

26. Williamson, *Penguin History of Latin America*, pp. 258–81.

27. Williamson, *Penguin History of Latin America*, p. 459; A. Maddison, *Economic Progress and Policy in Developing Countries*, London, Allen & Unwin, 1970, p. 18. Argentina's GDP/capita in 1870 was $1,700, compared to $2,000 in the USA, $2,700 in the UK and $1,600 in Germany. In 1900, although it had fallen way behind the USA ($2,800 compared to $4,000), it was still 40 per cent higher than Spain, more than double that of Russia, Mexico and Japan ($1,100) and four times that of Brazil ($700). See also C. F. D. Alejandro, *Essays on the History of the Argentine Republic*, New Haven CT, Yale, 1970.

28. Williamson, *Penguin History of Latin America*, pp. 142, 204–5, 218.

29. See P. J. Cain and A. G. Hopkins, *British Imperialism: Crisis and Deconstruction 1914–1990*, London, Longman, 1993, p. 147.

30. Williamson, *Penguin History of Latin America*, pp. 459–60; R. Munck, R. Falcon and B. Galitelli, *Argentina: From Anarchism to Peronism. Workers, Unions and Politics 1855–1985*, London, Zed Press, 1987, pp. 7, 13–14, 43, 71.

31. S. Levitsky, *Transforming Labour Based Parties in Latin America: Argentine Peronism in Comparative Perspective*, Cambridge University Press, 2003, p. 38.

32. Williamson, *Penguin History of Latin America*, pp. 459–62.

33. Munck, Falcon and Galitelli, *Argentina: From Anarchism to Peronism*, pp. 75–89.

34. The quote is from Cain and Hopkins, *British Imperialism*, p. 157. See their analysis pp. 154–61.

35. Munck, Falcon and Galitelli, *Argentina: From Anarchism to Peronism*, pp. 106–34.

36. The quote is from Munck, Falcon and Galitelli, *Argentina: From Anarchism to Peronism*, p. 193, see pp. 153–93

37. Munck, Falcon & Galitelli, *Argentina: From Anarchism to Peronism*, pp. 207–14; Williamson, *Penguin History of Latin America*, pp. 464–83.

38. Levitsky, *Transforming Labour Based Parties in Latin America*, pp. 50–3, 91–105, 123–46.

39. The quote is in Levitsky, *Transforming Labour Based Parties in Latin America*, p. 147. See also pp. 134, 183, 209–25.

40. See J. Petras and M. Morley, *Latin America in the Time of Cholera – Electoral Politics, Market Economics and Permanent Crisis*, London, Routledge, 1992, p. 15.

41. This section extensively draws upon D. Rock, 'Racking Argentina', *New Left Review* 17, September–October 2002, pp. 55–86.

42. See www.zmag.org, especially pieces by Roger Burbach, Alan Ciblis, Daniel Morduchowicz, James Petras and Gustavo Rubles.

43. E. Cozarinsky, 'Letter From Buenos Aires', *New Left Review* 26, March–April 2004, pp. 105–16.

44. Zinn, *A People's History*, does tell the story of violence against the common people in the USA; on slavery and land ownership (pp. 49, 59, 98); on building 'new' capitalism in the South (pp. 188–204); and on the defeat of the early US socialist and trade union movement (pp. 239–75).

45. M. Davis, *Prisoners of the American Dream. Politics and Economy in the History of the US Working Class*, London, Verso, 1986; *Dead Cities*. New York, New Press, 2002; 'Poor, Black and Left Behind', www.zmag. org, 24 September 2004. H. G. Wells wrote *War in the Air* in 1909, envisaging a Zeppelin attack on Manhattan leaving it 'a furnace of crimson flames [and] blazing conflagrations' (Davis, *Dead Cities*, pp. 1–2). On the rapture, see M. Northcott, *An Angel Directs the Storm: Apocalyptic Religion and American Empire*, London, I. B. Tauris, 2004, pp. 12–15, 46 whose chapter on this is also entitled 'the fading of the dream'.

46. P. Anderson, *A Zone of Engagement*, London, Verso, 1992 argues that Fukuyama's explanation is 'cavalier to a degree' (p. 334) in making 'cultural' factors central to his analysis of the black problem in the USA. Fukuyama is analysed in Chapter 4. Also see Znet (www.zmag.org/weluser.htm) writers on Hurricane Katrina, especially Michael Albert, Michael Cohen and Tom Engelhardt.

47. C. Myers, *Who Will Roll Away the Stone? Discipleship Queries for First World Christians* (1994), Maryknoll, Orbis, 1995. The two quotes are from p. xvi and p. 48. The Great Disruption is an oblique reference to Fukuyama.

Chapter 3

1. Solzhenitsyn's *August 1914* was his first major work after the 'Gulag' series, published in 1971. It was followed by *Lenin in Zurich* (1975). See also E. Hobsbawm, *Age of Extremes: The Short Twentieth Century 1914–1991* (1994), London, Abacus, 2001, p. 3.

Notes

2. Stockwell quoted in J. Turner, *Britain and the First World War*, London, Unwin Hyman, 1988, p. 36.

3. D. French, *British Strategy and War Aims: 1914–16*, London, Allen & Unwin, 1986, p. 233; and Turner, *Britain and the First World War*, p. 2.

4. A. J. P. Taylor, *Essays in English History* (1950), London, Hamilton, 1976, pp. 221–2; and Turner, *Britain and the First World War*, pp. 24–50.

5. On Barth, see T. J. Gorringe, *Karl Barth: Against Hegemony*, Oxford University Press, 1999, pp. 4, 35–6. On Temple, see A. Marrin, *The Last Crusade: The Church of England in the First World War*, Durham NC, Duke University Press, 1974, p. 94.

6. A. Wilkinson, *The Church of England and the First World War*, London, SPCK, 1978 quotes Virginia Woolf on the chasm (p. 13); J. Joll, *The Origins of the First World War*, London, Longman, 1984 p. 123 on Hardie.

7. Christopher Hill's work was important from the 1950s onwards in building on Tawney and providing a radical perspective on the English Revolution of the seventeenth century. Hill, *A Nation of Change and Novelty: Radical Politics, Religion and Literature in 17ᵀʰ Century England* (1990), London, Bookmarks, 2001, p. 72.

8. See N. Ferguson, *The Pity of War*, London, Penguin, 1998, pp. 32–3, 462. Stephen Poliakov's play *The Lost Prince* (18 Jan 2003 and 25 Jan 2003). The quotes from W. C. Sellar and R. J. Yeatman, *1066 And All That* (1930), London, Methuen, 1941 are pp. 113–14.

9. George Orwell quoted in J. Pilger, *Hidden Agendas*, London, Vintage, 1998, Preface; David Howell, *A Lost Left: Three Studies in Socialism and Nationalism*, Manchester University Press, 1986; F. Jamieson, *Postmodernism: Or, The Cultural Logic of Late Capitalism*, London, Verso, 1991 p. ix.

10. See Anderson, *Lineages of the Absolutist State*, p. 113–37, Barrington Moore, *Social Origins of Dictatorship and Democracy*, p. 420.

11. C. Hill brings this point out in his first published work: *The Economic Problems of the Church: from Archbishop Whitgift to the Long Parliament*, Oxford University Press, 1956, p. 343.

12. P. Anderson, in his seminal piece 'Origins of the Present Crisis' in 1964, now published in *English Questions*, London, Verso, 1992, pp. 15–21 especially. There is also a good summary of the thesis in G. Elliott, *Perry Anderson: The Merciless Laboratory of History*, University of Minnesota Press, 1998, p. 15.

13. 'Blatcherism' is used by J. Atherton, *Public Theology for Changing Times*, London, SPCK, 2000, p. 31, like 'Butskellism', to show the essential continuity of many of the policies – particularly with regard to global capital – under both Conservative and Labour governments since 1979.

14. Anderson, *Lineages of the Absolutist State*, pp. 236–66 explains how it came to be that Prussia was the dominant state in rebuilding the German Empire from 1525 to 1870.

15. Barrington Moore, *Social Origins of Dictatorship and Democracy*, p. 35.

16. R. Terrill, *R. H. Tawney & His Times: Socialism as Fellowship*, London, Harvard University Press, 1973 makes this point about Tawney (p. 84).

17. This is the theme of T. A. Brady, *Turning Swiss: Cities and Empire* 1450–1550, Cambridge University Press, 1985, Also see Anderson, *Lineages of the Absolutist State*, pp. 88, 301–2.

18. P. Blickle, *The Revolution of 1525: The German Peasants War from a New Perspective* (1977), Baltimore, Johns Hopkins, 1981, pp. xi–xii; and Barrington Moore, *Social Origins of Dictatorship and Democracy*, pp. 460–6.

19. The path-breaking account here was F. Engels, *The Peasant War in Germany* (1850), Moscow, Progress Publishers, 1977, but it was not translated into English until 1926. This is my summary of Engels p. 48 and Blickle, *The Revolution of 1525*, pp. xxii–xxiii.

20. Blickle, *The Revolution of 1525*, pp. 190 and 185. The destruction of the Radical Reformation elsewhere is described at great length in the classic piece by G. H. Williams, *The Radical Reformation* (1962), Missouri, Sixteenth Century Journal Publishers, 1992.

21. Engels, *The Peasant War in Germany*, p. 130; Blickle, *The Revolution of 1525*, p. 9.

22. Engels' second serfdom comes out of his analysis of *The Peasant War in Germany*, p. 172; Barrington Moore, *Social Origins of Dictatorship and Democracy*, pp. 436–7; Anderson, *Passages*, pp. 262–3.

23. E. J. Hobsbawm, *The Age of Revolution* (1962), London, Abacus, 1996, pp. 190–2 makes this point. Anderson, *Passages*, pp. 268–71 shows that although the Junker army was crushed by the revolutionary French army, the Junkers took most of the benefits of the new freedom, by buying much of the land released. (Much the same happened in Russia after 1861.)

24. Barrington Moore, *Social Origins of Dictatorship and Democracy*, quotes are pp. 38, 437 and 34–5; Bismarck is p. 440.

25. R. Dahrendorf, *Society and Democracy in Germany*, New York, Anchor, 1967, quotes are pp. 52, 61; K. D. Bracher, *The German Dilemma*, London, Weidenfeld & Nicholson, 1974, p. 119.

26. Z. S. Steiner, *Britain and the Origins of the First World War*, London, Macmillan, 1977, pp. 22–8, 70, 95–126, 216–24, 262; Joll, *Origins of the First World War*, pp. 34–46, 59–62, 105–16.

27. Bracher, *The German Dilemma*, p. 86.

28. Dahrendorf, *Society and Democracy in Germany*, p. 418; C. Fischer, *The German Communists and the Rise of Nazism*, London, Macmillan, 1991, p. xii; W. L. Shirer, *The Rise and Fall of the Third Reich. A History of Nazi Germany* (1959), Trowbridge, Secker & Warburg, 1985, p. 196.

29. On Germany, see K. Scholder, *A Requiem for Hitler and Other New Perspectives on the German Church Struggle* (1988), London, SCM Press, 1989. On England, see A. Hastings, *A History of English Christianity 1920–1990*, London, SCM Press, 1991, particularly pp. 377–80, 399–400.

30. B. Semmel, *Imperialism and Social Reform: 1895–1914*, London, Allen & Unwin, 1960, pp. 13, 23, 55.

31. W. Kent, *John Burns: Labour's Lost Leader*, London, Williams & Norgate, 1950, p. 98; R. P. Price, *An Imperial War and the British Working Class*, University of Toronto, 1972, pp. 1, 12.

32. The quote is from Joll, *Origins of the First World War*, p. 2. See also pp. 34–47; Steiner, *Britain and the Origins of the First World War*, pp. 40–6, 65–93, 127–9; and French, *British Strategy and War Aims: 1914–16*, p. 1.

33. French, *British Strategy and War Aims: 1914–16*, p. 15 and Steiner, *Britain and the Origins of the First World War*, pp. 125–6 on a short war; Stockwell in Turner, *Britain and the First World War*, pp. 36–41 on the Imperial War Cabinet.

34. A credit of £3.7 billion in the USA in 1914, for example, was turned round in four years to an equivalent level of debt. See R. W. D. Boyce, *British Capitalism at the Crossroads: 1919–32. A Study in Politics, Economics and International Relations*, Cambridge University Press, 1987, p. 131.

35. The Anglo-French Entente of 1904 had led to a joint military study of a possible German attack through Belgium as early as 1905 (Joll, *Origins of the First World War*, p. 84).

36. See for all of this part, G. Simons, *Iraq from Sumer to Saddam*, London, Macmillan, 1994; on the Wahhabis' violent history, p. 180. For a recent Christian theologian's overview see Northcott, *An Angel Directs the Storm*, especially pp. 32–3, on the Wahhabis in his section from the Cold War to the Holy War.

37. The Iraqis could claim with some justice in 1990 that, to use Saddam's phrase, 'Kuwait was a State built on an oil well.' Simons, *Iraq from Sumer to Saddam*, p. 342; see also pp. 208–10, 341–5.

38. Simons, *Iraq from Sumer to Saddam*, pp. 184–7, 196–7.

39. N. Ferguson, 'Clashing Civilizations or Mad Mullahs: the United States Between Formal and Informal Empires' in S. Talbott and N.

Chanda (eds), *The Age of Terror. America and the World after September 11*, New York, Basic Books, 2001, p. 116.

40. The 'proclamation' of Baghdad reads: 'our armies do not come into your cities and lands as conquerors and enemies, but as liberators', quoted by Robert Fisk in the *Independent*, 17 June 2004.

41. The quote from Churchill is Simons, *Iraq from Sumer to Saddam*, p. xvi and his own p. 216; see also pp. 210–16. See Curtis, *The Great Deception* for the Bomber Harris quote (p. 136). Curtis also notes that in the same era Afghanistan, Somaliland and the Nuer in the Sudan were bombed (pp. 135–7).

42. Simons, *Iraq from Sumer to Saddam*, quote is p. 201; see also pp. 217–20, 232, 244 and p. 18 (for Saddam).

43. Even then, the CIA arranged a coup in Syria in 1958. Curtis, *The Great Deception*, pp. 129, 250; Simons, *Iraq from Sumer to Saddam*, p. 267.

44. Simons, *Iraq from Sumer to Saddam*, pp. 55–7, 256–63, 269–86, 334, 345–9, 353. On Bin Laden, see Northcott, *An Angel Directs the Storm*, pp. 31–5.

45. I look at the history of globalization in Chapter 5.

46. W. Hutton, *Observer*, 3 July 2005.

47. This debate is briefly summarized in Lenin's *Imperialism* pp. 10–12.

Chapter 4

1. F. Fukuyama, *The End of History and the Last Man*, London, Hamish Hamilton, 1992.

2. F. Fukuyama, *The Great Disruption: Human Nature and the Reconstruction of Social Order*, London, Profile, 1999. On Fukuyama's career, see the Guardian Education website. It is worth noting that Blair was especially keen to speak on his new interventionist foreign policy at the Economic Club of Chicago. See J. Kampfner, *Blair's Wars* (2003), London, Free Press, 2004, p. 50.

3. On Fukuyama, see N. Chomsky, *Hegemony or Survival. America's Quest for Global Dominance* (2003), London, Penguin, 2004, p. 29. Tariq Ali, *The Clash of Fundamentalisms – Crusades, Jihad and Modernity*, London, Verso, 2002, pp. 246, 272–3, 283.

4. For more on Wolfowitz, see Kampfner, *Blair's Wars*, pp. 18, 24,138 and www.en.wikipedia.org

5. UK Department for International Development, *Eliminating World Poverty: Making Globalization Work For the Poor*, London, HMSO, 2000 pp. 4–5, 10–11, 15. Rawnsley, *Servants of the People*, p. xiv

6. See Yao Graham, 'Africa's Second Last Chance', *Red Pepper*, July

2005 p. 24–6. J. Markakis, *National and Class Conflict in the Horn*, Cambridge University Press, 1987, p. xvi comments that he had to go back 100 years to understand the origins of current conflicts.

7. See W. Rodney, *How Europe Underdeveloped Africa* (1972), London, Bogle L'Ouverture Publications, 1978, p. 71. The quote from Churchill is in S. McCarthy, *Africa: The Challenge of Transformation*, London, I. B. Tauris, 1994, p. 93. Likewise, McCarthy pointed out ten years ago that the usual explanations for Africa's problems – trade, debt and corruption – are too 'simplistic' (p. xvi).

8. McCarthy, *Africa*, pp. 76–7. The quote on India is from Marx and Engels, *On Colonialism*, p. 81.

9. McCarthy, *Africa*, p. 131 and World Bank Development Reports. Coffee exports from Ethiopia (population 30 million) between 1965 and 1975 were barely greater than El Salvador's (population 5 million). F. Halliday and M. Molyneux, *The Ethiopian Revolution*, London, Verso, 1981, p. 69.

10. The Somalis were spread around Somalia itself, French Djibouti, British Somaliland, Italian Somalia and British Kenya. Markakis, *National and Class Conflict in the Horn*, p. 30.

11. On African elites with a rural interest, see McCarthy, *Africa*, p. 145. A typical financial city of antiquity – Tyre – is discussed theologically in Chapter 6.

12. F. Morrison, *Who Moved the Stone?* (1930), London, Faber, 1958; D. K. Fieldhouse, *Economics And Empire: 1830–1914* (1976), London, Macmillan, 1984, pp. 118–23; L. James, *Rise and Fall of the British Empire* (1994), London, Abacus, 2001, p. 269.

13. Fieldhouse, *Economics And Empire*, pp. 261–68, 381; G. Brown, *Maxton* (1986), Edinburgh, Mainstream, 2002, pp. 51–72.

14. D. F. Calhoun, *Hungary and Suez, 1956. An Exploration of Who Makes History*, Lanham MD, University Press of America, 1991, p. 8; P. Mansfield, *The British in Egypt*, London, Weidenfeld & Nicholson, 1971, p. xi.

15. R. L. Tignor, *Capitalism and Nationalism at the End of Empire. State and Business in Decolonizing Egypt, Nigeria and Kenya 1945–63*, New Jersey, Princeton University Press, 1998, pp. 27–30; M. Hussein, *Class Conflict in Egypt: 1945–70* (1969), New York, Monthly Review Press, 1977, p. 55. D. Hopwood, *Egypt: Politics and Society 1945–90* (1982), London, Harper Collins, 1991, pp. 1, 14, 17–21; Mansfield, *The British in Egypt*, pp. 101–11, 211–48. Rural landlessness continued to increase from 24 per cent of the population in 1929 to 38 per cent in 1938 to 44 per cent in 1950.

16. On Qutb and the Muslim Brotherhood in Egypt, see Northcott, *An Angel Directs the Storm*, pp. 38–9; Tariq Ali, *The Clash of Fundamentalisms*, pp. 95–6, 101–3. On Sadat and Mubarak, see J. K. Cooley, *Unholy Wars. Afghanistan, America and International Terrorism* (1999), London, Pluto, 2002, pp. 22–3, 159–60.

17. J. M. Jok, *War and Slavery in the Sudan*, Philadelphia, University of Pennsylvania Press, 2001 pp. viii, 1, 153; D. H. Johnson, *The Root Causes of Sudan's Civil Wars*, London, The International African Institute, 2003, pp. 2–7; L. B. Deng, 'The Sudan Famine of 1998', Brighton, *Institute of Development Studies Bulletin*, October 2002, Volume 33 Number 4, p. 28. On Bin Laden's role in the Sudan, see Cooley pp. 95–102.

18. B. Vandervort, *Wars of Imperial Conquest in Africa, 1830–1914*, Bloomington, Indiana University Press, 1998, pp. 179–82; R. O. Collins, *Shadows in the Grass. Great Britain in the Southern Sudan, 1918–56*, New Haven, Yale University Press, 1983, pp. 9–11, 21–31; James, *Rise and Fall of the British Empire*, pp. 283–6.

19. R. First, *The Barrel of a Gun. Political Power in Africa and the Coup D'Etat*, London, Penguin, 1970. The quote is p. 125 and see pp. 125–7.

20. Johnson, *The Root Causes of Sudan's Civil Wars*, pp. 21–77; Fieldhouse, *Economics and Empire*, p. 363; Cain and Hopkins, *British Imperialism*, p. 21; Collins, *Shadows in the Grass*, p. 455.

21. Markakis, *National and Class Conflict in the Horn*, pp. 28–9, 77. First, *The Barrel of a Gun*, p. 127–42, 222, 228, 242–62.

22. Markakis, *National and Class Conflict in the Horn*, pp. 82–4, 161, 344–6; M. Barratt-Brown, *Africa's Choices after Thirty Years of the World Bank*, London, Penguin, 1995, p. 104.

23. First, *The Barrel of a Gun*, pp. 272–7; Johnson, *The Root Causes of Sudan's Civil Wars*, pp. 58–69.

24. M. Meredith, *The State of Africa. A History of Fifty Years of Independence*, New York, Free Press, 2005, pp. 35, 344–5, 595. Jok, *War and Slavery in the Sudan*, pp. 5, 12–27, 46, 69, 107, 127, 147–8; Markakis, *National and Class Conflict in the Horn*, pp. 208–15; Johnson, *The Root Causes of Sudan's Civil Wars*, pp. 58–60, 82–114. On Garang see the *Guardian* 3 August 2005. On oil, *BP Statistical Review of the World Oil Industry* and Deng, 'The Sudan Famine of 1998', p. 34.

25. C. Leys, *Underdevelopment in Kenya: The Political Economy of Neo-Colonialism*, London, Heinemann, 1975, pp. 28–40. Barratt-Brown, *Africa's Choices*, p. 53

26. Christian Aid, *Taking Liberties*, p. 8.

27. M. Mamdani, *Politics and Class Formation in Uganda*, New York,

Notes

Monthly Review Press, 1976, pp. 23–54; J. J. Jorgensen, *Uganda: A Modern History*, London, Croom Helm, 1981, pp. 35–56.

28. Fieldhouse, *Economics And Empire*, pp. 381–3; Mamdani, *Politics and Class Formation in Uganda*, pp. 73–127; Jorgensen, *Uganda*, pp. 61–88.

29. Simons, *Iraq from Sumer to Saddam*, pp. 360–1, 368. Markakis, *National and Class Conflict in the Horn*, suggests Ethiopia expanded to twice its old size in the late nineteenth century (p. 91). On the British Protectorate, see Cain and Hopkins, *British Imperialism*, p. 212.

30. Halliday and Molyneux, *The Ethiopian Revolution*, pp. 51–6, 214–5. J. Young, *Peasant Revolution in Ethiopia – The Tigray Peoples Liberation Front 1975–91*, Cambridge University Press, 1997 shows how the regionally based TPLF overthrew the Derg.

31. Halliday and Molyneux, *The Ethiopian Revolution*, pp. 61–9.

32. See S. Hodkinson, 'Make the G8 History', *Red Pepper*, July 2005, pp. 20–23; Chomsky, *Hegemony or Survival*, p. 11. On Barbara Stocking, see the Oxfam website.

33. P. Cammack, 'Blair's Commissioners', *Red Pepper*, July 2005, p. 25; L. Michaels, 'Our Corporate Interest', *Red Pepper*, July 2005, pp. 28–30.

34. The vampire state is Barratt-Brown, *Africa's Choices*, quoting Frimping Ansah (on Ghana), p. 369.

Chapter 5

1. Mayo's Foreword quoted in A. Pettifor (ed.), *Real World Economic Outlook: The Legacy of Globalization – Debt and Deflation*, London, Palgrave, 2003 pp. xiii–xiv.

2. M. Northcott, *Life After Debt: Christianity and Global Justice*, London, SPCK, 1999, pp. 12–13.

3. Jubilee Plus, *How It All Began; Causes Of the Debt Crisis*, Beginners Guide, 2001, www.jubileeresearch.org.

4. S. George and F. Sabelli, *Faith and Credit: The World Bank's Secular Empire*, Boulder, Westview Press, 1994, pp. 40–51. Curtis also looks at the World Bank and WTO, *The Great Deception*, pp. 75–80.

5. The critique of Christian Aid here draws on *Trade Justice: A Christian Response to Global Poverty*, Church House Publishing, 2004 and *Taking Liberties: Poor People, Free Trade and Trade Justice*, Christian Aid, 2004.

6. The dangers of appealing to the 'better nature of the strong' comes ironically from Michael Taylor, ex-director of Christian Aid, in M. Taylor, *Not Angels But Agencies: The Ecumenical Response to Poverty: A Primer*, London, SCM Press, 1995, p. 87. Curtis, *The Great Deception*, p. 213.

7. E. J. Hobsbawm, *Industry and Empire* (1968), London, Penguin, 1990, pp. 135–8, 144–52, 479. For the impact of imperial preference on Argentina, see Chapter 2.

8. Marx and Engels first use the term the 'heavy artillery of cheap commodities' as early as in *The Communist Manifesto* (1848), in *Political Writings Volume 1*, London, Penguin, 1973, p. 71.

9. See P. Q. Hirst and G. Thompson, *Globalization in Question: The International Economy and the Possibilities of Governance*, London, Polity, 1999. In the most extreme case, in the UK mercantile trade as a percentage of GDP was still lower in 1990 than in 1913 (63 vs. 76 per cent) (p. 64).

10. See E. Mandel, *Late Capitalism* (1972), London, Verso, 1980, pp. 58–9.

11. E. J. Hobsbawm, *The Age of Empire* (1987), London, Abacus, 1995 on prices and tariffs pp. 35–9.

12. C. P. Kindleberger, *The World in Depression 1929–39*, London, Allen Lane, 1973, p. 139. Kindleberger remains the best international monetary and economic historian of this era.

13. See Hobsbawm's excellent discussion in *The Age of Empire*, pp. 56–73.

14. See R. W. D. Boyce, *British Capitalism at the Crossroads: 1919–32. A Study in Politics, Economics and International Relations*, Cambridge University Press, 1987, p. 58.

15. Roberts, *Penguin History of the World*, p. 879; Kindleberger, *World in Depression*, p. 66.

16. See D. Rothermund, *The Global Impact of the Great Depression*, London, Routledge, 1996, pp. 33–51, Kindleberger, *World in Depression*, p. 83–8, and Hobsbawm, *Industry and Empire*, p. 211.

17. See J. Atack and P. Passell, *A New Economic View of American History from Colonial Times to 1940*, New York, Norton, 1994, pp. 575–6; Kindleberger, *World in Depression*, pp. 77–97, Boyce, *British Capitalism at the Crossroads* pp. 62–3.

18. See J. K. Galbraith's *Great Crash 1929* (1954), London, Penguin, 1992, pp. 31–37, 45, 60–3, 88–91, 155, 191. This is still the classic read on the 1929 Stock Market Crash. But it is too US dominated in its thinking to cover both the international preludes (other European markets fell earlier) or implications. See also Kindleberger, *World in Depression*, pp. 59–74; Atack and Passell, *New Economic View of American History*, pp. 579–80, 607.

19. See Boyce, *British Capitalism at the Crossroads* p. 70–1; Hobsbawm, *Industry and Empire*, p. 213.

20. See Kindleberger, *World in Depression*, pp. 34, 41–3, 79–80; Galbraith, *Great Crash*, pp. 48–9.

21. Stiglitz in Pettifor, *Real World Economic Outlook*, p. 42.

22. For a British analysis of the domestic political implications see an old classic, R. Skidelsky, *Politicians and The Slump: The Labour Government of 1929–1931*, London, MacMillan, 1967, esp. pp. 371–83; and a newer one, P. Williamson, *National Crisis and National Government: British Politics, the Economy and Empire 1926–32*, Cambridge University Press, 1992, pp. 286–301. Also see Atack and Passell, *New Economic View of American History*, p. 600–11; and Kindleberger, *World in Depression*, p. 122.

23. Pettifor, *Real World Economic Outlook*, pp. 7–8. The tendency towards a conspiracy theory is very strong in this book and particularly reflected in the analysis of finance. On Hitler, the Jews and Finance, see Hobsbawm, *The Age of Empire*, p. 89.

24. The IMF Charter sums this up well in its very first Article. The IMF aimed to 'facilitate the expansion and balanced growth of international trade'. See H. James, *International Monetary Co-operation Since Bretton Woods*, New York, IMF, OUP, 1996, p. 1.

25. See Pettifor's executive summary, *Real World Economic Outlook*, p. xxv.

26. See D. Harvey, *Spaces of Hope*, p. 13.

27. Tariq Ali (ed.), *Masters of the Universe: Nato's Balkan Crusade*, London, Verso, 2000, p. 24.

28. See N. Harris, *The End of the Third World: Newly Industrialising Countries and the Decline of an Ideology*, London, Penguin, 1986, pp. 70–92.

29. See A. G. Frank, *Capitalism and Underdevelopment in Latin America: Historical Studies in Chile and Brazil* (1967), London, Penguin, 1971.

30. Atherton, *Marginalisation* points to Sweden and Japan (pp. 158–60); Heslam, *Unravelling the New Capitalism*, especially pp. 5–11.

31. W. Hutton, *The State We're In* (1995), London, Vintage, 1996 is the basis for my critique of Hutton's work on Japan (pp. 268–77) and Germany (pp. 262–8). For a far better historical analysis of Japan, see Barrington Moore, *Social Origins of Dictatorship and Democracy*.

32. This paragraph stems from a critique of Duchrow's attempt to read across from East Asia to Latin America. See Duchrow and Hinkelammert, *Property For People Not Profit*, pp. 149–50.

33. For a historical background to the recent incorporation of Georgia and the Ukraine see S. Goldenberg, *The Pride of Small Nations: The Caucasus And Post Soviet Disorder* London, Zed 1994; A. Wilson, *The Ukrainians: Unexpected Nation*, Yale University Press, 2000.

34. See R. Evans, *Deng Xiaoping and the Making of Modern China* (1993), London, Penguin, 1995, p. 215.

35. See A. Shastri and A. J. Wilson, *The Post Colonial States of South Asia*, Richmond, Curzon, 2001 on the Indian turn to further liberalization after the balance of payments crisis of 1991 and the lower middle-class support base of the BJP (pp. 224–31).

36. One quick summary of the role of the Brazilian military to 'manage' an industrializing coalition is in J. Sheahan, *Early Industrialization and Violent Reaction*, Brighton, Institute of Development Studies, University of Sussex Discussion Paper 176, 1982, pp. 19–20. Sheahan also notes how such repressive military governments cling to protection (p. 14).

37. McCarthy, *Africa*, p. 144 makes precisely the point as to what happened when markets were protected in Africa.

38. This is taken from Peter Heslam's 2003 attempt for JustShare to summarize the case against capital liberalization and for 'financial recovery', in common with much of the Christian Aid and Trade Justice material.

39. See Northcott, *Life After Debt*, p. 169; and J. Stiglitz, *Globalization and its Discontents*, London, Penguin, 2002. Stiglitz's analysis of the reasons for the East Asian crisis of 1997–8 only takes a few pages (pp. 88–94) and has no real history. Most of his work concentrates on the IMF policy reactions after the event (pp. 94–132). Hirst and Thompson, *Globalization in Question*, pp. 143–50.

40. P. Selby, *Grace and Mortgage; The Language of Faith and the Debt of the World*, London, Darton, Longman and Todd, 1997, p. 68.

41. See S. George, *The Lugano Report: On Preserving Capitalism in the 21ˢᵗ Century*, London, Pluto, 1999.

42. See Northcott, *Life After Debt*, p. 16; and Luke 4.14–30.

Chapter 6

1. Chris Rowland writes that the 'boundaries of acceptable exegesis begin to crumble' (p. 5) and sees social ethics as being of the essence of the gospel, not just its consequence. See C. Rowland and M. Corner, *Liberating Exegesis. The Challenge of Liberation Theology to Biblical Exegesis*, London, SPCK, 1990, pp. 2–12.

2. See Moltmann's essay on 'Theology and its Problems Today' in *The Experiment Hope: Collected Essays*, London, SCM Press, 1975.

3. W. R. Herzog, *Jesus, Justice and the Reign of God. A Ministry of Liberation*, Louisville, John Knox Press, 2000, pp. xi–xii, 3–9.

4. Along with C. Myers, *Binding the Strong Man: A Political Reading*

of Mark, Maryknoll, Orbis, 1988, Horsley's work has been a major influence, first through R. A. Horsley and J. S. Hanson, *Bandits, Prophets and Messiahs – Popular Movements in the Time of Jesus*, Harrisburg, Trinity Press International, 1985. It has been a great disappointment that although Tom Wright has done pioneering work on Paul and *The Challenge of Jesus*, London, SPCK, 2000, his own recent 'popular' commentary on *Mark For Everyone*, London, SPCK, 2001, completely fails to recognize the implications for a gospel commentary raised even by his own work.

5. J. Milbank, *Theology and Social Theory. Beyond Secular Reason*, Cambridge University Press, 1994, in his last chapter, speaks of the theoretical need for a Christian/theologically based social theory. Unlike Milbank who approaches this task philosophically via intellectual history, I have begun through the practice of a material history of contemporary global capitalism. So, as with Herzog, the gospels are 'proto-types of an on-going task' (*Jesus, Justice and the Reign of God*, p. 252).

6. See Michael Taylor, 'How to Overcome: A Third Way?' Paper presented at Sarum College, Summer 2004.

7. Clinton Black's recent survey *Mark: Images of an Apostolic Interpreter*, Edinburgh, T. & T. Clark, 2001, on the history of Mark exegesis has no reference to Myers' work. Horsley is not mentioned either but since his work on Mark was in the same year, this is perhaps understandable. Mainstream academic exegesis has simply not taken on board radical work like this.

8. Rowland and Corner, *Liberating Exegesis*, speak in a British tradition of the 'sad distancing' of 'new methods' from the people and of the 'arcane enterprises of the academic elite' (pp. 38–9). I would argue that it is not just about methods, but also about essence, attitudes and hermeneutics.

9. R. P. Martin, *Mark: Evangelist and Theologian* London, Paternoster, 1972. Martin, however, can only see the subversion in the scandal of a gospel being used to refer to a written book for the first time (pp. 12, 22–8).

10. Rowland and Corner, *Liberating Exegesis*, also write of Matthew's Gospel recalling a 'subversive memory' that 'sits light' on doctrinal purity (p. 141).

11. For the best description of the political meaning of 'gospel' in the Roman Empire, see C. Myers and others, *Say To This Mountain: Mark's Story of Discipleship*, Maryknoll, Orbis, 1996, pp. 5–6.

12. The idea that 'anointing' stresses a king's popular legitimacy I first came across in Horsley and Hanson, *Bandits, Prophets and Messiahs*, p. 94. In this sense, a messiah is closer to being a president or a prime minister – by popular acclamation like King David – while today we tend to think of a king as hereditary.

13. Both quotes are from Myers, *Binding the Strong Man*, pp. 39 and 40.

14. R. A. Horsley, *The Message and the Kingdom. How Jesus and Paul Ignited a Revolution and Transformed the Ancient World* (1997), Augsburg Fortress, 2002, p. 5 and in *Hearing the Whole Story: The Politics of Plot in Mark's Gospel*, Louisville, John Knox Press, 2001 R. A. Horsley compares Galilee with Afghanistan (pp. 27, 37). Herzog using Paulo Freire's phrase, calls it a 'pedagogy of the oppressed' (*Jesus, Justice and the Reign of God*, p. 47).

15. Myers, *Binding the Strong Man* emphasizes the importance of Galilee in Jesus' ministry in Mark; this subsequently influences all the Synoptic Gospels. Horsley argues that Mark is about 'the people of Galilee' not the 'Jews' (*Hearing the Whole Story*, pp. 37–8). He argues that it was the Romans who lumped all these people together as 'Jews'; rather like the USA with regard to 'Iraqis' (p. 46).

16. Black argues that despite the traditional attempt to link 'Mark' to the John Mark of Acts, the 'personality of Mark is irretrievable' (*Mark*, p. xiii). Martin stresses that Mark reads like an eyewitness account. In the second century, the link with Peter was first made by Papias and helped give the Gospel apostolic authority. See V. Taylor, *The Gospel According to St Mark*, London, Macmillan, 1951 pp. 1–8, 26–30 and Black, *Mark*, pp. 82–5, 118–27, 200, 242.

17. Horsley, *Hearing the Whole Story*, pp. vii, 3. More conventional commentators like Martin also emphasize that Mark should be seen as a 'literary whole' (*Mark*, p. 47).

18. M. Hooker, *The Message of Mark*, London, Epworth, 1993, p. 17; Taylor quoting Torrey on Aramaic (*Gospel According to Mark*, pp. 21, 31); Myers, *Say to this Mountain*, p. 1. The poor quality of Mark's Greek may explain the disdain of ancient and modern scholars, so often classically trained, and the preference for Matthew.

19. These quotes are the starting points of Myers' books: on apocalyptic (*Binding the Strong Man*, p. xxvii) and from Isaiah (*Say to this Mountain*, p. xv).

20. In Kee's analysis of five chapters of Mark (11—16), there are 57 Old Testament allusions: 12 from Daniel, 21 from other prophets, 12 from the Psalms and 2 from the historical books. This is reflected in the rest of the Gospel. Of the 160 allusions to the Old Testament in the Gospel, 50 per cent are from the prophets and 12 per cent from Daniel alone with roughly similar proportions to Daniel from the Torah and the Psalms (Myers, *Binding the Strong Man*, p. 98).

21. The critical early twentieth-century debate on Mark was first estab-

lished by Wrede's work on *The Messianic Secret*, written in 1903. Wrede argued that Jesus did not see himself as the Messiah so the early church belief, as represented in the Gospels, was to make it appear that his messianic role had to be kept a secret.

22. The argument I present here instead is a harshly realistic political one: whatever one's view about the nature of this messiah, the 'messianic secret' stems from the fact that it was far too dangerous for Jesus to proclaim it loudly.

23. See Myers, *Binding the Strong Man*, pp. 101–3. Even Myers tends to slide back into seeing apocalyptic as a 'literary tradition'. His own analysis implies that although the politics of the protest tradition clearly has literary outcomes, it is not just a 'literary strategy'.

24. The Latinisms are discussed in Myers, *Binding the Strong Man*, p. 95; 'Empire America' is from pp. 6–7 and the quote on the present-day usage of apocalyptic is p. xxvi.

25. Horsley notes that in 1.21–8 there are 10 'ands' (*Hearing the Whole Story*, p. 15) and appends to his book a literal translation (p. 255).

26. The Myers quote is *Binding the Strong Man*, p. 91 and his analysis, pp. 92–7.

27. Hooker makes the point that this is Mark's only direct Old Testament quote. Horsley, stressing the impact of what would have been an oral delivery in the early church, argues that in fact Mark has run together remembered quotes from Malachi 3.1 and Isaiah 40.3 (*Hearing the Whole Story*, pp. 183, 232).

28. Hooker's introduction here is excellent (*Message of Mark*, pp. 4–5, 9–16, 24). After such a brilliant beginning, the rest of Hooker's work falls back into convention. She does in passing light up the importance of the Strong One – the eschatological deliverer – which is the basis of Myers' title. However, the links between apocalyptic and eschatology are not followed up in any consistent fashion; a problem partly created by the commentary genre.

29. Myers, *Say to this Mountain*, p. 7 points out that in 1.10, Mark is alluding to Isaiah's hopes that God would come down and 'rend the heavens' and that 'the mountains would tremble'.

30. This uses Myers extensively (*Binding the Strong Man*, pp. 141–7). The Myers quotes are pp. 141–2 (including that from Kee) and p. 147; and from G. Thiessen, *The Gospels in Context: Social and Political History in the Synoptic Tradition*, Edinburgh, T. & T. Clark, 1992, p. 144.

31. Myers, *Binding the Strong Man* p. 117. Hooker manages to get half way to this analysis. She notes that in the 'conflict' stories of Mark 2, the 'Jewish authorities' refuse to accept Jesus' authority (*Message of Mark*,

p. 22). She goes on that Jesus' message divides the world into two camps and wanders off into sermon mode (p. 30) quite missing the point that at least in Mark's early chapters it is the 'authorities' against the people that are the two camps divided.

32. Myers translates Jesus' in an even stronger manner: Jesus literally 'snorts with indignation' (*Say to this Mountain*, p. 18). F. Belo, *A Materialist Reading of the Gospel of Mark* (1975), Maryknoll, Orbis, 1981, p. 106 points out that it is the leper ironically who is the first to 'proclaim' the good news.

33. Quote is Myers, *Binding the Strong Man*, pp. 153–4.

34. Myers, *Binding the Strong Man*, pp. 151–6, 165–6, 421–3; *Say to this Mountain*, p. 48; Herzog, *Jesus, Justice and the Reign of God*, p. 253

35. Myers, *Binding the Strong Man* p. 191–3, Myers (2001) p. 58–9.

36. D. Nineham, *The Gospel of St Mark* (1963), London, Penguin, 1992, p. 150. Horsley, *Hearing the Whole Story*, p. 140–1.

37. Horsley, *Hearing the Whole Story*, pp. 88, 106, 235, 248; Horsley, *The Liberation Of Christmas*, p. 24; N. K. Gottwald, *The Hebrew Bible* Philadelphia, Fortress, 1985, p. 344, 352.

38. Theissen, *Gospels in Context*, pp. 26–42, 81–5; Myers, *Binding the Strong Man*, pp. 112, 215–16.

39. Theissen, *Gospels in Context*, pp. 61–2. For understanding 'Canaan' in today's terms, see N. K. Gottwald, *The Tribes of Yahweh: A Sociology of the Religion of Liberated Israel 1250–1050 BCE*, London, SCM Press, 1979, pp. 32–43, 192–3, 409, 576–87, who argues that the key to the Israelite revolution was the transformation of the Canaanite city states, whose 'religion' was overthrown by the new believers in Yahweh. He goes on to criticize the Old Testament writers, like Bright, *A History of Israel* (1959), London, SCM Press, 1972, who see the revolution but fail to follow through the theological and political consequences (pp. 592–607).

40. Theissen, *Gospels in Context*, pp. 63–5. The fact that this pericope is difficult to interpret is shown by the fact that neither Horsley nor Myers seriously attempt it. For Nineham, the woman accepts the 'divinely ordained division between God's people and the gentiles'(*Gospel of St Mark*, p. 199). This is very much exegesis of its time; today it is dangerously poor, if misused.

41. The quote is Bright, *History of Israel*, p. 218, see also pp. 199–218; Horsley, *Archaeology, History and Society*, pp. 17–21; and Gottwald, *Tribes of* Yahweh, pp. 528, 542.

42. Theissen, *Gospels in Context*, pp. 65–7. He comments (p. 79) that this reads like a Palestinian pericope.

43. Theissen, *Gospels in Context*, pp. 69–70, 73–6 and Horsley, *Archaeology, History and Society*, p. 81.

44. Theissen, *Gospels in Context*, pp. 61, 69, 73–5, 84. The quote is p. 79.

45. M. Polley, *Amos and the Davidic Empire*, Oxford University Press, 1989, pp. 128–9, 135, 206.

46. Negri and Hardt, *Empire*, p. xviii.

47. Myers, *Say to this Mountain*, pp. 7, 89.

Chapter 7

1. Reflecting the late 1960s counter-culture, J. H. Yoder, *The Politics of Jesus*, Grand Rapids, Eerdmans, 1972 called his initial quest for the politics of Jesus 'looking for a messianic ethic' (pp. 11–25).

2. This rulers/ruled class difference is vital to Horsley and is established in his preface to Horsley and Hanson, *Bandits, Prophets and Messiahs* (p. xii). Following him, I stress here the messianic expectation was linked to the 'peasant', or popular, culture in which Jesus was rooted (p. xx), not the general culture. Horsley calls these the great and little traditions (pp. 4–5). He also argues convincingly that the literary elite did not have a general expectation of the Messiah at this time, so that what has been constructed as a Jewish (all-class alliance, my words) against Roman rule was in fact a popular movement (which presumably included opposition to its own ruling classes).

3. The quotes on the Magnificat are from J. B. Green, *The Theology of the Gospel of Luke*, Cambridge University Press, 1995, p. 1; that on the birth of a child from S. Farris, *Hymns of Luke's Infancy Narratives*, Sheffield, Journal for the Study of the New Testament Press, 1985, pp. 20–1.

4. On the Magnificat as a liberation song, see Horsley, *The Liberation of Christmas*, pp. 107–10; and on Gabriel and Daniel, pp. 24, 65, 77.

5. The quote is Horsley, *The Liberation of Christmas*, p. 110. On the role of women as liberators see pp. 87–116.

6. The quote is Horsley, *The Liberation of Christmas*, p. 112. Also see p. 24.

7. The quote is Yoder, *Politics of Jesus*, p. 26, also see pp. 27–34; Myers, *Binding the Strong Man*, p. 112; Horsley, *The Liberation of Christmas*, p. 115.

8. K. E. Bailey, *Through Peasant Eyes: The Parables of Luke* (1976), Grand Rapids, Eerdmans, 1997, p. 25. Bailey takes the quote about politics and religion from Manson, *The Servant Messiah*. For the quote on the Parable, see p. 44.

9. On Antipas in Rome and tax, see Perowne, *The Later Herods*, pp. 10, 47; on the issue of migrant labour, Horsley, *The Liberation of Christmas*, pp. 71–3.

10. Horsley and Hanson, *Bandits, Prophets and Messiahs*, pp. 34–9; Horsley, *The Liberation of Christmas*, pp. 49, 73; Horsley, *Archaeology, History and Society*, p. 33; Perowne, *The Later Herods*, pp. 8, 13–14, 22–3, 48–54. Theissen argues that the house divided for Mark could also refer to the Empire with a civil war raging in 69 CE (*Gospels in Context*, p. 261).

11. Belo, *Materialist Reading of Mark*, pp. 178–80. Belo points out that the word used for 'driving' out the money changers is the same one used for driving out the demons in the early exorcisms.

12. N. T. Wright, *Jesus and the Victory of God*, London, SPCK, 1996, p. 483. On rebuilding the Temple, see Horsley, *Archaeology, History and Society*, p. 31. On the Temple Robbers, see Horsley and Hanson, *Bandits, Prophets and Messiahs*, pp. 15–20, 53–60.

13. The quote is Horsley, *Hearing the Whole Story*, p. 41. Luke does not place Jesus on the Mount of Olives for the discourse (21.5–36), but does so later (22.39–45).

14. Myers, *Binding the Strong Man*, pp. 119, 313, 425–6.

15. Wengst, *Pax Romana*, pp. 57–9. Also, See Chapter 1 on New Labour's political theology.

16. Myers, *Binding the Strong Man*, p. 320; *Archaeology, History and Society*, p. 165. Belo's work first alerted me to the importance of the widow's story. He points out that the Temple is mentioned three times in relation to money here (*Materialist Reading of Mark* pp. 193–5). Belo correctly points to the theological void in understanding the political economy of the New Testament which liberation theology attempts to fill (p. 2). His 'materialist' reading is overly philosophical – full of Althusserian circuits – and adds surprisingly little to conventional exegesis.

17. As a good example of old-style exegesis, Taylor argues that the 'widow's story is told for its own sake' (*Gospel According to Mark*, p. 496) disagreeing with Montefiore, who believes it to be non-authentic and what's more, to have no 'religious value' (quoted in Taylor, p. 499). With a historical understanding, and a closer theological and sociological perspective, nothing could be seen to be further from the truth and nowhere more clearly shows the poverty of conventional exegesis. In fact, Mark's Gospel here now comes to its discursive and apocalyptic climax using Malachi. On this, see Myers, *Say to this Mountain*, p. 6.

18. T. J. Geddert, *Watchwords: Mark 13 in Markan Eschatology*, Sheffield, 1989, p. 114. The quotes are from Nineham, *Gospel of St Mark*,

p. 329 and p. 342. Each of the theologians provides a slightly different context to the 'Temple discourse' for the purposes of their Gospel. Although Mark has a brief attack on the Jewish leadership (12.38–40), Matthew places his revelations in the context of a sustained denunciation of the Pharisees in the Seven Woes of chapter 23. He links the coming signs to Jerusalem's fate to be left 'desolate' (vv. 37–8). In Luke, the story comes as a culmination of the Parables and Jesus in effect becomes a living Parable. The signs of the end – of Jerusalem – are there (in vv. 40–4) before Jesus clears the temple (vv. 45–8) and despite his entry in apparent triumph (19.28–38).

19. I found this the most political – and the best – part of G.R. Beasley Murray, *Jesus and the Last Days*, London, Hendrikson, 1993 pp. 381–6. On the 'awed' disciples, see Myers, *Say to this Mountain*, p. 165 and *Binding the Strong Man*, p. 304. Ironically, Beasley Murray falls into the same trap as the disciples: the Temple was 'probably the most awesome building in the ancient world' (p. 383).

20. See Horsley, *The Liberation of Christmas*, p. 42–4, 94–5, on the costs to the people of Herod's security and of the Temple rebuilding. Myers, *Binding the Strong Man*, p. 375 makes the economic point.

21. C. S. Keener, *A Commentary on the Gospel of St. Matthew*, Grand Rapids, Eerdmans, 1999. His quote is from p. 560, Myers, *Binding the Strong Man*, p. 320. Despite Geddert's excellent analysis of the leadership condemnation (*Watchwords*, p. 124), he still fails to see that the Temple represents more than a religious establishment (pp. 116–25).

22. Beasley Murray makes the excellent point about Jesus leaving the Temple (*Jesus and the Last Days*, p. 381). On Barclay, see his *The Bible and History*, pp. 314–21.

23. See Theissen, *Gospels in Context*, pp. 137, 141–55, 158, 164–5.

24. Myers, *Say to this Mountain*, p. xv.

25. Myers, *Binding the Strong Man*, p. 369 and Herzog, *Jesus, Justice and the Reign of God*, pp. 218–9, 240–3. Herzog quotes Crossan on the use of 'State terrorism' (p. 243).

26. Myers, *Say to this Mountain*, pp. 183–5, *Binding the Strong Man*, pp. 372–3. The parallel with John the Baptist's martyrdom is also stressed by Myers, *Say to this Mountain*, p. 194 and *Binding the Strong Man*, pp. 112–13, 211–16. The 'binding' without its implications for Mark's Gospel is the only worthwhile point made by E. Bammel and C. F. Moule, *Jesus and the Politics of His Day*, Cambridge University Press, 1984, p. 415, in reference to John's Gospel (18.12, 24).

27. Like binding, handing over is another crucial term to Mark; being handed over to the powers is usually the implication. Beasley Murray notes

that it is used 10 times in Mark's 'passion' (*Jesus and the Last Days*, pp. 398–9). On Barabbas, see Myers, *Binding the Strong Man*, pp. 380–1. The word used by the crowd 'asking' for Barabbas, uses the same Greek word as Herodias' daughter asking for John the Baptist's head (6.24 and 15.8).

28. See Myers, *Binding the Strong Man* p. 387 and, especially on social banditry, Horsley and Hanson, *Bandits, Prophets and Messiahs*, pp. 48–51. Horsley's down-playing of the 'Zealot party', to make it only in existence at the time of the last Jewish revolt from 68 CE (p. xxvi), seems to me to undermine the power of his historical argument about the extent of popular resistance. (To take a modern analogy, the existence of a popular working class labour politics from the 1790s in England does not have to be identical to the Labour Party, only founded in 1900.) The popular Jewish peasant culture of Jesus' time looked for the overthrow of the existing order. In the New Testament this desire is sometimes equated with Zealots and does not have to equate with a later 'political party' of the same name.

29. C. Rowland, *Radical Christianity: A Reading of Recovery*, London, Polity, 1988, p. 23. The importance of the Samaritans in John is drawn out by a number of theologians. O. Cullmann, *The Johannine Circle*, London, SCM Press, 1976, pp. x, 55–61, notes the importance of John 8.48 (p. 90).

30. O. Cullmann, *The State in the New Testament*, London, SCM Press, 1957, pp. 14–17. The two quotes from Wright, *Jesus and the Victory of God*, are p. 544 and p. 541.

31. Wright, *Jesus and the Victory of God*, p. 543. Myers emphasizes: 'Crucifixion was a political and military punishment ... it was inflicted above all on the lower classes ... slaves, violent criminals and the unruly elements in the rebellious provinces. These were primarily people who had no rights [who] had to be suppressed by all possible means to safeguard law and order in the State' (*Binding the Strong Man* p. 247), see also pp. 380–3, 392–3.

32. Black, *Mark* p. 4. W. Marxsen, *Mark the Evangelist: Studies on the Redaction History of the Gospel* (1956) Abingdon Press, 1969 in his early redaction critique made much of the Galilee motif, which I have adapted here to be far more human and far less 'eschatological'.

33. Wengst, *Pax Romana*, pp. 2–3, Myers, *Binding the Strong Man*, p. 414.

Chapter 8

1. Christian Smith begins his book, as I begin this chapter with this assassination, see *The Emergence of Liberation Theology: Radical Religion*

And *Social Movement Theory,* London, University of Chicago Press, 1991, pp. 1–2, 239. See also O. Romero, *Voice of the Voiceless. Four Past Letters and Other Statements,* edited by I. Martin-Baro with an introduction by J. Sobrino, Maryknoll, Orbis, 1985, p. 191.

2. W. LaFeber, *Inevitable Revolutions: The US in Central America* (1983), London, W. W. Norton, 1993, p. 14. LaFeber also points out that 'no area in the world is more tightly integrated into the US' (p. 5).

3. Graham Greene in D. Keogh (ed.), *Church and Politics in Latin America,* London, Macmillan, 1990, p. xv–xvi.

4. Romero describes the reforms in El Salvador after 1979, for example, as 'reforms with a big stick' (*Voice of the Voiceless,* p. 42), but such has been common in Latin America.

5. See J. Sobrino, *Jesus the Liberator: A Historical-Theological View* (1991), Maryknoll, Orbis, 2004. He argues (p. 265) that more people have died a violent death in Latin America that in any other continent, particularly so since Vatican Two.

6. R. Bauckham, *Messianic Theology in the Making,* London, Marshall Pickering, 1987 p. viii; J. Moltmann, *The Crucified God. The Cross of Christ as the Foundation and Criticism of Christian Theology,* London, SCM Press, 1974, pp. 1–5.

7. W. Wink, *Naming The Powers: The Language of Power in the New Testament,* Minneapolis, Augsburg Fortress Press, 1984 p. ix; Horsley, *The Liberation of Christmas,* pp. 127–41; Rowland and Corner, *Liberating Exegesis,* pp. 8–52.

8. See Smith, *Emergence of Liberation Theology,* pp. 11–24 and in more detail from 1955 to 1968, see pp. 89–164. Also see J. Dunkerley, *Warriors and Scribes. Essays on the History and Politics of Latin America,* London, Verso, 2000.

9. See Sobrino in Romero, *Voice of the Voiceless,* p. 24 and *Jesus the Liberator,* p. 195.

10. P. Wade, *Race and Ethnicity in Latin America,* London, Pluto Press, 1997, pp. 2–58, argues in favour of using the term 'Indian' rather than 'native' or 'indigenous', which I have followed here, while also occasionally using all three.

11. J. Dunkerley, *Power in the Isthmus. A Political History of Modern Central America,* London, Verso, 1988, p. 431.

12. Christian Aid, *Taking Liberties* pp. 5, 50–3.

13. LaFeber, *Inevitable Revolutions,* pp. 28–9, 41–2, 63–9, 125. 'If Honduras was dependent on fruit companies before 1912 (the first major US invasion), it was virtually indistinguishable from them after' (p. 46). Dunkerley, *Power in the Isthmus,* p. 527 notes that the US agreement on

military aid was to be paid for by the Hondurans themselves (shades of the British in India).

14. Dunkerley, *Power in the Isthmus*, pp. 519–20, 572–4, 583. The USS Honduras is from LaFeber, *Inevitable Revolutions*, p. 310.

15. D. Browning, *El Salvador: Landscape and Society*, Oxford, Clarendon Press, 1971, pp. 66–77 has the most detailed descriptions of the development of indigo production and pp. 157–71, 222 the taking of Indian land for coffee. His descriptions of the dense population and of the relationship of the Indians to the land are excellent (pp. x, 5–21).

16. Dunkerley, *Power in the Isthmus*, on land ownership, pp. 65, 180. On the tribute and the politics up to the 1930 census, see L. Zamosc, 'Class Conflict in Export Economies. The Social Roots of the Salvador Insurrection of 1932' in J. L. Flora and E. Torres-Rivas (eds), *Sociology of Developing Societies: Central America*, London, Macmillan, 1989, pp. 58–71.

17. Farabundo Marti, born in 1893, founded the Communist Party in Guatemala in 1925, supported Sandino in Nicaragua and was shot in El Salvador in February 1932. See P. Berryman, *The Religious Roots of Rebellion. Christians in the Central American Revolutions*, London, SCM Press, 1984, p. 93.

18. On the course of the 1932 revolt see Dunkerley, *Power in the Isthmus*, pp. 65–6, 90–7, Zamosc 'Class Conflict in Export Economies', pp. 64–72, Berryman, *Religious Roots of Rebellion*, p. 92–6 and Browning, *El Salvador*, pp. 272–3.

19. Dunkerley, *Power in the Isthmus*, pp. 94–8, 118, 154.

20. Dunkerley, *Power in the Isthmus*, on income distribution, p. 178; see also pp. 352–3; LaFeber, *Inevitable Revolutions*, pp. 147, 175.

21. The LaFeber quote is *Inevitable Revolutions*, p. 289, see also pp. 243–3 and Berryman, *Religious Roots of Rebellion*, pp. 112–13.

22. Dunkerley, *Power in the Isthmus*, pp. 343–4, 55–60 and T. L. Karl, 'The Christian Democrat Party and the Prospects for Democratization' in Flora and Torres-Rivas, *Sociology of … Central America*, p. 141.

23. The hegemonic crisis is Berryman's concept, which fits El Salvador in 1972–89 very well, although there is no explicit reference to Gramsci (*Religious Roots of Rebellion*, p. 115). The point is made by Dunkerley as a bourgeois crisis of how to handle the 'oligarchic bloc' and linked to falling coffee profits (*Power in the Isthmus*, pp. 373–4, 417). Also see LaFeber, *Inevitable Revolutions*, pp. 194–5 on land reform.

24. Both terms for Guatemala are from Dunkerley, *Power in the Isthmus*, pp. 61, 134 The pressure on El Salvador from Guatemala is a traditional one given that Guatemala was the centre of Spanish rule in Cen-

tral America. The liberal regimes based on El Salvador's cocoa, indigo and coffee wealth had been put down by Guatemala in the nineteenth century. See Browning, *El Salvador*, pp. 57–8, 65 and R. L. Woodward, *Central America: A Nation Divided*, Oxford University Press, pp. 152–3.

25. Berryman, *Religious Roots of Rebellion*, pp. 97–105. Also see M. Lowy, *The War of Gods. Religion and Politics in Latin America*, London, Verso, 1996, p. 104. The US ambassador – no less – accused D'Aubuisson of Romero's murder. See Berryman, *Religious Roots of Rebellion*, p. 150.

26. The quote is from Dunkerley, *Power in the Isthmus*, p. 376. On land reform see Romero, *Voice of the Voiceless*, p. 3. For a detailed analysis of the church situation, see Berryman, *Religious Roots of Rebellion*, pp. 114–24.

27. The quote is Berryman, *Religious Roots of Rebellion*, p. 113; also see pp. 107–13, 126–34. The Archbishops' third pastoral letter on the Church and Popular Organizations reflected the conflict; see Romero, *Voice of the Voiceless*, pp. 86–113. Also see Lowy, *The War of Gods*, pp. 103–6.

28. Berryman, *Religious Roots of Rebellion*, pp. 146–9; Dunkerley, *Power in the Isthmus*, pp. 389–96; Romero, *Voice of the Voiceless*, p. 9. On the lack of justice under Reagan-controlled Central America, see LaFeber, *Inevitable Revolutions*, p. 365.

29. The quote is from Berryman, *Religious Roots of Rebellion*, p. 145; see also pp. 140–5. Dunkerley, *Power in the Isthmus*, p. 402.

30. The quote is Berryman, *Religious Roots of Rebellion*, p. 155, see also pp. 140–55; Dunkerley, *Power in the Isthmus*, pp. 351, 360, 373, 393; and LaFeber, *Inevitable Revolutions*, p. 252.

31. LaFeber is excellent on this, see *Inevitable Revolutions*, pp. 313–17; and Berryman, *Religious Roots of Rebellion*, pp. 151–60.

32. On the Pope see Berryman, *Religious Roots of Rebellion*, pp. 152–3.

33. J. Dunkerley, *The Pacification of Central America. Political Change in the Isthmus*, London, Verso, 1994, p. 145 on US aid; also see Dunkerley, *Power in the Isthmus*, pp. 404–5, 410–11 and Karl 'The Christian Democrat Party', pp. 147–8.

34. Dunkerley, *Power in the Isthmus*, p. 338 and *Pacification of Central America*, p. 145; LaFeber, *Inevitable Revolutions*, pp. 249–50, 354.

35. Dunkerley, *Pacification of Central America*, pp. 67–71 and *Power in the Isthmus*, p. 412; Karl 'The Christian Democrat Party', p. 148.

36. The best book summary I have seen on the background and course of the Nicaraguan Revolution is T. W. Walker, *Nicaragua: Land of Sandino* (1981), Boulder, Westview, 1991. On the 1990 election see pp. 52–5 and Dunkerley, *Pacification of Central America*, pp. 57, 150.

37. J. Petras, 'El Salvador Elections. Polarization in the Post Peace Accords' Z Net, 1997 (www.zmag.org). Dunkerley, *Pacification of Central America*, pp. 67–76.

38. Morris is quoted to this effect in the preface to Negri and Hardt's *Empire*.

39. The quote from Duarte is in Dunkerley, *Power in the Isthmus*, p. 335; the concept of recomposition is Dunkerley's (p. 338). He also explains why he uses the word pacification – the term used by the Spanish for the conquest after 1573 (*Pacification of Central America*, pp. 3–4).

40. The quote from Romero is in Sobrino, *Jesus the Liberator*, p. 255. Sobrino argues that Yahweh's suffering servants are like the remnants of Israel in Second Isaiah's vision. The poor of the 'third world' are the Galilee of today (pp. 255–6).

41. Geddert, *Watchwords*, pp. 255, 200, 15, 146; Myers, *Say to this Mountain*, pp. 100, 170–1.

42. Wengst, *Pax Romana*, pp. 55–56; Myers, *Say to this Mountain*, pp. 116, 133, 279.

43. M. Hooker, *The Gospel According to St Mark*, London, A. & C. Black, 1991, p. 119.

44. C. Myers, *Who Will Roll Away the Stone? Discipleship Queries for First World Christians* (1994), Maryknoll, Orbis, 1995, pp. 337, 339 and *Binding the Strong Man* p. 144.

45. Herzog, *Jesus, Justice and the Reign of God*, pp. 193–5.

46. The El Salvador quote is in LaFeber, *Inevitable Revolutions*, p. 246; that from Romero, *Voice of the Voiceless*, p. 43; see also pp. 44–5.

47. See www.veteransagency.mod.uk for the significance of 10 July 2005.

Chapter 9

1. See Hobsbawm, *Industry and Empire*, especially pp. 89–90.

2. Elliott, *Perry Anderson*, pp. 13–15, 36.

3. Anderson quoted in Elliott, *Perry Anderson*, p. 191. On working class defeats, see p. 28. P. Anderson, *English Questions*, London, Verso, 1992, pp. 4–5 admits in dialogue with E. P. Thompson, *The Poverty of Theory*, London, Merlin Press, 1978 that in 1964 he had underestimated the importance of radical English political culture, as represented by theorists like Morris.

4. See G. Dale, *God's Politicians: The Christian Contribution To 100 Years of Labour*, London, Harper Collins, 2000 with a Foreword by Tony Blair and an introduction by Stephen Timms. See also C. Bryant, *Possible*

Dreams, London, Hodder & Stoughton, 1996 and A. Wilkinson, *Christian Socialism: Scott Holland To Tony Blair*, London, SCM Press, 1998.

5. Anderson quoted in Elliott, *Perry Anderson*, p. 21. Ideally my critique of the 'new economics' foundation in particular (with Stiglitz as another populist representative of the art) should be more theoretical than this throwaway line.

6. The two key works on Morris used extensively here are P. Meier, *William Morris: The Marxist Dreamer*, Brighton, Harvester, 1978, pp. 4–14, 21–4 and E. P. Thompson, *Morris: Romantic to Revolutionary* (1955), London, Lawrence and Wishart, 1976, pp. 2–3.

7. The quote on Disraeli is in Thompson, *Morris* p. 215 and on war p. 429. On the Afghan War in 1878, see p. 259.

8. Thompson, *Morris*, pp. 384, 457, 778.

9. See Meier, *Morris*, pp. 219–22 and Thompson, *Morris*, pp. 293–7, 777.

10. Thompson, *Morris*, pp. 805, 816. The quote on Rome is from p. 778.

11. Thompson, *Morris*, p. 799–800.

12. W. Morris, *Selected Writings* edited by G. D. H. Cole, London, Bloomsbury, 1934 on State Socialism as 'quasi socialist machinery' (p. 663); on dung, see W. Morris, *News From Nowhere. Or an Epoch of Rest being some chapters from a Utopian Romance* (1890), London, Routledge, 1970, p. 63. Later he calls Parliament part of the 'machinery of tyranny' (p. 67) and MPs 'sham kings' (p. 139).

13. Morris, 'How I Became A Socialist' *Selected Writings* pp. 660, 664.

14. Cromwell and Ireton's disagreements with the 'Levellers' centred on the franchise – a debate that was not to be effectively repeated for nearly a further 200 years. See D. Manning, *The English People and the English Revolution*, London, Heinemann, 1976, pp. 261–7, 278; C. P. Hill, *The World Turned Upside Down. Radical Ideas During the English Revolution* (1972), London, Penguin, 1991, pp. 58–72; and M. Cowling, *1867: Disraeli, Gladstone and Revolution: The Passing of the Second Reform Bill* Cambridge University Press, 1967, pp. 2–47.

15. R. McKibbin, *The Evolution of the Labour Party: 1910–24*, Oxford University Press, 1974 points out that the issue of workers' control was fudged in the Labour Party Constitution's famous Clause 4 and reflected more of the trade unions' increasing incorporation during the Great War (pp. xiv, 94–110).

16. Royal Dutch Shell still is the closest example of a trans-national company, both in management structure and ownership. The Dutch still see Royal Dutch as Dutch, the British see Shell as British, the Americans

think Shell Oil is American; even Shell Canada is seen as Canadian. In fact, it is all and none of these. This is also part and parcel of the problems of Shell Nigeria – driven rather more by Nigerian than by Shell's corruption.

17. Churchill took a 51 per cent stake in what was then the Anglo Persian Oil Company (now BP) in 1914, three months before the outbreak of war, to safeguard British oil supplies for the Navy. See A. Sampson, *The Seven Sisters: the Great Oil Companies and the World They Made* (1975), London, Hodder & Stoughton, 1977, pp. 68–74.

18. W. Hutton, *The Stakeholder Society: Writings on Politics and Economics*, London, Polity, 1999, pp. 2, 79, 269–71. The quote on a 'new economics struggling to be born' is p. 9.

19. See A. Nove, *Economics of Feasible Socialism*, London, Allen & Unwin, 1983 on Yugoslavia pp. 135–9.

20. P. Frolich, *Rosa Luxemburg: Ideas in Action*, London, Pluto Press, 1972, p. 167.

21. Quoted by Nove, *Economics of Feasible Socialism*, p. 212.

22. Negri and Hardt, *Empire*, p. xv.

23. My son recently bought me a copy of a book on the Italian campaign and the description of an attempted US crossing of the Rapido is remarkably similar to my dad's (without, of course, his own escape story). See E. Morris, *Circles of Hell: The War in Italy 1943–45*, New York, Crown Publishers, 1993, pp. 249–53.

24. Sobrino, *Jesus the* Liberator, p. 256. See the descriptions in Berryman, *Religious Roots of Rebellion*, p. 156, and Dunkerley, *Power in the Isthmus*, p. 398.

25. Romero, *Voice of the Voiceless*, p. 50–1.

26. C. Rowland, quoting Sobrino in *The Cambridge Companion to Liberation Theology*, Cambridge University Press, 1999, pp. 250–1. Sobrino uses not only the language of Exodus, but 'goes global', as Archbishop Romero also spoke of the cries of the oppressed of El Salvador.

Suggestions for Further Reading

Part 1

Global Capital and Political Economy

Anderson, P. *Passages From Antiquity To Feudalism*, London, New Left Review, 1974; Verso, 1978.

Curtis, M. *The Great Deception: Anglo American Power and World Order*, London, Pluto Press, 1998.

Harvey, D. *Spaces of Hope*, Edinburgh University Press, 2000.

Marx, K. and Engels, F. *The Communist Manifesto* (1848) in *Political Writings Volume 1*, London, Penguin, 1973.

Moore, Barrington Jr *Social Origins of Dictatorship and Democracy. Lord And Peasant in the Modern World* (1966), London, Penguin, 1973.

Negri, A. and Hardt, M. *Empire*, Harvard University Press, 2000.

Thompson, E. P. *Morris: Romantic to Revolutionary* (1955), London, Lawrence and Wishart, 1976.

History – Africa and the Americas

Dunkerley, J. *Power in the Isthmus. A Political History of Modern Central America*, London, Verso, 1988.

First, R. *The Barrel of a Gun. Political Power in Africa and the Coup D'Etat*, London, Penguin, 1970.

Frank, A. G. *Capitalism and Underdevelopment in Latin America: Historical Studies in Chile and Brazil* (1967), London, Penguin 1971.

Johnson, D. H. *The Root Causes of Sudan's Civil Wars*, London, The International African Institute, 2003.

Jorgensen, J. J. *Uganda: A Modern History*, London, Croom Helm, 1981.

Markakis, J. *National and Class Conflict in the Horn*, Cambridge University Press, 1987.

Rock, D. 'The Racking of Argentina', *New Left Review*, 17, Sept/Oct 2002.

Simons, G. *Iraq from Sumer to Saddam*, London, Macmillan, 1994.

291

Williamson, E. *The Penguin History of Latin America*, London, Penguin, 1992.

Zinn, H. *A People's History of the United States. From 1492 to the Present* (1980), Harlow, Pearson Education, 1999.

History – Europe

Blickle, P. *The Revolution of 1525: The German Peasants War from a New Perspective* (1977), Baltimore, Johns Hopkins, 1981.

Engels, F. *The Peasant War in Germany* (1850), Moscow, Progress, 1977.

Hobsbawm, E. J. *Industry and Empire* (1968), London, Penguin, 1990.

Joll, J. *The Origins of the First World War*, London, Longman, 1984.

Rawnsley, A. *Servants of the People: The Inside Story of New Labour*, London, Penguin, 2000.

Semmel, B. *Imperialism and Social Reform: 1895–1914*, London, Allen and Unwin, 1960.

Steiner, Z. S. *Britain and the Origins of the First World War*, London, MacMillan, 1977.

Part 2

Mark's Gospel

Hooker, M. *The Message of Mark*, London, Epworth, 1993.

Horsley, R. A. *The Liberation of Christmas*, New York, Crossroad, 1989.

Horsley, R. A. *Hearing the Whole Story: the Politics of Plot in Mark's Gospel*, Louisville, John Knox Press, 2001.

Myers, C. *Binding the Strong Man: A Political Reading of Mark*. Maryknoll, Orbis, 1988.

Myers, C. and others. *Say to This Mountain: Mark's Story of Discipleship*, Maryknoll, Orbis, 1996.

Theissen, G. *The Gospels in Context: Social and Political History in the Synoptic Tradition*, Edinburgh, T. & T. Clark, 1992.

Public Theology

Atherton, J. *Marginalization*, London, SCM Press, 2003.

Berryman, P. *The Religious Roots of Rebellion. Christians in the Central American Revolutions*, London, SCM Press, 1984.

Duchrow, U. and Hinkelammert, F. J. *Property For People Not Profit: Alternatives to the Global Tyranny of Capital*, London, CIIR, Zed Press 2004.

Suggestions for Further Reading

Herzog, W. R. *Jesus, Justice and the Reign of God, A Ministry of Liberation* Louisville, John Knox Press, 2000.

Howard-Brook, W. and Gwyther, A. *Unveiling Empire: Reading Revelation Then and Now*, Maryknoll, Orbis, 1999.

Northcott, M. *Life after Debt: Christianity and Global Justice*, London, SPCK, 1999.

Northcott, M. *An Angel Directs the Storm. Apocalyptic Religion and American Empire*, London, I. B. Tauris, 2004.

Wengst, K. *Pax Romana and the Peace of Jesus Christ*, Minneapolis, Augsburg Fortress, 1987.

Yoder, J. H. *The Politics of Jesus*, Grand Rapids, Eerdmans, 1972.